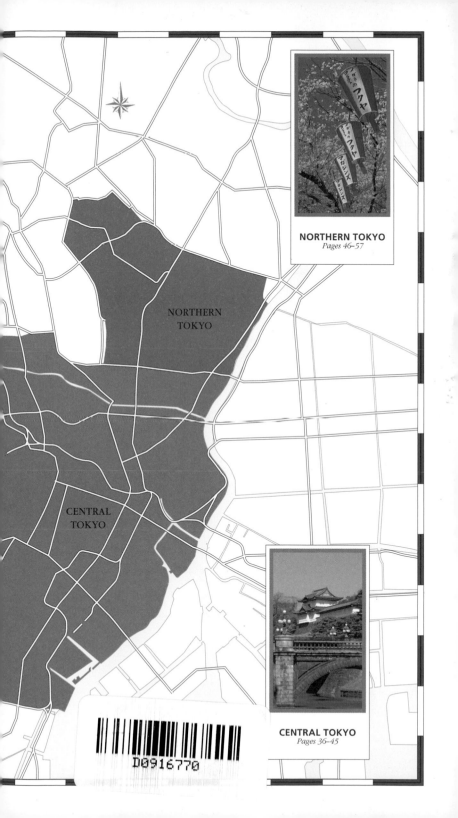

NORTHERN
TOKYO

NORTHERN TOKYO
Pages 46–57

CENTRAL
TOKYO

CENTRAL TOKYO
Pages 36–45

EYEWITNESS TRAVEL

TOKYO

LONDON, NEW YORK,
MELBOURNE, MUNICH AND DELHI
www.dk.com

MANAGING EDITOR Aruna Ghose
EDITORIAL MANAGER Joseph Mathai
DESIGN MANAGER Priyanka Thakur
PROJECT EDITOR Arundhti Bhanot
PROJECT DESIGNER Rajnish Kashyap
DESIGNER Anchal Kaushal
SENIOR CARTOGRAPHIC MANAGER Uma Bhattacharya
CARTOGRAPHER Alok Pathak
SENIOR DTP DESIGNER Vinod Harish
SENIOR PICTURE RESEARCHER Taiyaba Khatoon
PICTURE RESEARCHER Sumita Khatwani

MAIN CONTRIBUTORS
Jon Burbank, Emi Kazuko, Stephen Mansfield, Robbie Swinnerton

PHOTOGRAPHER
Martin Hladik

ILLUSTRATORS
Richard Bonson, Gary Cross, Richard Draper, Paul Guest, Claire
Littlejohn, Maltings Partnership, Mel Pickering, John Woodcock

Reproduced in Singapore by Colourscan
Printed and bound by South China Printing Company
Limited, China

First published in Great Britain in 2008
Dorling Kindersley Limited
80 Strand, London WC2R 0RL

Front cover main image: Shibuya crossing, Western Tokyo

◁ **Cherry trees in full bloom, Tokyo**

CONTENTS

Great Buddha statue at Kamakura

INTRODUCING
TOKYO

**Post-modernist masterpiece, Glass
Hall, Tokyo International Forum**

TOKYO
AREA BY AREA

The expansive Yokohama Bay Bridge, Central Honshu

A typical selection of Japanese food
in a *bento* box

1825 print by Hokusai depicting the
stages of woodblock printing

Imperial figure at Yomeimon
Gate, Tosho-gu Shrine, Nikko

Toshu-go Shrine, Nikko

HOW TO USE THIS GUIDE

This guide helps you to get the most from your visit to Tokyo. It provides detailed practical information and expert recommendations. *Introducing Tokyo* maps the city and the region, sets it in its historical context, and guides you through the succession of significant cultural events. *Tokyo Area By Area* is the main sightseeing section, giving detailed information on all the major sights, with photographs, illustrations, and detailed maps. *Farther Afield* looks at major sights of interest outside the city center, and *Beyond Tokyo* explores other places to visit within easy reach of the city. Carefully researched suggestions for restaurants, hotels, and shopping are found in the *Travelers' Needs* section of the book, while the *Survival Guide* contains useful advice on everything from changing money to traveling on the extensive Tokyo subway network.

TOKYO

The center of Tokyo has been divided into three sightseeing areas, each with its own chapter, color-coded for easy reference. Every chapter opens with an introduction to the part of Tokyo it covers, as well as an Area Map. This is followed by a Street-by-Street map illustrating the heart of the area.

Sights at a Glance lists the area's key sights by category, such as Notable Districts, Historic Buildings, Parks and Gardens, and Markets.

1 Area Map
The sights are numbered and located on a map. City center sights are also marked on the Street Finder maps.

A locator map shows where you are in relation to other areas in the city center.

Each area has color-coded thumb tabs.

2 Street-by-Street map
This map gives a bird's-eye view of interesting and important parts of each sightseeing area.

A suggested route takes in some of the most interesting streets in the area.

The Visitors' Checklist provides detailed practical information.

3 Tokyo's main sights
These are given two or more full pages. All top sights in Tokyo are described individually.

Stars indicate the sights that no reader should miss.

TOKYO AREA MAP
The colored areas shown on this map *(see inside front cover)* are the five main sightseeing areas used in this guide. Each is covered in a full chapter in *Tokyo Area by Area (see pp36–103)*. They are highlighted on other maps throughout the book. In *Tokyo at a Glance*, for example, they help you locate the top sights. They are also used to help you find the position of the three walks *(see pp78–83)*.

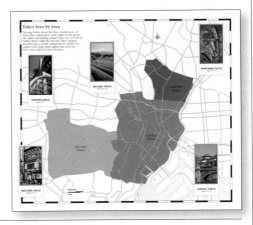

4 Farther Afield
This section covers those sights of interest to visitors that lie just outside the city of Tokyo and are easily accessible from the city center.

A key outlines the symbols used to read the map.

A map of the city shows the location of Farther Afield sights in relation to the city center.

The introduction outlines the areas covered in this section and their historical context.

5 Beyond Tokyo
Places worth visiting that are within a day's travel of Tokyo are described here. The general introduction is followed by a map which gives an illustrated overview of the region, with major roads marked and useful tips on getting around by bus and train.

Special features, such as this one on Zen Buddhist Temples, are highlighted with maps or illustrations.

6 Detailed Information
All the important sights are listed in order, following the numbering on the Area Map. Practical information, including map references, opening hours, and telephone numbers, is also provided.

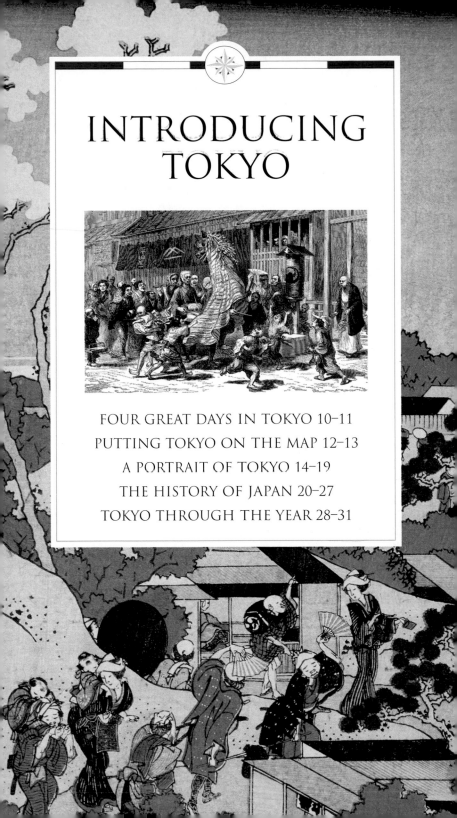

INTRODUCING
TOKYO

FOUR GREAT DAYS IN TOKYO

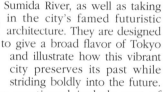
Clay mask, Tokyo National Museum

In little more than 400 years Tokyo has grown from being an impoverished fishing village to the world's largest metropolis. These itineraries sample both the traditional sights of Edo *(see p25)*, such as the Imperial Palace and its moats, and the historically important Sumida River, as well as taking in the city's famed futuristic architecture. They are designed to give a broad flavor of Tokyo and illustrate how this vibrant city preserves its past while striding boldly into the future. Prices mentioned include cost of travel, food, and admission fees.

Akihabara or "Electric Town" lined with hi-tech stores

ARCHITECTURE AND ELECTRONICS

- **A museum of the future**
- **Majestic Rainbow Bridge**
- **Lunch in Akihabara**
- **Tokyo International Forum, an architectural marvel**

FAMILY OF 4 allow at least ¥10,000

Morning
Start at the **Miraikan** *(see p82)*, a superbly designed museum dedicated to science and the latest in cutting-edge Japanese technology. Follow the elevated monorail across Dream Bridge to **Tokyo Big Sight** *(see p82)*, an exhibition and convention center. A gravity-defying structure, the center building consists of four inverted pyramids standing on a deceptively small base. Take the Yurikamome line monorail to Daiba station. Stop at one of the outdoor cafés at **Decks Tokyo Beach** *(see p83)*, where the walkways look down onto the sandy strip of Odaiba Marine Park and the picturesque Rainbow Bridge.

Afternoon
Take the monorail to Shimbashi station, changing to the JR Yamanote line for **Akihabara** *(see p45)*. Enjoy a tasty, no-frills lunch at **Jangara Ramen** *(see p181)*, a popular noodle shop. Explore the area's electronic emporiums and mangaesque buildings before visiting the **Tokyo Anime Center** *(see p45)*, a colorful, interactive space dedicated to anime culture. Return to the station and take the Yamanote line

Post-modernist masterpiece, Glass Hall, Tokyo International Forum

to Yurakucho, site of the **Tokyo International Forum** *(see p43)*, one of the city's most striking examples of post-modernist architecture.

A FAMILY DAY

- **Fun at the Children's Castle**
- **Toys at Kiddyland**
- **Thrills at Tokyo Dome**
- **Sunset at a Shinjuku skyscraper**

FAMILY OF 4 allow at least ¥18,000

Morning
Begin this day, centered around kids, low teens, and young-at-heart adults, at the **Children's Castle** *(see p181)*. Each floor has a different theme from chutes and slides for the very young to music rooms where kids can try out musical instruments. Do not miss the rooftop play garden with its go-karts and jungle gyms. If the kids want more, the **Tokyo Metropolitan Children's Hall** *(see p183)* is a short walk away. Take the JR Yamanote line from Shibuya to Harajuku station and then walk down Omotesando-dori to **Hiroba** for a vegetarian lunch, a floor beneath Crayon House *(see p181)*, a great children's bookstore.

Afternoon
Next stop is **Kiddyland** *(see p149)*, a multi-story toy shop. Take the train or subway to Suidobashi station and **Tokyo Dome** *(see p153)*, an amusement park with a roller-coaster that passes through a giant ferris-wheel, and over the rooftops of nearby buildings.

◁ Woodblock print from the series *Thirty-Six Views of Mount Fuji* by Katsushika Hokusai (1790–1849)

Evening

Take the Toei Oedo line to Shinjuku station and walk to the west exit of the **Tokyo Metropolitan Government Building** (see pp14–15). Its high speed elevator goes up to the 45th-floor observation gallery for the city's best sunset and night views.

AN OUTDOORS DAY

- **A relaxing river cruise**
- **A grand tour of the historic Imperial Palace**
- **A stroll in Shinjuku-Gyoen Garden**
- **Shopping and a *shabu-shabu* dinner**

TWO ADULTS allow at least ¥10,000

Morning

Board the Suijo Bus (river cruise) at Asakusa's Azuma Bridge. The Sumida River provides the setting for one of the most interesting concentrations of bridges in Japan. On alighting walk straight into the grounds of the **Hama Detached Palace Garden** (see pp40–41), a stunning, spacious, landscape garden dating from the 1650s that includes an elegant tea pavilion on the edge of its tidal salt pond. Walk through the Ginza district or take the metro to **Hibiya Park** (see p43), a spacious, green Western-style park, full of shady arbors. Stroll along the outer moat of the Imperial Palace to the Marunouchi Building (see p182) and lunch at Kua'Aina, a popular Hawaiian burger restaurant.

Imperial Palace Garden, a pleasant retreat in the heart of the city

The restaurant is right in front of **Tokyo Station** (see p42) and its redbrick, Queen Anne-style façade.

Afternoon

Return to the palace moat and Otemon gate, the main entrance to the **Imperial Palace Garden** (see p43). The green of manicured lawns contrast with gigantic stones and a ruined keep that give a vivid sense of the grandeur of the original castle grounds. Head for JR Yurakucho station to **Shinjuku-Gyoen Garden** (see p183), a cherry blossom-viewing spot. The former estate of a feudal lord, this is the closest you can get to a great outdoors experience in Tokyo. Stroll over to **Takashimaya Times Square** (see p145) for window shopping before stopping at Imahan, a *shabu-shabu* restaurant (see p123), upstairs from the **Tokyu Hands** store (see p145).

ART BROWSING

- **Treasures at the Tokyo National Museum**
- **A fine art museum and garden**
- **A craft museum**

TWO ADULTS allow at least ¥10,000

Morning

Begin this day of museums, galleries, and cultural sights with the world's largest collection of Japanese art and antiquity at the **Tokyo National Museum** (see pp50–3). The cafés around nearby Shinobazu Pond, with the Benten shrine sitting on an islet surrounded by lotuses, are a good place for a coffee break. Take the Ginza Line to Omotesando for the next cultural treat, the **Nezu Museum of Fine Arts** (see p68). Stop next at Maisen, (see p137) a *tonkatsu* (pork cutlet) Japanese restaurant.

Afternoon

It is just two stops from Shibuya on the Keio-Inokashira line to Komaba-Todaemae and the **Japan Folk Craft Museum** (see p77), housed in a wonderful 1936 residence. Return to Shibuya station and the **Bunkamura** (see p66) cross-cultural center, which houses regular exhibitions. After spending an hour or two here, you will be well positioned for a night out in Shibuya.

Exhibition of flag models at the Japan Folk Craft Museum

Putting Tokyo on the Map

Tokyo, Japan's capital city since 1868, lies on the
Japanese archipelago's largest island, Honshu. This
island chain is situated to the east of mainland Asia,
in the northwest of the Pacific Ocean. Tokyo is
located at the southern end of the Kanto Plain and
is bordered by Tokyo Bay and Chiba, Yamanashi,
Kanagawa, and Saitama prefectures.

Satellite image of Tokyo and Tokyo Bay

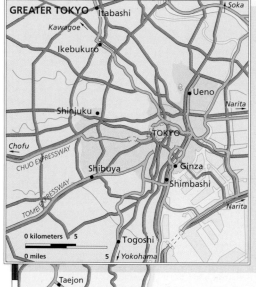

GREATER TOKYO

Itabashi
Soka
Kawagoe
Ikebukuro
Ueno
Narita
Shinjuku
Chofu
TOKYO
CHUO EXPRESSWAY
Shibuya
Ginza
Shimbashi
TOMEI EXPRESSWAY
Narita
Togoshi
Yokohama

0 kilometers 5
0 miles 5

SEA   OF
(EAST

Taejon
SOUTH
KOREA
Taegu
Sunch'on
Pusan
Fuku
Matsue
Tottori
Maizur
9
9   CHUGOKU EXPWY
Himeji   Kyoto
27
Kobe   Osaka
Hiroshima   SANYO EXPWY   Kurashiki   Okayama
Yamaguchi
Kokura   Tokuyama   Imabari   Takamatsu   Na
Fukuoka   Matsuyama   Tokushima   Wakayama
Saga   OITA EXPWY   Beppu   Kochi   Tanabe   42
Kurume   Oita   33   SHIKOKU   55
3
Nagasaki   Shimanto
Kumamoto   10   Nobeoka   56
Yatsushiro   KYUSHU
EAST   Sendai   Miyazaki
CHINA   3
SEA   Kagoshima   Miyakonojo
269

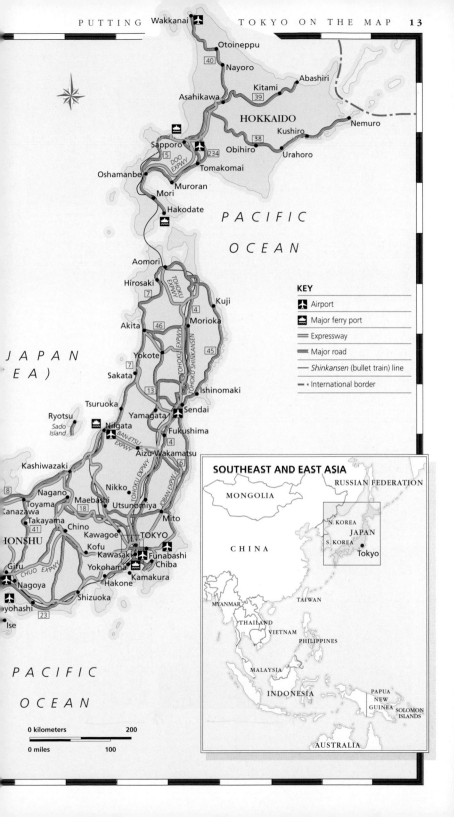

Wakkanai

Otoineppu

40

Nayoro

Kitami

Abashiri

Asahikawa

39

HOKKAIDO

Nemuro

Kushiro

Sapporo

38

Obihiro

DOO EXPWY

5

Urahoro

234

Tomakomai

Oshamanbe

Muroran

Mori

Hakodate

PACIFIC

OCEAN

Aomori

Hirosaki

TOHOKU EXPWY

7

Kuji

4

Akita

46

Morioka

TOHOKU SHINKANSEN

45

JAPAN

(... EA)

Yokote

TOHOKU EXPWY

7

Sakata

13

Ishinomaki

Tsuruoka

Yamagata

Sendai

Ryotsu

Sado Island

Niigata

BAN-ETSU EXPWY

Fukushima

Kashiwazaki

TOHOKU EXPWY

Aizu-Wakamatsu

4

6

8

Nikko

JOBAN EXPWY

Nagano

Toyama

Maebashi

Utsunomiya

Kanazawa

18

HONSHU

Takayama

41

Chino

Mito

Kawagoe

TOKYO

Kofu

Kawasaki

Funabashi

Gifu

CHUO EXPWY

Yokohama

Chiba

Nagoya

Kamakura

...yohashi

23

Hakone

Shizuoka

Ise

PACIFIC

OCEAN

KEY

✈ Airport

⛴ Major ferry port

═══ Expressway

━━━ Major road

—— *Shinkansen* (bullet train) line

–·–· International border

SOUTHEAST AND EAST ASIA

RUSSIAN FEDERATION

MONGOLIA

N. KOREA

JAPAN

CHINA

S. KOREA

Tokyo

MYANMAR

TAIWAN

THAILAND

VIETNAM

PHILIPPINES

MALAYSIA

INDONESIA

PAPUA NEW GUINEA

SOLOMON ISLANDS

AUSTRALIA

0 kilometers   200

0 miles   100

Architecture in Tokyo

Tokyoites have been obliged to rebuild their city so many times that what meets the eye is a mishmash of architectural styles. First impressions suggest chaos, but there is a dynamism, perhaps even a hidden order, to Tokyo's macramé of older wood and mortar buildings and its hi-tech modernity. From the splendid futuristic creations of Odaiba *(see p75)* to the triangulated rooftops and glass sheets of Tadao Ando's new 21 Design Sight in Roppongi *(see pp68–9)*, visitors sense perpetual renewal. In the midst of innovation are traditional structures, but Tokyo's heart, one suspects, is firmly in the future.

Prada Aoyama, *the dazzling creation of Jacques Herzog and Pierre de Meuron, has tinted, diamond-shaped outer panels which reveal a stylish interior.*

SHINJUKU SKYSCRAPER DISTRICT

Shinjuku district in Tokyo epitomizes the modern Japanese urban labyrinth. Most skyscrapers are clustered to the west of Shinjuku station. Built of materials such as aluminium, steel, and concrete, the buildings use flexible-frame technologies to withstand powerful earthquakes.

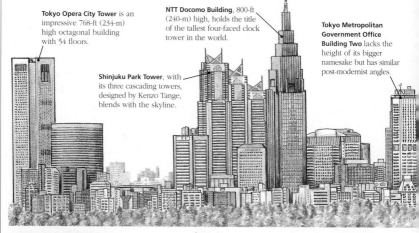

Tokyo Opera City Tower is an impressive 768-ft (234-m) high octagonal building with 54 floors.

NTT Docomo Building, 800-ft (240-m) high, holds the title of the tallest four-faced clock tower in the world.

Tokyo Metropolitan Government Office Building Two lacks the height of its bigger namesake but has similar post-modernist angles.

Shinjuku Park Tower, with its three cascading towers, designed by Kenzo Tange, blends with the skyline.

Asahi Super Dry Hall, *an amusing cartoon-like building, was built by French architect Philippe Starck in 1989 for the Asahi beer company.*

St Mary's Cathedral, *an early Kenzo Tange masterpiece, is covered in sparkling sheets of stainless steel, designed to symbolize the light of Christ.*

Fuji-TV Building, *another Kenzo Tange creation and a signature building of Odaiba, is a design marvel of girders, sky corridors, and a titanium-clad sphere.*

TRADITIONAL ARCHITECTURE

Traditional Japanese architecture is based on the use of wood, combined with interiors consisting of paper screens, paper and wood doors, and *tatami* mat flooring *(see p108)*.

In Tokyo's older temples and shrines, architectural aesthetics survive in the polished wood floors, ceramic roof tiles, movable partitions, and the sliding panels and opaque screens that create an interaction between the exterior and interior. Gokoku-ji temple *(see p73)*, which dates from 1681, remains gloriously intact, as does the even older Sanmon Gate at Zojo-ji temple *(see p41)*. Though a post-war reconstruction, the Meiji shrine *(see p64)*, located at the centre of a sacred forest, keeps faith with the pure, austere lines and aesthetics of traditional Shinto architecture.

Famous Sanmon Gate, Zozo-ji temple

Tokyo Metropolitan Government Office, with its stunning walls of granite and digital-like windows, towers above the Citizen's Plaza. Its 45th-floor observatory is a great sightseeing spot.

The Olympic Pavilion's *sweeping curved roof of tensile steel helped Kenzo Tange to win architecture's most coveted award, the prestigious 1967 Pritzker Prize.*

Sumitomo Building has an impressive atrium running the entire height of the building.

Sompo Japan Building

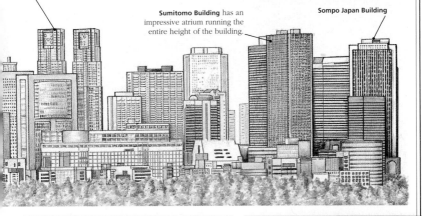

Tokyo International Forum, *one of Tokyo's architectural marvels designed by New York-based architect Raphael Viñoly, has a soaring 197-ft (60-m) high glass atrium, crisscrossed by walkways and curving walls resembling a crystal ship.*

Aoyama Technical College, *a sci-fi montage of posts, lightning rods, poles, and capsules by contemporary architect Watanabe Makoto, is an example of just how far Tokyo can go into the architectural beyond.*

Japanese Traditional Theater

Four major types of traditional theater are still performed regularly in Japan – Noh, Kyogen, Kabuki, and Bunraku *(see pp154–5)*. Originating in Shinto rites, Noh was first performed by Kan'ami Kiyotsugu (1333–84) and developed by his son Zeami. Adopted by the *daimyo* (feudal lords), Noh became more ritualistic and ceremonial. Gradually its farcical elements were confined to a separate form, Kyogen. By the 17th century, people wanted a more comprehensible and entertaining form of drama, and Kabuki evolved from Noh, starting in Kyoto. A form of puppet theater, Bunraku, was aimed at the general populace.

A Noh play *is being performed for the imperial household in this 1863 woodblock print by Taiso Yoshitoshi.*

The backdrop is a single pine tree, epitomizing the simplicity of Noh staging.

Slow rhythmic movements, subtle expressions, and sonorous music characterize a Noh performance.

NOH

An austere, restrained, and powerful theatrical form, Noh is performed on a bare, three-sided cypress-wood stage roofed like a shrine, with an entrance ramp to one side. One or two masked characters appear at a time. Their slow, choreographed actions *(kata)* are performed to music.

Musicians playing traditional drums and flutes sit at the back of the stage and accompany the actors.

Noh actors may be men or women but the majority are men.

Kyogen *evolved from comic interludes devised as relief from the demanding nature of Noh. A down-to-earth, colloquial form, its characters highlight human foibles and frailties. Masks are rarely used, and costumes are plain. The actors wear distinctive yellow tabi socks.*

Noh masks *are worn by the leading characters; the greatest masks are classified as National Treasures. The mask on the right represents a samurai, and on the far right, a demon.*

Noh costumes *are usually richly decorated and heavy. Many layers are worn to make the actors seem larger and more imposing.*

Kabuki actors *were popular subjects for Edo-era woodblock prints. The tradition can still be seen in this modern poster advertising a Kabuki play.*

BUNRAKU

Bunraku puppets are about 1.2 m (4 ft) tall with carved wooden heads, movable hands, and elaborate costumes. The main puppeteer wears traditional formal dress; his two assistants, one on each side, are clothed in black. *Shamisen (see p155)* music accompanies the action, and a narrator both tells the story and speaks all the parts. Many Kabuki plays were originally written for puppets; Bunraku has in turn borrowed a number of of Kabuki dramas.

Bunraku puppet with his manipulator

Stage right is where less important characters are usually located.

Costumes and wigs are highly elaborate, indicating the status and personality of each character.

The pine trees on Kabuki stage backdrops are a reference to its evolution from Noh.

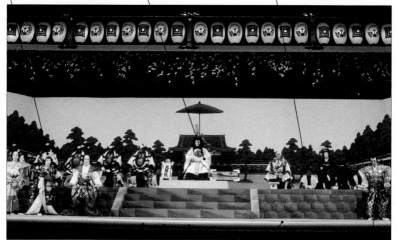

KABUKI

Kabuki is flamboyant and colorful with a large stage and cast. The major actors are stars, often from famous acting dynasties. Elaborate make-up replaced Noh masks, and a curtain allowed set changes. The musicians and chorus sit behind screens on either side or on stage.

Stage sets often incorporate special effects including trapdoors, revolving sections, and overhead cables for flying.

Stage left is usually occupied by characters of high rank or importance.

The hanamichi *(flower path) is a raised walkway running from the stage right through the audience and is used for dramatic entrances and exits.*

Aragoto, *or "rough-style" acting, is used in certain plays by male characters who move in exaggerated, choreographed ways and wear stylized makeup. Eye and facial movements are crucial to an actor's success.*

Although Kabuki *was founded by a woman, Izumo no Okuni, female actors were soon banned as immoral. All actors are now male, and female roles are played by highly skilled* onnagata.

Sumo and the Martial Arts

Now more of a professional sport than a martial art, sumo traces its origins back 2,000 years to Shinto harvest rites, and retains strong links with Shinto in many of its rituals. There are six sumo tournaments in Japan every year *(see p152)*, broadcast live on TV and followed enthusiastically. Training is a way of life for sumo wrestlers, and if a tournament is not on, it may be possible to watch practice sessions. Martial arts are known as *budo*, or the "martial way." They aim to cultivate balance, control, speed, and accuracy in a spiritual, mental, and physical sense. Kendo and kyudo, the least changed since the days of the samurai, are seen as the purest of the martial arts.

A karate kick

Sumo wrestlers *were a highly popular subject for Edo-period woodblock prints.*

Throwing salt *to purify the ring and the fight to come is part of a complex pre-match ritual that the wrestlers undertake. They also stamp, clap, and raise their hands before crouching down in front of their opponent ready to start.*

The *gyoji* (referee) wears traditional court costume and uses a fan to signal when to begin.

SUMO WRESTLING

Despite their size – there are no weight restrictions – sumo wrestlers *(rikishi)* move quickly and with agility, and so matches are often short (10 seconds or so). The loser is the first to touch the ground with any part of his body, except the soles of his feet, or to step out of, or be pushed from, the ring. The referee declares the winner.

Grand champions (yokozuna) *perform pre-match rituals wearing a richly decorated ceremonial apron and a white hemp-rope belt hung with folded paper (as seen at Shinto shrines). This champion is performing* shiko, *lifting his leg and stamping his foot to banish evil spirits and intimidate his opponent.*

A referee pours an offering *of sake onto the ring as part of the dedication ceremony before a tournament. The ring is a platform of clay edged by a square of sunken rice-straw bales, with an inner ring (where the match is fought) also marked by sunken bales.*

Banners *announce a sumo tournament – here at the National Sumo Stadium in Tokyo (see p153). Each tournament lasts 15 days. The lower-ranking wrestlers fight early in the day, while higher-ranking ones appear from mid-afternoon onward.*

The wrestlers' hair is oiled and fastened into a topknot *(mage).*

Only 48 winning techniques are commonly used, but many more have been identified.

A loincloth *(mawashi)* is worn for bouts, along with a thin belt *(sagari)* hung with threads similar to those seen at Shinto shrines.

The ring stands *under a suspended roof resembling that of a Shinto shrine. A different-colored tassel hangs from each corner of the roof, representing the four seasons.*

MARTIAL ARTS

Originally developed as traditional arts of war by the samurai, the martial arts have evolved into forms of austere discipline *(shugyo)* aimed at spiritual improvement; some are also competitive sports. The modern forms of kendo and kyudo trace their origins to methods practiced in Japanese antiquity.

Kendo *means the "way of the sword." Originating from samurai fencing, kendo now uses bamboo swords. Contestants wear extensive padding and protection. In a match, points are gained for hitting the head, torso, forearm, or throat.*

Kyudo, *or the "way of the bow," has close associations with Zen Buddhism. Although accuracy in hitting a target is important, the emphasis is also on concentration of mind and body.*

Judo *developed from jujitsu. A system of self-defense, it is well established as a sport in which throwing and grappling techniques are used to subdue an opponent.*

Karate *("empty hand") reached Japan in 1922 from Okinawa. A form of self-defense as well as spiritual and physical training, it has become a sport, consisting of explosive yet controlled kicks, punches, or strikes, and blocking moves.*

Aikido – *the "way of harmonious spirit" – uses an opponent's strength and speed against them. Training unites spiritual awareness and physical flexibility.*

THE HISTORY OF JAPAN

From the origins of the Japanese race to its military behavior in World War II, Japan's history is still subject to conjecture. What is indisputable is that the people of this archipelago were able to avail themselves of the fruits of continental civilization even as their isolation protected them from attack. As a result, Japan has one of the most distinct of all the many Chinese-influenced cultures in Asia.

During glacial epochs when the sea level was low, Japan's first inhabitants may have reached the archipelago overland from Sakhalin and Siberia, China and Korea, or the Okinawa islands. Crude stone tools found at sites across Honshu, Japan's main island, may date back 40,000 years.

Recent discoveries posit the emergence of the hunting and gathering society known as Jomon around 14,500 BC. Jomon pottery is among the world's oldest and includes vessels and figurines, particularly of women. Mounds of shells and other evidence indicate that the diet included fish, shellfish, deer, wild pigs, and wild plants and seeds. In the Kanto Plain (near Tokyo), the Jomon culture in its later stages included village-like groupings.

Rice agriculture and bronze, iron, and other crafts are believed to have reached Japan via Korea during the Yayoi period. The Yayoi people spread from the southern island of Kyushu to Honshu over time, pushing the earlier inhabitants north. Chinese histories record a visit by an envoy of Himiko, queen of Yamatai,

Clay figurine from the Kofun period

to the Chinese kingdom of Wei in 239, but Yamatai's location is still open to debate. Aristocratic orders emerged, including that of the emperor, said to be descended from the sun goddess Amaterasu. Figures of high rank were buried in *kofun* (tumuli), along with clay sculptures, armor, mirrors, and jewelry.

By the late 6th century, tribes that had migrated to the fertile lands of the Yamato Plain in Western Honshu were engaged in a power struggle over the introduction of Buddhism. Prince Shotoku, appointed regent by Empress Suiko in 593, helped seal victory for the pro-Buddhist camp.

In 701, the Taiho code, a penal and administrative system based on the Chinese model, was in place. Founded in 710 on the Yamato Plain, the city of Nara became the grand diocese of Buddhism and one of Asia's most splendid cities in its 74-year spell as Japan's first capital. With the completion of the *Man'yoshu*, the earliest known Japanese poetry, in 759, the culture began to establish a clear voice of its own.

PERIODS AT A GLANCE

Jomon	14,500–300 BC
Yayoi	300 BC–AD 300
Kofun/Asuka	300–710
Hakuho	645–710
Nara	710–794
Heian	794–1185
Kamakura	1185–1333
Muromachi	1333–1568
Momoyama	1568–1600
Tokugawa (Edo)	1600–1868
Meiji	1868–1912
Taisho	1912–1926
Showa	1926–1989
Heisei	1989–present

TIMELINE

300 BC–AD 300 Continental methods of farming, metalworking, pottery, and other skills reach southwestern Japan via Korea, and spread through the islands

710 Heijo-kyo (Nara) made capital

701 Taiho code put in place, the basis of the first Japanese legal system

AD 1	200	400	600

Yayoi earthenware

239 Himiko, queen of Yamatai, sends envoy to kingdom of Wei in China

587 Power struggle over introduction of Buddhism from China

712 *Kojiki*, Japan's oldest historical account, complete

◁ **Detail from a 16th-century screen painting, showing customs month-by-month in the Momoyama period**

COURT LIFE AND THE TALE OF GENJI

Court life in the Heian period focused on romance, aesthetic pursuits, and fastidious observation of precedent and ritual, as documented in the *Pillow Book* of court lady Sei Shonagon in the late 10th century. The *Tale of Genji*, written in the early 11th century by Sei Shonagon's rival, Murasaki Shikibu, a court lady of the Fujiwara clan, is possibly the world's oldest novel. It depicts the loves and sorrows of a fictitious prince, Genji, and, after he dies, the amorous pursuits of a man whom Genji thought was his son. The story has been illustrated in countless scrolls.

Tale of Genji scroll

HEIAN PERIOD

The Fujiwara family and Emperor Kammu built a new capital in Western Honshu known as Heian-kyo, now Kyoto, in 794. The new system, also based on Chinese models, held that the land and people were the property of the emperor. Tax-exempt status was granted to Buddhist institutions, large landholders, and settlers who would expand the state's frontiers. Meanwhile, the Fujiwara clan gained influence by acting as regents, and intermarriage with the imperial family. A pattern emerged in which emperors would abdicate, name a younger successor, enter a monastery, then exercise power from behind the scenes.

Buddhism's immense influence continued as proponents such as the Japanese Buddhist monk Saicho adapted it, launching hundreds of separate movements and sects.
Powerful temples grew militant in faceoffs with other temples and the government, creating armies of warrior-monks. Ironically, Buddhism's abhorrence of killing fed the nobility's contempt for the farmer-warriors – the early samurai – on the frontier, who battled the indigenous people and each other. After 1100, the court could no longer control infighting, and tensions rose between two clans of farmer-warriors from the northeast – the Taira and the Minamoto. By 1160, the ruthless Taira no Kiyomori was the most powerful man in Japan. But the Minamoto, led by the brothers Yoshitsune and Yoritomo, fought back to defeat the Taira and establish the first military shogunate at Kamakura *(see pp90–93)* in 1185.

Heian-period fan

KAMAKURA SHOGUNATE

Deliberately basing his government far from the imperial court in the village of Kamakura, Minamoto no Yoritomo carefully crafted a system that benefited his *bushi* (warrior) peers and brought 150 years of relative peace and stability. Yoritomo's direct heirs were shoguns only in name, however, as they were dominated by hereditary regents from the military Hojo family of Kamakura. The Hojo assumed the prerogatives of power while granting the imperial institution and nobility the privilege of signing off on policy.

Wooden statue of Minamoto no Yoritomo

TIMELINE

Portuguese in Kyushu – the "Southern Barbarians" who introduced firearms and Christianity to Japan

The *Tale of the Heike*, a chronicle of the war between the Taira and Minamoto clans, was first recited to lute accompaniment at this time. Temples and works of art were created in Kamakura, reflecting Yoritomo's warrior ideals of stoicism, self discipline, frugality, and loyalty. Zen Buddhism as imported from China was popular with the samurai, while the Pure-Land, True-Pure-Land, and Nichiren Buddhist sects promoted salvation to the common people.

Mongol invasions were repelled twice in the 13th century, but weakened the resources and command of Kamakura. The end came in 1333, when the Ashikaga clan, led by Takauji, toppled the Kamakura shogunate. However, the power systems instigated by Yoritomo and the Hojo influenced Japanese life for five more centuries.

Muromachi-period sword guard

MUROMACHI SHOGUNATE

With military power back with the imperial court in Kyoto, arts such as Noh drama and the tea ceremony flowered under the patronage of Shogun Ashikaga Yoshimasa. However, a succession dispute split the court into southern and northern factions. With leaders engaged in power struggles, chaos and famine were common. The nadir was reached during the Onin War (1467–77), when arson and looting destroyed much of Kyoto.

The Muromachi period, named for the Kyoto district where the Ashikagas built their palace, was a time of craven ambition that unleashed every class in society to vie for advantage. Warfare, once the exclusive business of samurai, now involved armies of footsoldiers (*ashigaru*) recruited from the peasantry, who could hope for promotion based on success in the battlefield.

In 1542, a trio of Portuguese from a shipwrecked junk emerged in Tanegashima, an island off Kyushu, and introduced firearms to Japan. Francis Xavier, a founding member of the Society of Jesus, established a Jesuit mission on Kyushu in 1549. The contact with Europeans further destabilized the political situation and set the stage for the first of the great unifiers, Oda Nobunaga, who entered Kyoto in 1568.

1180–85 Minamoto clan defeats the Taira and establishes Kamakura shogunate

Great Buddha statue at Kamakura

c.1400 Noh theatrical form flourishes under Shogun Ashikaga

1467 Devastating Onin War begins. Vast sections of Kyoto are burned over the next decade

| 1200 | 1300 | 1400 | 1500 |

1160 Ascendant Taira clan under Taira no Kiyomori suppresses its rivals, the Minamoto, and dominates court life

1281 Second Mongol invasion

1274 First Mongol invasion

1242 Emperor Shijo dies without naming an heir, setting off succession dispute

1560–80 Oda Nobunaga victorious in battles for hegemony of Japan

1428 Peasant uprising in Kyoto

1401 Formal relations with China reestablished

Screen depicting the Battle of Nagashino in 1575, won by Oda Nobunaga's 3,000 musketeers

MOMOYAMA PERIOD

After Japan had been racked by over a century of debilitating, inconclusive warfare, Oda Nobunaga, who rose through military ranks in the provinces, set out to unify the nation under his rule. From 1568–76 Nobunaga defeated rival warlord Asai Nagamasa; burned down Kyoto's main temple complex, where militant monks had long challenged the court and their Buddhist rivals; drove Ashikaga Yoshiaki into exile; and deployed 3,000 musketeers to massacre the Takeda forces at the Battle of Nagashino. In 1580, in his last great military exploit, Nobunaga

Momoyama-period detail at Nishi Hongan-ji, Kyoto

obtained the surrender of Ishiyama Hongan-ji, a nearly impregnable temple fortress in today's Osaka in Western Honshu. The temple had been the power base of the Buddhist True-Pure-Land sect. By 1582, when he was forced to commit suicide by a treasonous vassal, Nobunaga was in control of 30 of Japan's 68 provinces. Nobunaga's deputy, a warrior of humble birth named Toyotomi Hideyoshi, continued the work of unification, launching epic campaigns that brought Shikoku (1585), Kyushu (1587), the Kanto region (1590), and Northern Honshu (1591) under his control. He followed up by destroying many of the castles and forts belonging to potential rivals, confiscating weapons belonging to peasants, and devising a system in which peasants held their own small plots and paid a fixed tax directly to the central government.

In his later years, Hideyoshi ordered two unsuccessful invasions of Korea and persecuted the Portuguese missionaries and their Japanese converts. Like Oda Nobunaga, however, Hideyoshi never claimed the title of shogun but became obsessed with ensuring the perpetuation of his line after his death. Two years after his death in 1598, however, dissension among his retainers led to the Battle of Sekigahara, in which Tokugawa Ieyasu emerged victorious.

THE TOKUGAWA SHOGUNATE

Named shogun by the emperor in 1603, Ieyasu split the population into rigidly defined hereditary classes. To end turf wars, samurai were forbidden to own

TIMELINE

Osaka Castle

1615 Siege of Osaka Castle

1635 All foreign commerce confined to the artificial island of Dejima in Nagasaki Bay. From 1641, only Dutch and Chinese allowed access

1689 Haiku poet Basho departs on his journey to the north

1707 Last eruption of Mour Fuji

1600	1625	1650	1675	1700

1590 Hideyoshi controls all Japan

1597 Violent persecution of Christians in Nagasaki

1614 Christianity banned

1600 Tokugawa Ieyasu wins battle of Sekigahara, achieves hegemony over Japan

1657 Meireki fire in Edo kills over 100,000

Statue of Basho

1703 Suicide of the 47 *ronin*

land and could reside only within certain quarters of castle towns. Farmers were allotted small plots, which they had to cultivate. Artisans formed the next class, merchants the bottom. Movement between regions was regulated, and families or whole villages could be punished for crimes by their kin or neighbors.

The *daimyo* or lords who governed regions, now subject to Tokugawa authority, were shuffled to different regions if their service was not approved. After 1635, the *daimyo* and their samurai retinue were forced to reside every other year in the city of Edo (Tokyo), the new seat of the shogunate.

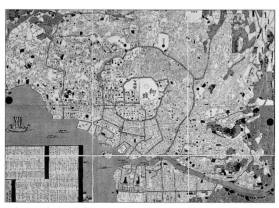

Fireman official's garment in Edo

ISOLATION AND THE RISE OF EDO
William Adams, an Englishman who reached Japan on a Dutch ship in 1600, served Ieyasu in various capacities over the next two decades (as portrayed in James Clavell's 1976 book *Shogun*). During this time, the English,

Dutch, Portuguese, Spanish, and New World governments made overtures to the shogunate on trade. However, the increasingly xenophobic Tokugawa regime restricted all foreign shipping to Nagasaki on the island of Kyushu from 1635; only Chinese and Dutch traders were allowed from 1641. This heralded 200 years of isolation from the rest of the world.

While Kyoto remained the official capital through the Tokugawa period, Edo eclipsed it in size and was probably the largest city in the world by around 1700. Edo also hosted an explosion of arts such as Kabuki and Bunraku theater *(see pp16–17)* and the *ukiyo-e* works *(see p55)* of Utamaro, Sharaku, Hokusai, and Hiroshige. Patrons included the merchant class and samurai.

In 1853 Commodore Matthew Perry steamed into Edo Bay leading a fleet of nine US vessels to challenge Japan's refusal to enter into international relations. Weakened by unrest from within its own and other ranks, the shogunate could only accede to Perry's demands. Samurai from the Satsuma, Choshu, and Tosa domains in Kyushu, Western Honshu, and Shikoku became the driving force behind a successful restoration of imperial power and a reorganization of the government carried out in 1868.

Early map of Edo, which outgrew Kyoto under the Tokugawa shogunate

A *Hokusai* view of Mount Fuji

1748 Kabuki drama *Chushingura* debuts, based on the suicide by 47 *ronin*

1831 Hokusai's *Thirty-Six Views of Mount Fuji* published

1725	1750	1775	1800	1825

1723 Love suicides *(joshi)*, spurred by rigid customs and hierachy during the Edo period, reach a peak

1782 Tenmei Famine claims as many as 900,000 lives

1853 Commodore Matthew Perry anchors in Edo Bay; Kanagawa Treaty between US and Japan signed

Woodblock print of Sino-Japanese War of 1894–5

MEIJI RESTORATION

Emperor Meiji (1852–1912) was 16 when the restoration of imperial rule was declared on January 3, 1868. Tokyo was swiftly made the new capital.

A new centralized system pressed for changes that would render Japan capable of competing with the West. Military conscription and the elimination of the hereditary samurai class were undertaken to create a modern fighting force, provoking furious resistance from samurai in 1874–6. *Daimyo* domains were gradually transformed into prefectures, although *daimyo* and court nobles lingered in the form of a new class called *kazoku*. Universal literacy became a goal. By 1884, tax and banking reforms, and an industrial strategy aimed at exports were underway. The Meiji Constitution of 1889, promulgated by the emperor, allowed the military direct access to the throne while creating a house of peers and a lower house.

Following disputes over control of the Korean peninsula, the Sino-Japanese War of 1894–5 ended with Japan's victory over China, but showed that greater military strength would be needed

Emperor Meiji (1852–1912), first Emperor of Japan

for the nation to contend as an imperial power equal with the West.

By the turn of the century, the transformation to an industrial economy, with textiles the chief export, was well underway. A second imperialist conflict, the Russo-Japanese war of 1904–5, ended with Japan aggrandizing its claims to Korea, which was annexed in 1910, and southern Manchuria in China.

During the final decade of Meiji's reign, the home ministry stressed reverence for the emperor, the family, the Shinto religion, and military and national heroes. Suppression of groups seen as enemies of the state became the government's prerogative.

WAR WITH CHINA AND WORLD WAR II

The attempt to transform Japan from a feudal to a modern industrial state caused severe dislocation. By 1929, when the stock market collapsed, resentment against those who had prospered from exports intensified. Young officers, chafing to restore national pride, began assassinating rich moderates, while militarists and oligarchs in the government believed that seizing land from China and Russia would secure raw materials and improve national security. At the same time, a Pan-Asianist movement, which saw Japan on a mission to lead Asia out of servility, construed the Chinese resistance to Japanese domination as an insult. By 1937, the country was embroiled in an unwinnable war with China that further estranged it from the rest of the world.

TIMELINE

1868 Meiji Restoration; Edo is renamed Tokyo and made capital	**1889** Imperial constitution promulgated	**1895** China cedes territory to Japan, ending war. Russia, France, and Germany force Japan to relinquish the territory

1910 Korea becomes Japanese colony

1932 In the May 15 incident, young naval officers assassinate prime minister and attempt coup

1865	1880	1895	1910	1925

1869 Colonization of Hokkaido begins

1890 Imperial Diet convenes for first time

Diet Building

1904 Russo-Japanese war begins

1894 Sino-Japanese war begins

1905 Treaty of Portsmouth ends war. Korea becomes a Japanese protectorate

1933 Japan withdraws from League of Nations

1923 Great Kanto Earthquake

Aftermath of the bombing of Tokyo in 1945

When the US cut off Japanese access to oil, Tokyo made the desperate decision to seize Pacific territory in a sneak attack on Pearl Harbor, Hawaii, in December 1941. A few months later, Japan took Southeast Asia.

By 1944, American bombers were decimating Japanese cities, but the Japanese army was determined not to surrender unconditionally, opting instead for a suicidal defensive strategy. In August 1945, the US dropped atomic bombs on Hiroshima and Nagasaki, and the Soviet Union entered the war in the Pacific. Emperor Hirohito ordered the cabinet to sue for peace.

Akihito, who was made emperor in 1989

JAPAN SINCE 1945

After World War II the Allied Occupation Force under General Douglas MacArthur began arriving as millions of homeless Japanese returned to bombed-out cities. The emperor renounced his divine status; land reform was promptly implemented; and war-crimes trials were soon underway.

By 1952, when the occupation ended, the neighboring war in Korea had turned into a boon for the Japanese economy. Industrial production surged

as the average household set its sights on obtaining a washing machine, refrigerator, and television.

In 1960, massive protests against the ratification of the US-Japan Security Treaty rocked Japan, leading to the cancellation of a visit by President Eisenhower. The prime minister resigned. His successors focused on economic growth. By the time of the Tokyo Olympics in 1964, annual growth was around ten percent and rising. Prosperity based on exports such as electronics, automobiles, and technological products made Japan one of the world's richest nations.

The recession of the 1990s was marked by unemployment, plummeting land values, and deflation. The effects of a shrinking economy were further conflated by the breakdown of the family, and rising crime. According to the media, the worst is over and the economy is now firmly back on track.

These days the products and artifacts of fashions, styles, and tastes are magnifying Japan's presence in the world, one which is elevating Japanese popular culture to a rank second in global terms only to that of the United States. As ever, Tokyo is the engine driving much of this change.

Tokyo skyline as seen from the Sumida River

1937 Sino-Japanese war of 1937–45 begins; 140,000 Chinese massacred in Nanjing

1945 Atomic bombs dropped on Hiroshima and Nagasaki; Japan surrenders

1995 Great Hanshin Earthquake in Kobe; fanatical cult releases sarin gas on Tokyo Subway

1997 Economic recession in Southeast Asia, spreading to Japan

2007 Shintaro Ishihara re-elected Tokyo Governor

1940	1955	1970	1985	2000	2015

武運長久 *Prayers of a soldier*

1964 Tokyo Olympics; first "bullet train"; government begins to promote computer industry

1989 Emperor Hirohito (Showa) dies; Akihito is new emperor

2008 Economy surges; Tokyo undergoes construction boom

Shinkansen ("bullet train")

1941 Japan enters World War II

TOKYO THROUGH THE YEAR

The seasons are closely observed in Japan. Many ritual observances are founded on traditional rural *matsuri* (festivals). There is nothing solemn about these events however, as hard-working, hard-playing Tokyoites enjoy nothing more than a good festival. The festivals, sports events, trade shows, flower exhibitions, and blossom-viewing all

New Year's sumo dedication ceremony

add up to a full cultural calendar. Each suburb also organizes its own festivals, more so during the summer months, when dancers in kimonos and Japanese drum groups perform, and clear skies explode with spectacular fireworks. In contrast, the winter months are devoted to travel, especially around New Year, and religious ceremonies.

SPRING

Spring symbolizes many important things in life. It is when the new economic year begins, students graduate, and projects are launched. While March and April can be rainy, May is usually sublime. The Japanese tend to value spring for its transience and the cherry, more than any other flower, embodies the imper-manence of life. However, there is nothing mournful or solemn about the vibrant cherry blossom-viewing parties held at parks throughout the city.

MARCH

Hina Matsuri (*Doll Festival, Mar 3*). Dolls dressed in traditional Heian-period imperial costumes are displayed in homes and public places.
Golden Dragon Dance (*Mar 18*). This colorful event takes place thrice in the day at Senso-ji temple in Asakusa.

APRIL

Hanami (*Cherry blossom-viewing, late Mar to Apr*). A glorious spring rite cele-brated wherever there are cherry trees, but most famously in Chidorigafuchi, Ueno Park, and Sumida Park.

Meiji Shrine Spring Festival (*Apr 2–May 3*). An extensive compendium of traditional cultural events attended by devotees, including colorful court dances, *yabusame* (horseback archery), and music performances.

Bugaku dancer, Meiji Shrine Festival

Hana Matsuri (*Buddha's Birthday, Apr 8*). Devotees pour sweet tea over a small image of the Buddha to honor his birth. Services are held at some temples.
Azalea Festival (*Apr 10–May 5*). Held at various venues, the best known is at the Nezu Shrine, where countless bushes grow along an embankment.
Tokyo International Anime Fair (*late Mar or early Apr*). Also known as Comiket, the world's largest event for fans of animation and manga. It is held at Tokyo Big Sight.

MAY

Kodomo no hi (*Children's Day, May 5*). Focusing largely on boys, families fly colorful *koi-no-bori* (carp streamers), symbolizing strength and determination.
Summer Sumo Tournament (*mid-May*). This 15-day event is held in the Kokugikan hall in Ryogoku.
Kanda Matsuri (*Sat & Sun before May 15, alternate, odd-numbered years*). One of the city's three big festivals. Floats and *mikoshi* (portable shrines) parade through the streets around the Kanda Myojin Shrine.
Sanja Matsuri (*3rd Fri–Sun in May*). A wild and heady mix of dance, music, ritual, and the jostling of heavy portable shrines, near Asakusa Jinja.
Design Festa (*mid–late May*). Asia's biggest art event. Thousands of people set up displays at this two-day fair at Tokyo Big Sight.

Visitors at the resplendent Azalea Festival

AVERAGE DAILY HOURS OF SUNSHINE

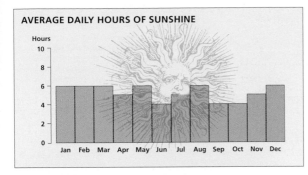

Sunshine Chart
The amount of sunshine per month in Tokyo does not vary greatly, even in the winter months. Winters can see temperatures drop to freezing but the clear skies are rarely disturbed by rain or snow.

Spectacular fireworks display on the Sumida River

SUMMER

When restaurants serve shaved ice, cold noodles, and glasses of chilled barley tea you know the humid summer days are upon the city. The clammy June rains can seem relentless. In August, as people return to their hometowns to celebrate O-Bon, the city is pleasantly quiet. Spectacular firework festivals along the banks of the Sumida and Edogawa rivers during the O-Bon festival add a splash of vivid color to the season.

JUNE

Iris Viewing *(early to mid-Jun)*. The iris garden in the grounds of the Meiji-jingu Shrine and at the Horikiri Iris Garden, Katsushika ward, offer the best viewing.

Sanno-Sai *(mid-Jun)*. In a festival that dates back to the founding of Edo, locals in historical costumes take out processions of *mikoshi*, accompanied by music and dancing at Hie Shrine.

JULY

Asagao Ichi *(Morning Glory Fair, Jul 6–8)*. Dozens of merchants set up stalls outside Iriya Kishibojin temple to sell flowers associated with the horticultural tastes of the Edo era.
Tanabata Matsuri *(Star Festival, Jul 7)*. Based on a Chinese legend; this is said to be the only day when two stars can meet as lovers across the milky way. Branches of bamboo are decorated with paper streamers inscribed with scribbled wishes, sometimes in the form of poetry.

Hanabl Taikai *(last Sat in Jul)*. A spectacular fireworks display on the Sumida river near Asakusa. The river turns into a sheet of red, green, and violet as lantern-lit boats take to the water.

AUGUST

O-Bon *(Festival of the Dead, mid-Aug)*. Family members return home at a time when, according to a Buddhist belief, the spirits also return to earth. Ancestral graves are visited and tended, and there are joyful Bon-Odori dances and festivals.
Koenji Awa Odori *(late Aug)*. Thousands of participants gather along Koenji's main street to join in the amusing Fool's Dance.
Samba Festival *(last Sat in Aug)*. Dancers from Rio join local samba devotees along Asakusa's Kaminarimon-dori, for an event that draws over half a million spectators.

Vibrantly costumed dancer at the Samba Festival

AVERAGE MONTHLY RAINFALL

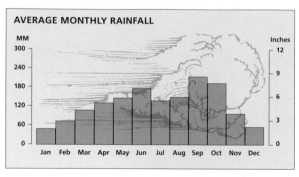

Rainfall Chart
Tokyo's rainy season lasts all through June and into the early days of July. September and October typhoons can bring squalls. Fall is generally a dry season. April has unpredictable rain showers.

FALL

Although the summer heat can linger through September, fall is a gentle season, with many fine, clear days and little rainfall. The ginkgo leaf is the symbol of Tokyo and avenues of the yellow-leaved trees can be seen throughout the city. Chrysanthemum festivals are held in temples and gardens. Open-air food stands called *yatai,* and convenience stores start to prepare *oden* (fish-cake stew) towards the end of the season signaling cooler days to come.

Women in traditional costumes at the Jidai Matsuri Festival

Visitors try the latest technology at the Tokyo Game Show

SEPTEMBER

Tokyo Game Show *(mid-Sep).* Held at the gigantic convention center at Makuhari Messe on Tokyo Bay, the three-day event attracts thousands of visitors.

Hachiman-gu Festival *(Sep 14–16).* Horseback archery and a procession of floats draw a large crowd to this important Kamakura shrine.
Ningyo-Kuyo *(late Sep).* Hopeful couples pray for children by offering dolls at the Kiyomizu Kannon-do temple in Ueno Park. Priests make a ritual fire, placing last year's dolls on the pyre.

OCTOBER

Tokyo International Film Festival *(late Oct).* The largest in Asia, the focus is on films from Asia and Japan.
Chrysanthemum Viewing *(late Oct–mid-Nov).* Chrysanthemum pavilions are erected in Shinjuku Gyoen Garden; flower dolls are displayed at Yushima Tenjin shrine.
Edo Tenka Matsuri *(late Oct, alternate, odd-numbered years).* A parade to commemorate the birth of Edo.

Sony's humanoid robot exhibit

NOVEMBER

Tokyo Designer's Week *(early Nov).* Art enclaves dotted around the city showcase the latest trends in the field of fashion, video graphics, furniture, and interior design.
Tokyo Jidai Matsuri *(Festival of the Ages, Nov 3).* Locals in period costumes representing figures from Japanese history parade around Asakusa's Senso-ji temple. This is a great photo opportunity.
Shichi-Go-San *(Seven-Five-Three Children's Festival, Nov 15).* Children of these ages are dressed up in kimonos for visits to shrines in appreciation of their health and to pray for further blessings.
International Robot Exhibition *(late Nov to early Dec, alternate, odd-numbered years).* Billed as the world's largest trade show focusing on robotics, it brings together an exciting array of the latest in technology and products.

AVERAGE MONTHLY TEMPERATURE

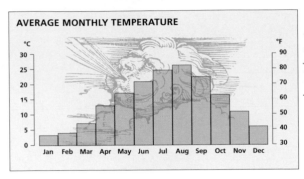

°C / °F

30	90
25	80
20	70
15	60
10	50
5	40
0	30

Jan Feb Mar Apr May Jun Jul Aug Sep Oct Nov Dec

Temperature Chart
Spring is comfortable for most visitors. Summer temperatures can be misleading. June to September are muggy with high levels of humidity. Winter temperatures can drop to freezing. May and October are the most pleasant months with crisp, clear skies.

WINTER

Winter can be cold in Tokyo, however there is only a day or two of snowfall. The return of *mochi* (rice cakes) and little jars of warmed up sake are seasonal signs. An exodus takes place at Oshogatsu (New Year), which is one of the year's peak travel times. For those who remain at home, it is a chance to enjoy traditional New Year dishes and to offer prayers for the coming year.

DECEMBER

Hagoita Ichi
(Battledore Fair, Dec 17–19). Ornate battledores, sold in the precincts of Senso-ji Temple, feature the faces of famous Kabuki actors, celebrities, and sports stars.

Kabuki actor in costume

Joya-no-Kane *(midnight Dec 31).* Temple bells begin to toll at midnight, 108 rings representing the 108 human sins that must be expunged.

JANUARY

Oshogatsu *(New Year's Day).* Japan's most important religious festival. The first few days are family-oriented. People pray at temples for the coming new year.
Water Purification Rituals *(Jan 10–12).* A ritual cleansing by both young and old. The best places to catch this event are at Kanda Myojin and Teppozu Inari shrines.
Seijin no hi *(Coming-of-Age Day, 2nd Mon in Jan).* Young people turning 20 this year celebrate their passage to adulthood.

FEBRUARY

Setsubun *(Feb 3 or 4).* Marking the first day of spring on the Buddhist calendar, temple priests and celebrities throw dried soy beans into crowds of onlookers, symbolizing the casting out of bad spirits.
Plum Viewing *(late Feb).* Yushima Tenjin shrine is a famous spot, though there are few plum trees here. Open-air tea ceremonies and floral exhibits are displayed, and plum bonsai are sold.

PUBLIC HOLIDAYS

If a public holiday falls on a Sunday, the following Monday is also a public holiday.

New Year's Day (Jan 1)
Coming-of-Age Day (2nd Mon in Jan)
National Foundation Day (Feb 11)
Vernal Equinox Day (Mar 21)
Showa Day (Apr 29)
Constitution Memorial Day (May 3)
Midori Day (May 4)
Children's Day (May 5)
Maritime Day (Jul 20)
Respect for the Aged Day (3rd Mon in Sep)
Fall Equinox Day (Sep 23)
Health-Sports Day (2nd Mon in Oct)
Culture Day (Nov 3)
Labor Thanksgiving Day (Nov 23)
Emperor's Birthday (Dec 23)

Braving the icy waters during a purification ritual

TOKYO AREA
BY AREA

Tokyo at a Glance

Japan's capital is situated on the banks of the Sumida
River, by Tokyo Bay. As the fishing village of Edo it
became the shogunate's center of power in 1590. The
Shitamachi (low city) of merchants and artisans served
the political and intellectual elite in the Yamanote (high
city) on the hills to the west. Renamed Tokyo and made
capital in 1868, the city was devastated by the Great
Kanto Earthquake of 1923, followed by World War II
bombing. It has since reinvented itself as one of the
world's most modern, exciting, and energizing cities.
Transportation is efficient – the easy-to-use JR Yamanote
line circles the city, subway lines crisscross the center
(*see* Back End Paper), and *shinkansen* lines link it with
the rest of the country. It can be difficult to find individual
buildings by their addresses *(see p171)*. The Tokyo
Street Finder *(see pp180–89)* locates all the sights,
restaurants, and hotels mentioned in this guide.

LOCATOR MAP

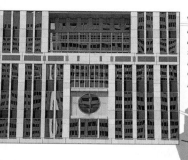

West Shinjuku (see pp62–3) *is an
area of soaring skyscrapers, providing
a visible manifestation of the corporate
wealth of Tokyo. The most impressive
buildings are the Tokyo Metropolitan
Government Offices, designed by
Kenzo Tange.*

**WESTERN
TOKYO**
(see pp58–69)

Shibuya (see pp66–7) *is a
mixture of large department
stores and smaller shops, all
catering to young consumers.
Adjacent to Shibuya are the
equally fashion-oriented
areas of Harajuku and
Minami-Aoyama.*

East Shinjuku (see
pp60–61) *comes alive
when West Shinjuku
shuts down. It
encompasses a red-
light area, countless
bars, and various
forms of entertain-
ment from movies to
pachinko parlors.*

◁ **A bustling shopping street in Shinjuku**

Ueno Park (see pp48–9) *is one of Tokyo's most extensive green spaces, always crowded with locals. Spectacular in the cherry blossom season, it also merits an unhurried visit at other times of the year for its boating ponds and many temples, shrines, and museums.*

Tokyo National Museum (see pp50–53) *consists of four main imperial buildings, dominating the northern reaches of Ueno Park, which exhibit a stunning array of Japanese art, and archaeological artifacts. It is the largest such collection in the world and includes some fascinating items from elsewhere in Asia including China and Korea.*

NORTHERN TOKYO
(see pp46–57)

CENTRAL TOKYO
(see pp36–45)

Senso-ji Temple (see pp56–7) *offers an insight into the traditional side of Tokyo. Still attracting thousands of worshipers daily, it also has many craft shops lining its main approach.*

| 0 kilometers | 2 |
| 0 miles | 1 |

Ginza (see pp38–9) *provides the archetypal Tokyo shopping experience, with its venerable department stores and small, exclusive shops, which have been joined by various international designer boutiques. Some excellent restaurants are also located here.*

CENTRAL TOKYO

Situated to the north and west of the Sumida River, this area has been at the heart of Tokyo since the first shogun, Ieyasu, built his castle and capitol where the Imperial Palace still stands today. Destroyed by a series of disasters, including the Great Kanto Earthquake of 1923 and the Allied bombing in World War II, the area has reinvented itself several times over. Ginza and Nihonbashi were commercial centers and are still prosperous, offering a mix of department stores and side-street boutiques. The new sky-scraper development, Shiodome, is another prominent commercial center. For more down-to-earth shopping, there is the Jimbocho area for books, Akihabara for electronics, and the early-morning Tsukiji Fish Market. Central Tokyo's continuing political importance is evident in the Hibiya and Marunouchi districts, and the area is also home to two very different shrines – Kanda and Yasukuni. A selection of green spaces provides a respite from the bustle elsewhere.

A kimono-clad woman at Kanda Myojin Shrine

SIGHTS AT A GLANCE

Notable Districts
Akihabara Electronics District **17**
Ginza *see pp38–9* **1**
Hibiya District **10**
Jimbocho Booksellers' District **14**
Marunouchi District **8**
Nihonbashi District **7**

Historic Buildings
Diet Building **10**
Imperial Palace **11**
Kabuki-za Theater **2**

Shrines
Kanda Myojin Shrine **16**
Yasukuni Shrine **13**

Modern Architecture
Tokyo International Forum **9**
Tokyo Tower **6**
Shiodome **5**

Parks and Gardens
Hama Detached Palace Garden **4**
Kitanomaru Park **12**
Koishikawa Korakuen Garden **15**
Shiba Park **6**

Market
Tsukiji Fish Market **3**

KEY

- Street-by-Street map *pp38–9*
- **S** Subway station
- **R** Train station
- Long-distance bus station
- **i** Tourist information

GETTING THERE

The best ways to get around are by Yamanote line or subway, or, for smaller distances, on foot. The Yamanote line stops at Akihabara, Kanda, Tokyo, and Shimbashi stations, while a number of subway lines crisscross the area.

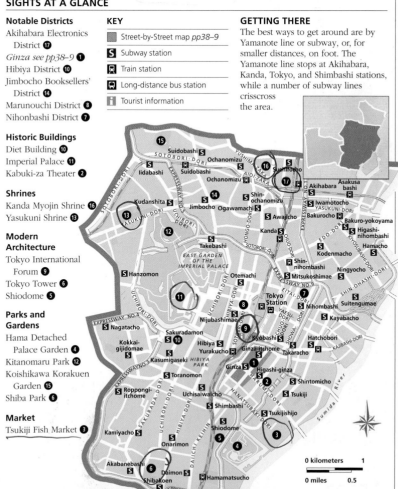

Street-by-Street: Ginza ❶
銀座

When Ieyasu moved his military capital to Edo in 1590, Ginza was all swamp and marshland. Once filled in, the area attracted tradesmen and merchants. The silver mint that provided Ginza's name, "silver place," was built in 1612. In 1872 fire destroyed everything and, with the Meiji Restoration in full swing, the government ordered English architect Thomas Waters to rebuild the area in red brick. From then on it was the focus for Western influences and all things modern, and is still one of Tokyo's prime market centers. Tiny shops selling local crafts mix with galleries, department stores, and the ultra-modern Sony showroom for an unrivaled shopping experience.

Shoppers at the landmark Ginza Yon-chome crossing

Mullion Building, housing Hankyu and Seibu department stores

Hankyu and Seibu department stores focus on fashions, with a mix of Japanese and international labels.

Gallery Center Building
On the second floor of this modern building are a number of exclusive galleries showcasing Japanese and Western art. On the fifth is an auction house, and the sixth has the Youkyo Art Hall, with exhibits by artists working in different media.

Ginza Noh Theater

Namiki-Dori and Chuo-Dori are now called "Brand Street" with boutiques such as Gucci, Dior, Louis Vuitton, and Cartier.

The Asahi Building contains a traditional kimono shop, silversmiths, and several boutiques.

HARUMI-DORI

SOTOBORI-DORI

NAMIKI-DORI

MIYUKI-DORI

SUZU-

Sony Showroom
Sony's latest technology and electronic gadgets are on display on several floors here, and many can be tried out.

KEY

- - - Suggested walk route

▬▬ Train line

Printemps is a branch of the French department store. Parisian influence came to Ginza in the 1930s and can also be seen in the nearby French cafés and boutiques.

LOCATOR MAP
See Tokyo Street Finder map 5

Wako Department Store
Opposite the San'ai Building, this enduring landmark was originally built in 1894. Its clocktower is a popular symbol of Ginza, and the window displays are always entertaining.

SOBORI-DORI

MIKI-DORI

CHUO-DORI

Matsuya department store is another huge store stocking everything from food to bonsai plants. Restaurant City offers a large range of cuisines.

Nihonbashi

Mikimoto
Visit the glittering interior of this shop, the original producer of cultured pearls.

Mitsukoshi Department Store
This classic Tokyo store retains an aura of glamor – some people still dress up to shop here. Do not miss the particularly luxurious kimono department.

S

Kabuki-za Theater *(see p40)*

Ginza Yon-chome crossing, one of the busiest in the world, is Ginza's main intersection.

0 meters 100

0 yards 100

San'ai Building
Made of glass, this building is at its best at dusk when the lights and neon signs inside shine through the glass, creating a magical effect.

The curved gable at the front of the Kabuki-za Theater

Kabuki-za Theater ❷
歌舞伎座

Map 5 C3. 4-12-15 Ginza. **Tel** (03) 3541-3131. 🚇 Higashi-Ginza stn, Toei Asakusa & Hibiya lines. 🖥 www.shochiku.co.jp/play/kabukiza/theater/index.html

Tokyo's principal theater for Kabuki (see p17) opened in 1889 during the reign of Emperor Meiji – a part of Kabuki's shift from popular daytime entertainment for the Shitamachi masses in Asakusa to a more highbrow art form.

The building is one of the striking examples of the use of Western building materials and techniques in traditional Japanese style. Its curved front gable was added in 1925 after earthquake damage in 1923. Partially destroyed by the Allied bombing of 1945, the theater was rebuilt in 1951. Afternoon matinees and evening performances are held almost daily (see p154–5).

Tsukiji Fish Market ❸
築地中央卸売市場

Map 5 C4. 🚇 Tsukijishijo stn, Toei Oedo line; Tsukiji stn, Hibiya line. ◯ 5am–noon Mon–Sat.

Officially known as Tokyo Central Wholesale Market, a visit to the world's largest fish market is an experience unique to Tokyo. It moved to this crowded location from Nihonbashi in 1935 after the 1923 Great Kanto earthquake and its subsequent fires destroyed the old one. Every morning except Sunday, auctions are held from about 5am to 10am. During this time 15,000 restaurateurs and food sellers from all over the city buy 450 types of sea produce from about 1,700 stalls. The market itself resembles a huge hangar filled with a maze of tiny stalls, each crammed with fish still dripping sea water. Despite the rush, people are tolerant of casual visitors. On the same site is a large wholesale vegetable market.

A small bridge marks the entrance to the market. Just before the bridge is **Namiyoke Inari Jinja** (Wave-repelling Fox Shrine), where fishermen and traders come to pray for safety and prosperity. Opposite is a street lined with shops selling everything from dried tuna to porcelain dishes. In the alleys to the right are more shops and stalls where excellent and cheap sushi, tempura, and even curry are sold.

When leaving the market, turn left before the bridge for a line of shops and small restaurants. The river wharf, where boats unload, is over the bridge to the left.

A box of fish from Tsukiji market

Hama Detached Palace Garden ❹
浜離宮庭園

Map 5 B4. **Tel** (03) 3541-0200. 🚇 Shiodome stn, Oedo line. 🚉 Shimbashi stn, Yamanote line. 🚢 Sumida River Trip. ◯ 9am–5pm. (Last adm 30 mins before closing.)

Situated where the Sumida River empties into Tokyo Bay, this 62-acre (25-hectare) garden was built in 1654 as a retreat for the shogun's family and opened to the public in 1945. US President Ulysses S. Grant stayed in a villa in the gardens during his visit in 1879 and sipped green tea with Emperor Meiji in Nakajima teahouse.

TUNA FISH SUPPLIES

Tsukiji market specializes in *maguro* (tuna) from as far away as New Zealand and the North Atlantic. Japan consumes about 30 percent of the annual global 1.7 million ton tuna catch, and eats 80 percent of its tuna raw, as sashimi, which requires the best cuts of fish. Suppliers can demand prices of up to 10–20 times that of the lower-grade tuna. The Pacific Ocean's South Blue Fin tuna, a favorite for sashimi, is endangered. The catch is managed and tuna numbers currently seem stable, although that may be due to the recession of the 1990s (from which Japan is now slowly recovering). If the economy in Japan starts to boom, South Blue Fin stocks could once again be put under pressure.

Rows of frozen tuna at Tsukiji fish market

The lovely garden grounds surrounding the duck ponds are still a pleasant place to stroll and sit. All of the original teahouses and villas, trees, and vegetation burned down after a bombing raid on November 29, 1944. **Nakajima Teahouse** has been rebuilt, seeming to float over the large pond. Green tea and Japanese sweets are available here.

Nakajima teahouse in Hama Detached Palace Garden

Shiodome **❺**

汐留

Map 5 C4, 4 F3. **S** *Shiodome stn, Toei Oedo line;* **R** *Shimbashi stn, Yamanote line, Toei Asakusa line;* **R** *Shiodome stn, Yurikamome line.*

Before industrialization, the ocean-facing parts of Tokyo Bay were famous for their *nori* (seaweed) cultivation. Twenty years ago, waterfront development became Tokyo's new frontier. The **Shiodome City Center** complex, opened in 2003, is one of the more successful of these waterfront developments. Within this grove of ultra-modern skyscrapers are the impressive, triangular **Shiodome Media Tower**, headquarters of Kyodo News, and **Acty Shiodome**,

the tallest residential building in Japan. Indoor malls and a spacious outdoor piazza provide exciting places to dine or shop. Nearby is **ADMT**, the Advertising Museum of Tokyo, located in the basement of the **Caretta Shiodome**, which has the offices of Japan's largest advertising agency – Dentsu. Beyond the northern boundary of Shiodome is the **Nagakin Capsule Tower**, a curious apartment complex based on the manned rocket designs of the 1970s. For greater exploration of the Tokyo Bay area, take the Yurikamome Line from Shiodome station in the direction of **Rainbow Bridge**, and enjoy great views of the Sumida River and the futuristic island of Odaiba *(see p75)*.

Shiba Park and Tokyo Tower **❻**

芝公園と東京タワー

Map 5 A4, 2 F5. **S** *Shiba-Koen stn, Toei Mita line.* **Tokyo Tower** **S** *Akabanebashi stn, Oedo line.* **Tel** *(03) 3433-5111.* ◯ *9am–10pm daily (to 9pm Aug).* 🎫 *(extra for higher viewpoint).*

Shiba Park is a rather fragmented green space. A large part of it is a golf driving range, but a portion in the east is pleasantly landscaped with woods and a water course. The park used to be the Tokugawa family's graveyard and at its center is **Zojo-ji**, the family

The soaring Tokyo Tower, the city's highest viewpoint

temple. It was founded in 1393 and Ieyasu moved it here in 1598 to protect his new capital. The present-day temple dates from 1974; nearby are the rebuilt Daimon (big gate) and the Sanmon (great gate), built in 1622, the oldest wooden structure in Tokyo.

To the west of the park is the striking **Tokyo Tower**, standing on the edge of the Roppongi District *(see pp68–9)*. Completed in 1958, at 1,093-ft (333-m) tall, it is higher than the Eiffel Tower in Paris, on which it is based. The ground floor has an aquarium and elevators to the observation deck. Other floors house amusements. Two viewpoints – the main one at 492 ft (150 m) and a higher one at 820 ft (250 m) – offer spectacular views of Tokyo Bay, the nearby districts of Shimbashi and Ginza, and Mount Fuji on a clear day.

The Shidome skyline from the vantage point of the Sumida River

View of Mitsukoshi's central hall in Nihonbashi

Nihonbashi District ❼

日本橋地区

Map 5 C1–2, 6 D1. **S** *Tokyo stn, Marunouchi line; Nihonbashi stn, Ginza, Tozai & Toei Asakusa lines; Mitsukoshimae stn, Ginza & Hanzomon lines.* **⎘** *Tokyo stn, many lines.* **Tokyo Stock Exchange Tel** *(03) 3665-1881.* **◯** *9am–4pm Mon–Fri.* **Kite Museum Tel** *(03) 3271-2465.* **◯** *11am–5pm daily.* **Bridgestone Museum of Art Tel** *(03) 3563-0241.* **◯** *10am–8pm Tue–Sat, 10am–6pm Sun & public hols.* 🅰

Once the mercantile center of Edo and Meiji Tokyo, Nihonbashi means "Japan's bridge," after the expansive bridge over the Nihonbashi River that marked the start of the five major highways of the Edo period. After the destruction of the 1923 earthquake, shops, businesses, and banks started relocating to Marunouchi and Ginza.

Although the area never regained its original stature, it is still a thriving commercial center, with dozens of bank headquarters as well as huge department stores and smaller traditional shops. **Mitsukoshi** *(see p142)* has its main store here, on Mitsukoshimae. It started as a kimono shop in 1673. Head for the basement food market with its free samples, and the sixth-floor bargain counters where you can jostle with Tokyo's thrifty elite. To the west of the store, the **Bank of Japan**, built in

1896 and modeled on the Neo-Classical Berlin National Bank, was the first Western-style building designed by a Japanese architect, Tatsuno Kingo.

On the north bank of Nihonbashi River, just before **Nihonbashi Bridge**, is the bronze marker from which distances to and from Tokyo are still measured. The bridge here today dates from 1911.

On the south bank of the river, east of the bridge, is the **Tokyo Stock Exchange**, which lists around 2,500 companies, making it one of the world's top five. This is a great place to see how important commerce remains in Tokyo. The visitors' observation deck overlooks the trading floor and has interesting exhibits comparing stock markets worldwide.

West of the Stock Exchange is the **Kite Museum**, located on the fifth floor of a well-known eatery, Tameikan. The restaurant's former owner, a kite enthusiast, founded the museum which exhibits kites from China and other Asian countries. To the south of Nihonbashi bridge, the **Bridgestone Museum of Art** holds one of Japan's best collections of Western art, including works by Manet, Picasso, Rouault, and Brancusi. To its north, the **Pokemon Center** is a shop devoted to the famous animation characters.

South of the museum, the **National Film Center** *(see p151)* hosts regular screenings of Japanese and foreign films. There are permanent exhibits of film equipment, and other film-related items. Books, film posters, and archival material are easily available in the center's bookstore and public library.

Marunouchi District ❽

丸の内地区

Map 5 B1–2. **S** *Tokyo stn, Marunouchi line.* **⎘** *Tokyo stn, many lines.* **Tokyo Station Gallery Tel** *(03) 3212-2485.* **◯** *10am–7pm daily.*

This district lies to the south and west of Tokyo Station. During the Edo era, it earned the name "Gambler's Meadow" as its isolation made it an ideal place to gamble secretly. In the Meiji period it was used by the army, who sold it in 1890 to Mitsubishi. The arrival of the railroad increased Marunouchi's appeal as a business site.

Tokyo Station, designed by Tatsuno Kingo and completed in 1914, is a brick building based on the design of Amsterdam station. Its handsome dome was badly damaged in the 1945 air raids and subsequently replaced by the polyhedron here today. It houses the small **Tokyo Station Gallery**.

Facing the station, the striking **Marunouchi Building** is the area's new landmark, housing shops, restaurants, and offices. A short walk west of the station over Wadakura Bridge leads to the **Wadakura Fountain Park**, with interesting water features. Returning over the bridge, cross Hibiya-dori and turn right to the **Meiji Seimeikan Building** (1934), with its huge Corinthian columns. Hiroshige, the woodblock print artist, was born on this site in 1797. Beyond, the **Imperial Theater** *(see p181),* founded in 1910, shows Broadway musicals and Japanese popular dramas.

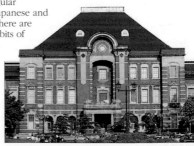

Tokyo Station's Western-style façade

Tokyo International Forum ❾

東京国際フォーラム

Map 5 B2. **S** *Yurakucho stn, Yurakucho line; Tokyo stn, Marunouchi line.* **R** *Tokyo & Yurakucho stns, many lines.* ◯ *8am–11pm daily.*

Designed by New York-based architect Rafael Viñoly, and completed in 1996, the Forum is one of downtown Tokyo's most distinctive buildings *(see p15)*. A cultural center, it is made up of two buildings – a curved, glass atrium soaring 200 ft (60m), and a cube-like, white structure housing four halls (the largest seating 5,012). A tree-shaded courtyard separates the two, while glass walkways provide an overhead link.

The interior of the huge atrium has a ceiling resembling a ship's hull. Inside the Forum are a number of shops, cafés, and restaurants, all with state-of-the-art facilities. The Cultural Information Lobby within the complex offers Internet facilities and has an audio-visual library highlighting Tokyo's attractions.

The imposing granite exterior of the Diet Building

Hibiya District and the Diet Building ❿

日比谷地区と国会議事堂

Map 2 F3, 5 A2, 5 B2. **S** *Kokkai-Gijidomae stn, Chiyoda & Marunouchi lines; Hibiya stn, Toei Mita, Chiyoda & Hibiya lines.* **Hibiya Park** ◯ *24 hours daily.* **Diet Building** ◯ *9am–5pm Mon–Fri.* 📷 *(compulsory, by reservation).* **Idemitsu Museum of Arts** *Tel (03) 5777-8600.* ◯ *10am–5pm Tue–Sun, (to 7pm Fri).*

Central Tokyo's only large, Western-style park, **Hibiya Park** is the focus of Hibiya district. The park's location, close to political centers, makes it a favorite place for public protests. The large bandstand is also used for concerts. Completed in 1936, the **Diet Building** houses the legislature of the Japanese government, originally established as the Imperial Diet in the Meiji era. Tours (in Japanese only) cover the Diet chamber, where you can see the deliberations of Diet members, and the extravagantly decorated rooms used by the emperor for official functions. Overlooking the Imperial Palace, in the Tei Geki building, the **Idemitsu Museum of Arts** features one of the city's finest displays of Japanese and Asian art.

The airy glass-and-metal interior of Tokyo International Forum

Imperial Palace ⓫

皇居

Map 3 A5, 3 B5, 5 A1, 5 B1. **S** *Nijubashi stn, Chiyoda line.* **R** *Tokyo stn, many lines.* **Imperial Palace** ◯ *Jan 2, Dec 23.* **East Garden of the Imperial Palace** *Tel (03) 3213-2050.* ◯ *9am–4pm Tue–Thu, Sat, Sun (Nov–Feb: to 3:30pm).*

Ieyasu, the first Tokugawa shogun, started building his castle here in 1590. In the Edo period his successors made this into the world's largest castle; now only the inner circle remains. The emperor and his family still live in the western part of the grounds in the **Imperial Palace**, rebuilt after the previous one was bombed during World War II. Public access is allowed twice a year – at New Year and on the emperor's birthday. The rest of the grounds, bounded by the moat, are divided into public parks.

The most famous landmark is the **Nijubashi**, a double-arched stone bridge, east of the palace. Completed in 1888, it was the palace's main entrance. The huge **Otemon** (Big Hand Gate), rebuilt in 1967, was the main gate before Nijubashi was built. Now it is the entrance to the **East Garden of the Imperial Palace**. Just inside is **Sannomaru Shozokan**, a collection of art and artifacts of the Showa Emperor. Beyond is the Edo-era **Hyakunin Basho**, where 100 samurai lived while standing guard in shifts. Behind is the **Honmaru**, the castle's main keep, now just massive stone walls with good views from the top. To the east of the Honmaru is the **Ninomaru** garden, landscaped by shogun Iemitsu in 1630.

A glimpse of the Imperial Palace over the stone bridge Nijubashi

fun, including virtual bike rides and electricity demonstrations (all explanations are in Japanese).

Five minutes beyond, over a main road, and left down the hill, is the **National Museum of Modern Art**. The permanent collection comprises Japanese works from the 1868 Meiji Restoration to the present day; visiting exhibits are often excellent. Nearby is the National Museum of Modern Art's **Crafts Gallery**. Inside this 1910 Neo-Gothic brick building is an exquisite collection of modern workings of traditional Japanese crafts – pottery, lacquerware, and damascene (etched metal artifacts). Some pieces are for sale.

Tokyoites enjoying an outdoor summer picnic in Kitanomaru Park

Kitanomaru Park ⑫

北の丸公園

Map 3 A5. Ⓢ *Kudanshita stn, Hanzomon, Toei Shinjuku & Tozai lines; Takebashi stn, Tozai line.* **National Museum of Modern Art Tel** *(03) 5777-8600.* ◯ *10am–5pm Tue–Sun.* 🖳 **www.momat.go.jp/english Crafts Gallery Tel** *(03) 3211-7781.* ◯ *10am–5pm Tue–Sun.* 🖳 **Science and Technology Museum Tel** *(03) 3212-8544.* ◯ *9:30am–4pm daily.* 🖳 **www.jsf.or.jp/english**

Lying to the north of the Imperial Palace, Kitanomaru Park is reached through the massive **Tayasumon** gate. A former ground for the Imperial Palace Guard, the area became a park in 1969. Before entering, walk past with Tayasumon on the left to reach **Chidorigafuchi** (the west moat), one of Tokyo's most beautiful cherry blossom-viewing spots. Row boats can be rented here.

Within Kitanomaru's pleasant grounds are a number of buildings. Near Tayasumon is the **Nippon Budokan** *(see p152)*. Built for the 1964 Olympics martial arts competition, it is now used mostly for rock concerts. A short walk farther on is the **Science and Technology Museum**. Some of the interactive exhibits are

Yasukuni Shrine ⑬

靖国神社

Map 2 F1. **Tel** *(03) 3261-8326.* Ⓢ *Kudanshita stn, Hanzomon, Tozai & Toei Shinjuku lines.* ◯ *24 hours daily.* **www.yasukuni.or.jp/english Yushukan** ◯ *9am–5:30pm daily Mar–Oct; 9am–5pm Nov–Feb.* 🖳

The 2.5 million Japanese, soldiers and civilians, who have died in war since the Meiji Restoration are enshrined at Yasukuni Jinja (Shrine of Peace for the Nation), which was dedicated in 1879. Its history makes it a sobering place to visit.

Until the end of World War II, Shinto was the official state religion, and the ashes of all who died in war were brought here regardless of the families' wishes. Unsettling for some of Japan's neighbors, the planners and leaders of World War II and the colonizers

of China and Korea are also enshrined here, including wartime prime minister, Tojo Hideki, and eight other Class-A war criminals. Visits by cabinet ministers are controversial.

Beside the shrine is the **Yushukan**, a museum dedicated to the war dead. Many exhibits put a human face to Japan at war; under a photograph of a smiling young officer is a copy of his last letter home, and there are mementos of a nurse who died from overwork. Romanticized paintings of Japanese soldiers in Manchuria and displays of guns, planes, and even a locomotive from the Thai-Burma Railroad may be disturbing to some.

Jimbocho Booksellers' District ⑭

神保町古本屋街

Map 3 B4–5. Ⓢ *Jimbocho stn, Toei Mita, Hanzomon & Toei Shinjuku lines.*

Three of Japan's prestigious universities, Meiji, Chuo, and Nihon, started out in this area in the 1870s and 1880s, and soon booksellers sprang up selling both new and used books. At one time 50 percent of Japan's publishers were based here. Although only Meiji University is still here, dozens of bookshops, several selling *ukiyo-e* prints, remain, all clustered around the junction of Yasukuni-dori and Hakusan-dori. For books in English on Oriental subjects try **Kitazawa Books** or **Issei-do**; for *ukiyo-e* prints, visit **Oya Shobo** – all are on the south side of Yasukuni-dori, walking away from Hakusan-dori.

The change in the economic status (and priorities) of students is evident here. Shops selling surf- or snowboards are everywhere. Music shops selling electric guitars seem as numerous as the bookshops.

Browsing in one of Jimbocho's bookshops

Tsutenkyo bridge in Koishikawa Korakuen Garden

Koishikawa Korakuen Garden ⑮

小石川後楽園

Map 3 A3–4. **Tel** (03) 3811-3015. S Korakuen stn, Marunouchi & Namboku lines. ◯ 9am–5pm daily.

Meaning "garden of pleasure last," Korakuen is one of Tokyo's best traditional stroll gardens, a delightful place to spend a few restful hours. The name Korakuen comes from the Chinese poem "Yueyang Castle" by Fan Zhongyan – "Be the first to take the world's trouble to heart, be the last to enjoy the world's pleasure."

Construction of the garden started in 1629 and finished 30 years later. Once four times its present size of almost 20 acres (8 hectares), it belonged to the Mito branch of the Tokugawa family. An exiled Chinese Scholar, Zhu Shun Shui, helped design the garden including the **Engetsukyo** (full-moon) **Bridge**, a stone arch with a reflection resembling a full moon. **Tsukenkyo Bridge** is a copy of a bridge in Kyoto; its vermilion color is a striking contrast to the surrounding deep green forest.

The garden represents larger landscapes in miniature. Rozan, a famous Chinese sightseeing mountain, and Japan's Kiso River are two famous geographic features recreated here. In the middle of the large pond is **Horai Island**, a beautiful composition of stone and pine trees.

Kanda Myojin Shrine ⑯

神田明神

Map 3 C4. **Tel** (03) 3254-0753. S Ochanomizu stn, Marunouchi line. R Ochanomizu stn, Chuo & Sobu lines. ◯ 24 hours daily. **Museum** ◯ 10am–4pm Sat, Sun & public hols. Kanda Matsuri (mid-May in alternate, odd-numbered years).

Myojin is more than 1,200 years old, although the present structure is a reproduction built after the 1923 earthquake. The gate's guardian figures are two beautifully dressed, tight-lipped archers – Udaijin on the right and Sadaijin on the left. Just inside the compound on the left is a large stone statue of Daikoku, one of the *shichi-fuku-jin* (seven lucky gods). Here, as always, he is sitting on top of two huge rice bales.

Lions on the gate to Kanda Myojin Shrine

The vermilion shrine itself and its beautiful interior, all lacquer and gold and ornate Chinese-style decoration, are impressive. Early morning is the best time to glimpse the Shinto priests performing rituals. The Kanda Matsuri *(see p28)* is one of the grandest and greatest of Tokyo's festivals – come early and be prepared for crowds.

Behind the main shrine is a **museum** containing relics from the long history of Myojin. There are also several small shrines, hemmed in by the surrounding office blocks.

Akihabara Electronics District ⑰

秋葉原電気店街

Map 3 C4. S Akihabara stn, Hibiya line. R Akihabara stn, Yamanote, Chuo & Sobu lines.

Akihabara electronics district surrounds Akihabara station. Under the station are tiny shops along narrow aisles selling any electronic device, simple or complex. The market grew out of the ruins of World War II when the Japanese army had surplus radio equipment they wanted to dispose of on the black market.

Akihabara and electronics have been synonymous ever since. The focus then changed to household electronic goods, and now the emphasis is on computers, cell phones, and video games. On Chuo-dori, **Laox** *(see p142)* is a great source of tax-free goods. **Radio Kaikan**, the site that housed the original radio spare parts dealers, remains with small operators. A redevelopment north and east of the station features flagship stores such as the Akihabara UDX and the Yodobashi Akiba Building.

The **Tokyo Anime Center** is a showcase for the very latest in Tokyo's popular anime culture. Its 3D digital theater holds regular screenings, live concerts, and other anime-related events.

Colorful shop fronts and advertisements in Akihabara district

NORTHERN TOKYO

The northern districts of Ueno and Asakusa contain what remains of Tokyo's old Shitamachi (low city). Once the heart and soul of Edo culture *(see p25)*, Shitamachi became the subject of countless *ukiyo-e* woodblock prints *(see p55)*. Merchants and artisans thrived here, as did Kabuki theater *(see p17)* and the Yoshiwara pleasure district near Asakusa. The last great battle in Japan took place in Ueno in 1868 when the Emperor Meiji's forces defeated the Tokugawa shogunate. Ueno and Asakusa are the best parts of Tokyo for just strolling and observing. Life in Asakusa still

In festival costume at Senso-ji Temple

revolves around the bustling Senso-ji Temple, its main approach packed with shops. Ueno is dominated by its huge park containing, among others, the National and Shitamachi museums. It is still possible to find pockets of narrow streets lined with tightly packed homes, especially in the Yanaka area, which escaped destruction by war and earthquake. Shopping is a pleasure in Northern Tokyo. As well as the traditional arts and crafts shops near Senso-ji Temple, there are specialists in plastic food in Kappabashi-dori, religious goods in neighboring Inaricho, and electronic items at Ameyoko Market.

SIGHTS AT A GLANCE

Temples
Senso-ji Temple pp56–7 **7**

Parks and Gardens
Ueno Park pp48–9 **1**

Notable Districts
Inaricho District and
Kappabashi-dori **5**

Museums
Drum Museum **6**
Shitamachi Museum **3**
Tokyo National Museum
pp50–53 **2**

Markets
Ameyoko Market **4**

KEY

S Subway station

R Train station

i Tourist information

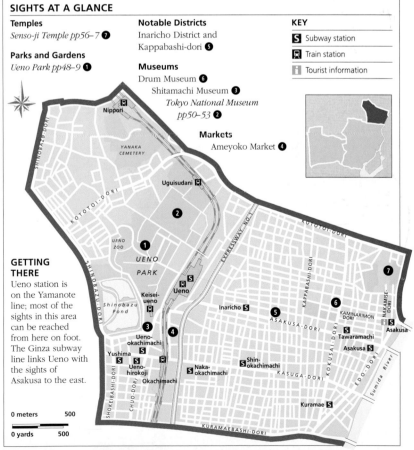

GETTING THERE
Ueno station is on the Yamanote line; most of the sights in this area can be reached from here on foot. The Ginza subway line links Ueno with the sights of Asakusa to the east.

0 meters 500
0 yards 500

◁ Lanterns hanging on Ueno Park's cherry trees to celebrate the cherry blossom-viewing festival

Ueno Park ❶

上野公園

Ieyasu, the first Tokugawa shogun, built the Kanei-ji temple and subtemples here in the 17th century to negate evil spirits that might threaten from the northeast. Judging by how long the Tokugawas lasted, it was a wise move. In 1873, five years after the Battle of Ueno, when the last supporters of the shogun were crushed by Imperial forces, the government designated Ueno a public park. A favorite since its earliest days, the park has figured in many popular woodblock prints and short stories. The Shinobazu pond (actually three ponds) is an annual stop for thousands of migrating birds. Several museums and temples are dotted around the park, and Japan's oldest and best zoo is here.

Boating on the Shinobazu pond

The Tokyo Metropolitan Art Museum, in a modern red-brick building, has a large collection of contemporary Japanese art, plus special exhibitions.

★ Pagoda

This landmark five-story pagoda dates from the 17th century and is a survivor from the original Kanei-ji temple complex. Today it stands in the grounds of Ueno Zoo, a popular destination for Japanese schoolchildren, among others, due to its giant pandas.

Ueno Zoo

★ Tosho-gu Shrine

This ornate complex of halls is one of Tokyo's few remaining Edo-era structures. Ieyasu was enshrined here and later reburied at Nikko (see pp98–9).

KEY

ℹ️ Tourist information

The Great Buddhist Pagoda was built in 1967. A Buddha statue formerly stood on the site; only its head remains.

The Gojo shrine is reached through a series of red *torii* (gates). Inside, red-bibbed Inari fox statues stand in an atmospheric grotto.

Benten Hall

Shinobazu pond

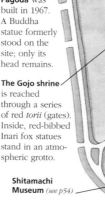

Shitamachi Museum (*see p54*)

STAR SIGHTS

★ Pagoda

★ Tosho-gu Shrine

★ Tokyo National Museum

KANEI-JI
TEMPLE

★ **Tokyo National Museum** (see pp50–53)

UGUISUDANI STATION

VISITORS' CHECKLIST

Map 3 C2–3, 4 D2. **S** Ueno stn, Hibiya & Ginza lines. **R** Ueno & Uguisudani stns, many lines. **Ueno Zoo** ☐ 9:30am–5pm Tue–Sun. **Tokyo Metropolitan Art Museum** ☐ 9am–5pm Tue–Sun. **National Science Museum** ☐ 9am–4:30pm Tue–Sun. **National Museum of Western Art** ☐ 9:30am–5pm Tue–Sun.

Rinno-ji Temple Imperial Cemetery

National Science Museum
A steam engine and life-sized blue whale model mark this museum's entrance. Inside are exhibits on natural history, science, and technology.

The main walkway is lined with hundreds of cherry trees. Boisterous *hanami* (blossom-viewing) parties are held here each spring.

National Museum of Western Art
Rodin's massive Gate of Hell *stands outside this building by Le Corbusier. On display are various Impressionist works, plus paintings by Rubens, Pollock, and others.*

Baseball ground

Tokyo Metropolitan Festival Hall

UENO STATION

The Tomb of the Shogi Tai is a small, leafy area containing two tombstones to the many samurai who died in the 1868 Battle of Ueno.

Japan Art Academy

Ueno Royal Museum

Saigo Takamori Statue
The leader of the victorious Meiji forces, Saigo subsequently instigated the Satsuma rebellion against the emperor in 1877, but killed himself when it failed. He was posthumously pardoned, and this statue was erected in 1899.

0 meters   100
0 yards   100

Kiyo-mizu Hall
Part of the original Kanei-ji temple, this dates from 1631 and is dedicated to Senju (1,000-armed) Kannon. Kosodate Kannon, the bosatsu of conception, is also here, surrounded by numerous offerings of dolls.

Tokyo National Museum ❷
東京国立博物館

The group of buildings that makes up the Tokyo National Museum is in a compound in the northeast corner of Ueno Park; tickets to all buildings are available at the entrance gate. The Honkan is the main building. To its east is the Toyokan *(see p52)*. The 1908 Beaux-Arts Hyokeikan is mainly used for special exhibitions. Behind it is the Gallery of Horyu-ji Treasures, containing stunning objects from Nara's Horyu-ji temple, and the Heiseikan *(see p53)*. More than 110,000 items make up the collection – the best assembly of Japanese art in the world – and the displays change frequently.

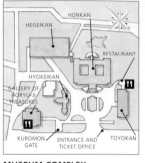

MUSEUM COMPLEX LOCATOR MAP

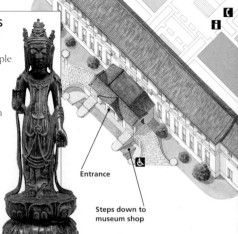

Noh and Kabuki
One of the exquisite kimonos that forms part of the textile and mask collection, this dates from the 16th century when it was used in a Noh play (see p16). *It depicts lilies and court vehicles.*

Heiseikan

First floor

The museum shop in the basement can be reached via twin staircases outside and a central one inside.

This building dates from 1938 and combines Japanese and Western features.

GALLERY OF HORYU-JI TREASURES

When the estates of the Horyu-ji temple complex in Nara were seized as part of the Meiji reforms, the impoverished temple gave a number of its exquisite treasures to the imperial family in exchange for money to finance its repairs. Over 300 of those priceless treasures are housed in this modern gallery, including rare and early Buddhist statues, masks used for Gigaku dances, and beautifully painted screens.

Rikishi mask, used for Gigaku dances, 8th century

7th-century gilt-bronze Kannon statue

Entrance

Steps down to museum shop

★ Ukiyo-e and Costumes
Popular from the mid-17th through the 19th century, these woodblock prints depicted everything from Kabuki stars to famous landscapes, details of market life to scenes from the pleasure quarters, like this 18th-century print of "Beauty with Clock."

VISITORS' CHECKLIST

Map 3 C2, 4 D2. **Tel** (03) 3822-1111. S Ueno stn, Hibiya & Ginza lines. R Ueno stn, many lines; Uguisudani stn, Yamanote line. ◯ 9:30am–5pm Tue–Sun. & www.tnm.jp

Courtly Art
This collection includes scrolls, woodblock prints, and screens. This 16th-century gold screen is illustrated with a procession of noblemen, a scene from the Tale of Genji *(see p22).*

★ National Treasures
The themed exhibition in the National Treasures room changes about every five weeks. Exhibits may be of calligraphy, Buddhist statues, tea utensils, or even armor, like this 16th-century Muromachi period Domaru *armor.*

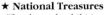

Second floor

★ Sculpture
This serene, wooden 12th-century sculpture of the Juichimen Kannon Bosatsu (11-faced goddess of mercy) is about 3 m (10 ft) high. Mainly Buddhist, the pieces in the sculpture collection range from miniature to monumental.

KEY TO FLOOR PLAN

- ☐ Donations Gallery
- ☐ Thematic Exhibition
- ☐ Sculpture
- ☐ Lacquerware and Ceramics
- ☐ Ainu and Ryukyu materials
- ☐ Modern Art
- ☐ Ukiyo-e, costumes, Noh & Kabuki
- ☐ National Treasures
- ☐ Military Attire
- ☐ Decorative Arts
- ☐ Interior Furnishings and Painting
- ☐ Courtly Art
- ☐ Swords

GALLERY GUIDE: HONKAN
The collection is on two floors. The second floor is a counterclockwise, chronological arrangement of Japanese art as it develops from the Jomon era (from 10,000 BC) clay figures to 19th-century Ukiyo-e woodblock prints. In between is everything from calligraphy and tea utensils to armor, as well as textiles used in Noh and Kabuki. The first floor also works best when viewed counterclockwise. Its rooms are themed, with stunning exhibits of sculpture, lacquerware, swords, and Western-influenced modern art.

STAR EXHIBITS

- ★ Ukiyo-e and Costumes
- ★ National Treasures
- ★ Sculpture

Tokyo National Museum: Toyokan

Opened in 1968, the Toyokan (Asian Gallery) has an excellent and eclectic collection of non-Japanese Eastern art, including textiles, sculpture, and ceramics. Many of the exhibits are from China and Korea – a result of their long ties with Japan. The layout of the three floors is in a rough spiral; a well-marked route takes visitors from the sculpture on the first floor up to the Korean collection at the top.

★ Korean Art
Dating from the Bronze Age (100 BC–AD 300), this dagger is one of the older pieces on display in the Korean collection.

★ Chinese Ceramics
Ceramics, such as this 8th-century Tang-dynasty camel, feature in the Chinese art section, along with bronzes, scrolls, jade, textiles, and glassware.

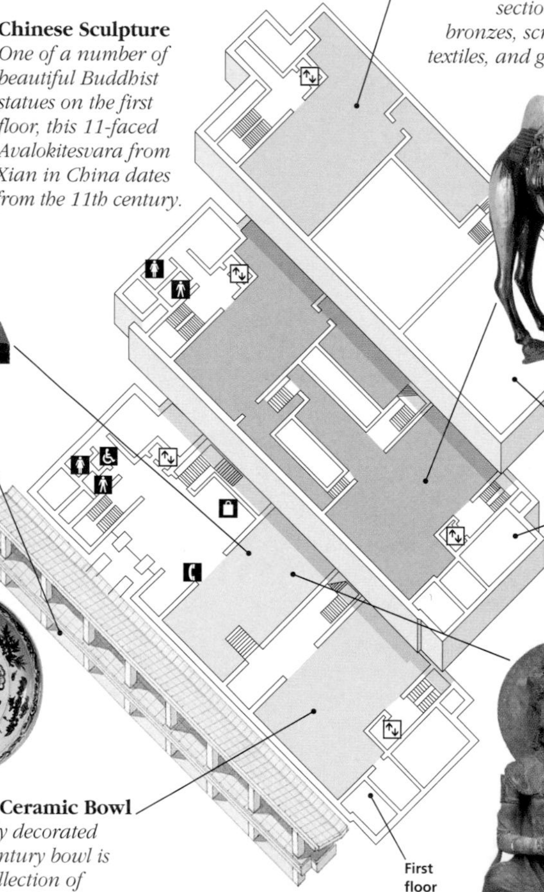

Chinese Sculpture
One of a number of beautiful Buddhist statues on the first floor, this 11-faced Avalokitesvara from Xian in China dates from the 11th century.

Entrance

Third floor

Second floor

First floor

Vietnamese Ceramic Bowl
This delicately decorated 15th–16th-century bowl is part of the collection of Asian art on the first floor, which also includes fabrics and statuary.

KEY TO FLOOR PLAN

- Chinese and Indian sculpture
- Egyptian and West, Southeast, and South Asian art
- Chinese art and antiquities
- Korean and Central Asian art and antiquities
- Non-exhibition space

STAR EXHIBITS

★ Korean Art

★ Chinese Ceramics

Indian Sculpture
This 2nd-century figure of a seated Bodhisattva, from Gandhara in Pakistan, is grouped with the Indian sculptures on the first floor.

Tokyo National Museum: Heiseikan

The Heiseikan opened in 1999 and was purpose-built to house major temporary exhibitions and a superb collection of Japanese archaeological artifacts. Its modern facilities do full justice to the fascinating displays. The first floor houses the Japanese archaeology gallery, with items from 10,000–7,000 BC onward. The temporary exhibitions on the second floor are of mainly – but not only – Japanese art. Captions are in English and Japanese.

KEY TO FLOOR PLAN

- Archaeological exhibits
- Temporary exhibitions
- Non-exhibition space

First floor

Second floor

Entrance

Honkan

★ Haniwa Horse

Haniwa *literally means "clay ring," and is used to describe earthenware sculptures that were made for 4th– 7th-century tombs and were thought to protect the dead. Many forms have been found, including horses and other animals.*

★ Haniwa Male Figure

This haniwa *is dressed as a warrior. Other human figures that have survived include singers, dancers, and farmers.*

STAR EXHIBITS

- ★ Haniwa Sculptures
- ★ Jomon Figures

Fukabachi Bowl

This large cooking pot is a fine example of Jomon pottery, which is among the oldest in the world. The curved, deep sides allowed the fire to be built up around it, while the flattened base ensured it could be balanced when in the hearth.

★ Jomon Figures

The prehistoric Jomon period (14,500–300BC) is thought to have produced Japan's first pottery, including dogu. This figurine is one of several female figures characterized by bulging eyes.

Shitamachi Museum ❸

下町風俗資料館

2-1 Ueno-koen, Taito-ku. **Map** 3 C3.
Tel (03) 3823-7451. **S** Ueno stn,
Hibiya & Ginza lines. **R** Keisei-Ueno
stn, Keisei line; Ueno stn, many lines.
◯ 9:30am–4pm Tue–Sun.

Dedicated to preserving the
spirit and traditional artifacts
of Shitamachi (see p47), this
museum is both fascinating
and fun. On the first floor are
re-creations of Edo-era shops
such as a candy store and a
coppersmith's. Second-
floor exhibits include traditional toys, tools, and photographs. All 50,000 exhibits
were donated by Shitamachi
residents. Performances of
kamishibai, storytelling using
large, hand-painted cards,
take place on weekends. The
nearby **Shitamachi Museum
Annex** (north of Ueno Park)
is in the traditional style of
shop-houses of the mid-Edo
period (late 17th century).

Ameyoko Market ❹

アメ横

Map 3 C3. **S** Ueno stn, Hibiya &
Ginza lines; Ueno-Okachimachi stn,
Oedo line. **R** Okachimachi stn,
Yamanote line; Ueno stn, many lines.

One of the great bazaars in
Asia, Ameyoko is a place
where anything is available,
at a discount. In Edo times
this was the place to come
and buy ame (candy). After
World War II black-market
goods, such as liquor, cigarettes, and nylons started
appearing here, and ame
acquired its second meaning
as an abbreviation for
American (yoko means alley).
An area of tiny shops packed
under the elevated train
tracks, Ameyoko is no longer
a black market, but still is the
place for bargains on foreign
brands, including Chanel and
Rolex. Clothes and accessories
are concentrated under the
tracks, while foods line the
street that follows the tracks.
Tropical fruits and exotic
imports fill the stalls inside the
Ameyoko Center Building.

**Appetizing colorful beer and food
models on display, Kappabashi-dori**

Inaricho District and Kappabashi-dori ❺

稲荷町地区とかっぱ橋通り

Map 4 D3, 4 E2–3. **S** Inaricho &
Tawaramachi stns, Ginza line.

Inaricho District is the Tokyo
headquarters for wholesale
religious goods. Small wooden
boxes to hold Buddhas and
family photos, paper lanterns,
bouquets of brass flowers
(jouka), Shinto household
shrines, and even prayer beads
can be found here. Most of
the shops lie on the south
side of Asakusa-dori, in the
stretch between Inaricho and
Tawaramachi stations.
   Kappabashi-dori, named after
the mythical water imps
(kappa) who supposedly
helped build a bridge (bashi)
here, is Tokyo's center for
kitchenware and the source of
the plastic food displayed in
almost every restaurant window.
Although the "food" such as

dessert dishes and palettes of
plastic sushi are for sale,
prices are much higher than
for the real thing. Connoisseurs hold two Kappabashi
stores, **Maizuru** and **Biken**
in high esteem.

Drum Museum ❻

太鼓館

Map 4 E3. **S** Tawaramachi stn,
Ginza line. **Tel** (03) 3844-2141.
◯ 10am–5pm Tue–Sun.

Over 600 drums from across
Japan and the world are on
display at the Drum Museum,
set up by Miyamoto Unosuke
Shoten, manufacturers of
wadaiko, traditional Japanese
drums used in festivals.
   Although none of the text
describing the instruments is
in English, it is not difficult to
identify the Diembe drums
from Mali, Cuicas from Brazil,
Chimes of Chinese origin, or
the complete set of wedding
drums from Benin. A world
map on the wall shows the
provenance of each drum.
   The museum has special
attractions for kids allowing
a hands-on appreciation of
many of the instruments on
display. All the unmarked
drums can be played with the
sticks and mallets provided. A
blue dot warns that a more
delicate handling is required;
a red dot signifies "do not
touch." The museum's first
floor gift shop sells a good
selection of local handicrafts,
traditional souvenirs, and
even a few drums. Look out
for flyers put up on the walls,
listing forthcoming drum
events around the country.

A worldwide collection of traditional drums, Drum Museum

The Floating World of Ukiyo-e

In the Edo period, woodblock prints, called *ukiyo-e*, or pictures of the pleasure-seeking "floating world," became the most popular pictorial art of Japan. They had a profound influence on artists such as Matisse and Van Gogh. Although today they are credited to individual artists, they were in fact a cooperative effort between the publisher, responsible for financing and distributing the work; the artist, who produced a fine line drawing; the carver, who pasted the drawings onto blocks of wood and

Two Kabuki actors by Sharaku

carved away what was not to appear on the print, making one block for each color; and the printer, who inked the wooden blocks and pressed them onto the paper – one for each color, starting with the lightest. Editions were limited to 100–200 copies. The first artist known by name was Moronobu, who died in 1694.

The golden age of *ukiyo-e* lasted from about 1790 to the 1850s. Beautiful women, Kabuki actors, scenes from Tokyo, including Shitamachi, and the supernatural were recurring themes.

A full-color *calendar of beautiful women published by Suzuki Harunobu in 1765 marked a transition from the earlier black-and-white techniques. Highly popular (and a moneymaker), the calendar's success attracted both financiers and artists to the medium*

Depictions of women *were eroticized by artists such as Kitagawa Utamaro and Torii Kiyonaga, after Harunobu's calendar. This print is by Utamaro.*

Landscape *prints were dominated by Hokusai (1760–1849) and his younger rival Hiroshige (1797–1858). This print is from the latter's Fifty-Three Stations of the Tokaido.*

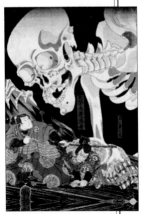

This 1825 print *by Hokusai shows the carving and printing stages of woodblock print making. Printers relied on vegetable dyes, some of which were very expensive. The red dye* beni, *derived from safflowers, could be worth more than its weight in gold. Some prints required up to a dozen colors.*

Ghosts and goblins *were a favorite theme, especially in summer (to be scared was thought to be cooling). Utagawa Kuniyoshi (whose print is shown here), Taiso Yoshitoshi, and Kobayashi Kiyochika were masters of the genre, which marked the end of ukiyo-e's golden age.*

Senso-ji Temple ⑦

浅草寺

Stroking the Nade Botokesan Buddha

Popularly known as Asakusa Kannon, this is Tokyo's most sacred and spectacular temple. In AD 628, two fishermen fished a small gold statue of Kannon, the Buddhist goddess of mercy, from the Sumida River. Their master built a shrine to Kannon, then in 645, the holy man Shokai built a temple to her. Its fame, wealth, and size grew until Tokugawa Ieyasu bestowed upon it a large stipend of land. The Yoshiwara pleasure quarter moved nearby in 1657 only increasing its popularity. The temple survived the 1923 earthquake but not World War II bombing. Its main buildings are therefore relatively new, but follow the Edo-era layout. While these buildings are impressive, it is the people following their daily rituals that make this place so special.

Awashima Hall is dedicated to a deity who looks after women.

The garden of Dembo-in (abbot's residence) is a tranquil stroll garden used as a training center for monks. It is a masterly arrangement of woods, bamboo groves, lawns, and water.

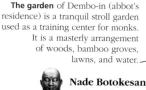

Nade Botokesan Buddha
This delicate statue has been polished smooth by the hands of those hoping for good luck and help with ailments.

Five-Story Pagoda
This replica of the original was constructed in 1973.

★ **Nakamise-dori**
This street is a treasure trove of traditional wares, including specialists in obi sashes, haircombs, fans, dolls, and kimonos.

Kaminarimon Gate
"Thunder Gate" burned down in 1865 and was not rebuilt until 1960. The guardian statues of Fujin (right) and Raijin (left) have old heads and new bodies.

For more details about individual shops here, see pages 142–5

To Asakusa stations and tourist information office

This **hexagonal temple** is a rare survivor from the 15th or 16th century.

★ **Main Hall**
Inside the hall (1958) the gold-plated main shrine houses the original Kannon image. Worshipers come to pay their respects by throwing coins and lighting candles.

Yougoudo Hall houses eight recent Buddha statues.

VISITORS' CHECKLIST

Map 4 E2, 4 F2–3.
ℹ️ by station (03) 3842-5566.
Ⓢ Asakusa stn, Ginza &
Toei-Asakusa lines. 🚃 Tobu-
Asakusa stn, Tobu-Isesaki line.
Temple ◯ 6am–5pm daily
Oct–Mar: from 6:30am).
Nakamise-dori ◯ 9:30am–7pm
daily. 🎴 Sanja Matsuri (3rd Fri–
Sun in May), Hagoita-Ichi
(Battledore Fair, Dec 17–19).

Asakusa Jinja, built in 1649, is a shrine dedicated to the men who found the Kannon statue.

★ **Main Hall**
Several large paintings hang inside the main hall. The painting of angels with lotus flowers is a 20th-century work by Domoto Insho.

Niten-mon Gate was built in 1618 as the entrance to the original Tosho-gu shrine.

Statues donated by a wealthy Edo merchant

Benten-yama Shoro belfry stands amid a group of temple buildings. The bell used to ring on the hour in Edo.

Incense Burner
One of the temple's focal points, this incense burner (joukoro) is constantly surrounded by people wafting the smoke over them to keep them healthy.

Hozo-mon Gate
Built in 1964 of reinforced concrete, this two-story gate has a treasure house upstairs holding a number of 14th-century Chinese sutras.

STAR SIGHTS

★ Nakamise-dori

★ Main Hall

WESTERN TOKYO

Shinjuku and Shibuya, the dual centers of Western Tokyo, three stops apart on the Yamanote line, started to boom only after the 1923 earthquake. This part of the city is new Tokyo – all vitality and energy, fast-paced, constantly changing, and challenging the more traditional pleasures of Central and Northern Tokyo. Modern architectural landmarks are dotted around, from the Olympic Stadiums of Yoyogi Park to the magnificent twin-towered home for the city government in West Shinjuku. Shibuya, along with neighboring Harajuku and Minami-Aoyama, is the epicenter of both young and haute-couture Japanese fashion. Nightlife is also in diverse and plentiful supply with Roppongi's cosmopolitan clubs, bars, and music venues, and the neon lights and *pachinko* parlors of East Shinjuku. In these overwhelmingly modern surroundings, historical sights are few and far between but include the popular Meiji Shrine and the nearby Sword Museum.

All dressed up in Harajuku

SIGHTS AT A GLANCE

Notable Districts
Akasaka District **12**
East Shinjuku pp60–61 **1**
Harajuku District **8**
Minami-Aoyama District **10**
Roppongi District **11**
Shibuya pp66–7 **9**
West Shinjuku pp62–3 **2**

Shrines
Meiji Shrine **6**

Museums
Bunka Gakuen Costume Museum **4**
Sword Museum **5**

Stations
Shinjuku Station **3**

Parks
Yoyogi Park **7**

GETTING THERE
Shinjuku, Shibuya, Harajuku, and Yoyogi are all on the Yamanote line. The Ginza and Hanzomon subway lines stop in or near Harajuku, Minami-Aoyama, and Akasaka, and the Hibiya line serves Roppongi.

KEY
Street-by-Street map *pp60–61*
Street-by-Street map *pp62–3*
Street-by-Street map *pp66–7*
S Subway station
🚆 Train station
🚌 Long-distance bus station

0 meters 500
0 yards 500

Street-by-Street: East Shinjuku ❶

東新宿

Façade of a café in Shinjuku

East Shinjuku is where Tokyo plays. The area has been a nightlife center from Edo times on, when it was the first night stop on the old Tokaido road to Kyoto. Since Shinjuku station opened in the 1880s, entertainments have been targeted at commuters (mainly men) en route back to the suburbs. Amusements are focused in the tiny bars of Golden Gai, and in the red-light district of Kabukicho. Daytime attractions include several art galleries, a tranquil shrine, and some department stores. A late-afternoon stroll as the neon starts to light up both sides of this fascinating, bustling area would be rewarding.

The Koma Theater specializes in Japanese historical melodramas.

Seibu-Shinjuku station

Movie Houses
This corner of Kabukicho is dominated by cinemas, many showing the latest blockbusters.

← **West Shinjuku**
(see pp62–3)

Kabukicho
Hostess bars and pachinko *parlors (see p67) flourish here alongside cafés and restaurants. In this area of contrasts, prices range from ¥500 for a bowl of noodles to ¥10,000 for a drink.*

Panasonic

ALTA

SAKURA–DO

YASUKUNI–DORI

Studio Alta
Instantly recognizable by its huge TV screen, Studio Alta stands opposite the crossing from Shinjuku station and is a favorite place for meeting up or just hanging out.

← **Shinjuku station**
(see p63)

↓ **Yoyogi**

Kinokuniya bookstore has one of Tokyo's best selections of foreign books.

KEY

– – – Suggested walk route

▬▬▬ Train line

Golden Gai

Viewed in the day-time these scruffy alleys look anything but golden. Most of the bars here are just wide enough for a bar, a counter, and a row of stools. Each has a set of regulars – from writers to bikers – but a few welcome strangers inside.

LOCATOR MAP
See Tokyo Street Finder Map 1

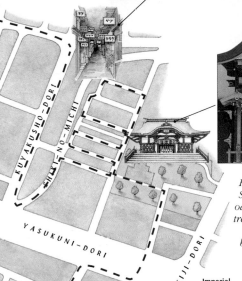

Hanazono Shrine

Founded in the mid-17th century, this Shinto shrine is a calm and surprising oasis among the concrete towers. In the tree-filled compound are a reconstructed traditional vermilion-and-white building and several Inari fox statues.

Flags café is a convenient coffee stop opposite Mistsukoshi Department store.

Isetan Department Store

Top Japanese and Western designer boutiques make this stylish store a favorite with Tokyo's affluent young. The food hall in the basement is also worth a visit. On the 8th floor of the Shinkan annex building, the Isetan Art Museum has interesting special exhibitions.

West Shinjuku ❷
西新宿

Most of Tokyo's skyscraper office blocks (and some of its most expensive land) are clustered just to the west of Shinjuku station. About 250,000 people work here each day. Many of the hotels and some office blocks have top-floor restaurants with views of the city. In 1960, the government designated Shinjuku a *fukutoshin* ("secondary heart of the city"); in 1991, when the city government moved into architect Kenzo Tange's massive 48-story Metropolitan Government Offices, many started calling it *shin toshin* (the new capital). Tange's building was dubbed "tax tower" by some outraged at its US$1 billion cost.

West Shinjuku seen from Tokyo Metropolitan Government Offices

Island Tower

Mitsui Building

Hilton Tokyo

KITA-DORI

GIJIDO-DORI

CHUO-DORI

Sumitomo Building
Inside this block are a shopping center and, at the top, a free observatory.

Dai-Ichi Seimei Building

Century Hyatt Hotel

KOEN-DORI

TOCHO-DORI

FUREAI-DORI

Tokyo Metropolitan Government Offices
This huge complex of two blocks and a semi-circular plaza is unified by the grid-detailing on its façades, recalling both traditional architecture and electronic circuitry. An observatory gives views from Mount Fuji to Tokyo Bay on a clear day.

Shinjuku Central Park

The Washington Hotel has flowing curves (inside and out) and tiny windows in its white façade.

MINAMI-DORI

Keio Plaza Hotel

The NS Building is recognizable by its rainbow-hued elevator shafts. In the 30-story atrium is a 29-m (95-ft) high water-powered clock.

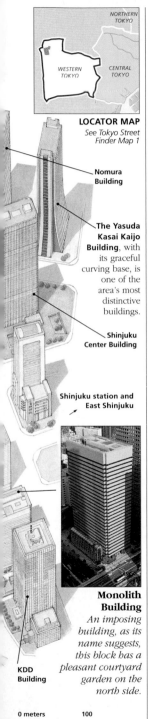

LOCATOR MAP
*See Tokyo Street
Finder Map 1*

Nomura
Building

**The Yasuda
Kasai Kaijo
Building**, with
its graceful
curving base, is
one of the
area's most
distinctive
buildings.

Shinjuku
Center Building

Shinjuku station and
East Shinjuku

**Monolith
Building**
*An imposing
building, as its
name suggests,
this block has a
pleasant courtyard
garden on the
north side.*

KDD
Building

0 meters   100

0 yards   100

Shinjuku Station ❸

新宿駅

Map 1 B1–2.

With over two million
people passing through
each day, this is the busiest
train station in the world. As
well as being a major stop on
both the JR and metropolitan
subway systems, Shinjuku
station is also the starting
point for trains and buses into
the suburbs. On the
Yamanote and Chuo line
platforms during the morning
rush hour (from about 7:30 to
9am), staff are employed to
gently but firmly push those
last few commuters on to the
train, making sure the odd
body part is not slammed in
the closing doors.

The corridors connecting all
the lines and train networks
together are edged with hundreds of shops and restaurants. It is easy to lose your
way in this maze of seemingly
identical passages, and often
simpler to find your bearings
at ground level. Look for the
nearest escalator or staircase
up, and then get oriented
once on the street.

Bunka Gakuen Costume Museum ❹

文化学園服飾博物館

Map 1 A2. **Tel** (03) 3299-2387.
Ⓢ *Shinjuku stn, JR, Odakyu, Keio
Shinjuku, Oedo lines.* ◯
10am–4:30pm Mon–Sat.

Opened in 1979, the
museum has been
building up its collection
of costumes and
accessories to over
20,000 exhibits today.

Clothing and dyed
articles from various
countries such as
Africa, the Middle
East, China, and India
are exhibited through-
out the year. Western
attire is represented by
a selection of dresses
typifying fashions of the 18th
to 20th centuries. Among the
permanent items in the
Japanese collection of interest

are modern court dresses,
kosode (short-sleeved kimono),
the lavish costumes worn
for Noh dramas, and bags.
The museum also exhibits
the creations of Japanese
Haute Couture designers.

**Late 19th-century Western wear,
Bunka Gakuen Costume Museum**

Sword Museum ❺

刀剣博物館

4-25-10 Yoyogi. **Map** 1 A3. **Tel** (03)
3379-1386. 🚃 *Sangubashi stn, Odakyu line.* ◯ *9am–4pm Tue–Sun.*

A little out of the way, this
museum is full of fine Japanese swords dating back to the
12th century. On the first
floor is an interesting display
of the process by which a
sword is produced.

The swords themselves are
exhibited on the second floor,
every detail carefully refined,
even down to the pattern of
burnishing on the blade's
face. There is also a display of
decorated hilts. English explanations trace the history of the
sword, and the processes of
sharpening, handling, and
maintenance. Old Japanese
texts, illustrated with beautiful drawings, explain the
finer points of sword-
making. Among the
ancient samurai
swords are examples
of works by modern
master swordsmiths,
who have kept alive
the tradition of refining
steel from pure iron
sand, painstakingly
manipulating the carbon content, then hammering, and
cross-welding the steel for
maximum strength.

**Ornate sword
handle**

Minami Shinmon gateway through a wooden *torii*, Meiji Shrine

Meiji Shrine **6**
明治神宮

Map 1 B3. **Tel** (03) 3379-5511.
🚉 *Harajuku stn, Yamanote line.*
Annex ⏰ *9am–4pm daily (4:30pm Mar–Oct).* **Treasure House** ⏰ *9am–4pm Sat, Sun, and public hols.* 📷
Meiji-Jingu Gyoen Garden
⏰ *daily (times vary).* 📷 📷 *Spring Festival (May 2–3), Fall Festival (Nov 1–3).* **www**.meijijingu.or.jp

The most important Shinto shrine in Tokyo, Meiji Jingu (Imperial shrine) dates from 1920. The Emperor Meiji (who reigned 1868–1912) and his wife the Empress Shoken are enshrined here. A focal point for right-wing militarists during Japan's colonial expansion prior to World War II, the shrine was destroyed by Allied aerial bombardment in 1945 but rebuilt with private donations in 1958. During the New Year holidays it is the most heavily visited place in Japan, with over three million people worshiping here and buying good-luck charms for the year ahead.

A wide graveled road under a huge *torii* (gate) and shaded by cedars leads into the shrine grounds. On the right is an abandoned entrance to the JR Harajuku station. Just beyond is a small entrance used by the emperor when he visits by train. Next on the right is the **Meiji Treasure House Annex**. The annex holds changing exhibitions of the royal couples' artifacts, including clothes, lacquerware, and furniture. A left turn takes you under the massive **Otorii** (big gate),

built in 1975 of huge logs that came from a 1,500-year-old Japanese cypress on Mount Tandai in Taiwan. A short distance beyond the gate, on the left, is the entrance to the **Meiji-jingu Gyoen Garden**, a favorite of the Meiji imperial couple. It is said that the Emperor Meiji designed it himself for his Empress. Inside there is a teahouse overlooking a pond stocked with water lilies and carp. To the right of the pond, a path leads to the beautiful **Minami-ike Shobuda** (iris garden), containing over 150 species.

Past the entrance to the garden, the road turns to the right and enters the **main shrine** area, set in the middle of a grove of cedars. Another large wooden *torii* leads to the Minami Shinmon (outer gate) through which is a spacious outer courtyard. Gracefully curving, the roof is in the Shinto style of architecture. Through a gateway to the right is the **Kaguraden**, a hall built in 1993 for sacred music and dance.

To reach the **Meiji Treasure House**, either return to the Otorii and turn left, following the signs, or walk through the woods to the left of the shrine. Lining the walls of the single high-vaulted room of the Treasure House are portraits of every emperor going back more than 1,000 years. Objects on display include the gorgeous kimonos worn by the Emperor Meiji and the Empress for court functions.

Yoyogi Park **7**
代々木公園

Map 1 A4, 1 B4. 🚉 *Harajuku stn, Yamanote line.*

Kenzo Tange's two **Olympic Pavilions** (*see p15*), the landmark structures in Yoyogi Park, were completed in 1964 for the Tokyo Olympics and are still used for national and international sports competitions. The impressive curves of the shell-like structures are achieved by using steel suspension cables.

For almost three decades the park filled with a fantastic array of performers and bands every Sunday. These events were stopped by the authorities in the mid-1990s, supposedly due to worries about the rise in criminal activities. The weekly flea market on Sundays is worth a visit. At the entrance to the park you can see members of the *zoku* (groups) who used to perform here, from punks to hippies and break-dancers. South of the park, on Inokashira-dori, **NHK Studio Park**, run by Japan's leading broadcaster, offers free tours of their TV studios.

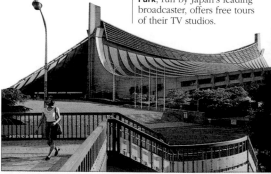

The main Olympic Stadium in Yoyogi Park

Harajuku District ⑧
原宿地区

Map 1 B4, 1 C4. **S** *Meiji-jingumae stn, Chiyoda line.* **R** *Harajuku stn, Yamanote line.* **Ukiyo-e Ota Memorial Museum** *Tel (03) 3403-0860.* ☐ *10:30am–5:30pm Tue–Sun.* ● *27th–end of each month.* 🌐

Harajuku station was the main station for the 1964 Tokyo Olympic village; that concentration of international culture left a great impact on the area, attracting the young and innovative of Tokyo. Today Harajuku remains a fashion center from high-end international stores to bargain boutiques. The neighboring chic and expensive Omotesando and Minami-Aoyama areas *(see p68)* cater to the more urbane shopper.

Takeshita-dori, a narrow alley between Meiji-dori and Harajuku station, is the place to find what is hot in teen fashion and culture. Prices range from cheap to outrageous, as do the fashions. Starting from the Harajuku station end, about 200 m (220 yards) down, a left turn leads up some stairs to the **Togo Shrine**, founded for Admiral Togo, the commander who defeated the Russian fleet at the straits of Tsushima in the 1904–5 war. Known as Nihonkai Kaisen (the Battle of the Sea of Japan), it was a huge naval victory, the first of an Asian country over a Western one. Admiral Togo remains a hero in Japan, and his shrine has a beautiful garden and pond. A **flea market** is held in the grounds of the shrine on the first, fourth, and fifth Sundays of the month. Back on Takeshita-dori, a short walk farther on is a right turn that leads to a life-sized statue of Elvis Presley. It stands at the entrance to the **Rock and Roll Museum**, which is a store filled with memorabilia for sale. The first floor is devoted to Elvis, the basement to rock 'n' roll items in general.

Large advertising screens in Harajuku

Street performer in Harajuku

Running parallel to, and south of, Takeshita-dori is the more sophisticated **Omotesando**. With its wide, tree-shaded sidewalks and dozens of boutiques showcasing top fashion designers and brands such as Celine, Fendi, and Dior, this is one of the best strolls in Tokyo. A recent addition to the district's fashion face is the **Omotesando Hills** mall complex. Designed by renowned architect Tadao Ando, the central atrium is encircled by a spiraling walkway, which replicates the angle and incline of the outside pavement, creating an effective interior-exterior flow of line and form. Many top brand stores such as Yves Saint Laurent are represented here. The complex's trendy restaurants and cafés provide respite from the intensive shopping experience.

Walking from Harajuku station, just before the intersection with Meiji-dori, a small street off to the left leads to the **Ukiyo-e Ota Memorial Museum of Art**, which houses one of the best collections of *ukiyo-e* prints *(see p55)* in Japan. A vivid image of a Kabuki actor portraying an *arogoto* (superhero)

by Sharaku and a masterful program of a memorial Kabuki performance by Hiroshige are among many familiar works. There is a small restaurant and a shop selling prints and other *ukiyo-e* related souvenirs. Just to the left down Meiji-dori is **LaForet**, a fashion mecca, with more than 150 boutiques. A lane leading off Omotesando, just before the pedestrian bridge, is lined with designer boutiques. Over the pedestrian bridge to the right is the landmark **Hanae Mori Building**. Designed by Kenzo Tange in 1974, it resembles a stack of glass blocks. Just before it is the **Oriental Bazaar**, many shops full of real and fake antiques and handicrafts *(see p145)*.

A group of teenagers, Harajuku

Street-by-Street: Shibuya 9

渋谷

Sign for a
pachinko parlor

Shibuya is the *sakariba* (party town) for Tokyo's youth. It has been so since the 1930s, when façades featured rockets streaking across the sky. Today this is the place to see the latest in fashion, food, music, and gadgets. Shibuya really started to grow after the 1964 Tokyo Olympics, and its continuing expansion has been spurred by the affluent youth of the world's second-biggest economy. The area, which lies to the northwest of Shibuya station and south of Yoyogi Park, is a mix of trendy boutiques, fashionable department stores, and record shops, plus a couple of interesting museums, and the Bunkamura cultural center. Adjoining this area is Dogen-zaka, a jumble of sloping streets and alleyways lined with nightclubs, bars, and love hotels *(see p107).*

VISITORS' CHECKLIST

S Shibuya stn, Hanzomon & Ginza lines. Shibuya stn, Yamanote, Tokyu Toyoko, Denentoshi & Keio Inokashira lines. **TEPCO Electric Energy Museum** *Tel* (03) 3477-1191. 10am– 6pm Thu–Tue. Thu if Wed is public hol. **Tobacco and Salt Museum** *Tel* (03) 3476-2041. 10am–5:30pm Tue–Sun. Tue if Mon is public hol.

Center Gai
The focus for youth entertainment in Tokyo, Center Gai is lined with shops, pachinko parlors, restaurants, and karaoke bars full of high-school and college-age kids.

Bunkamura
A popular site for rock and classical concerts, this cultural center has movies, an art gallery, and a theater.

Tokyu Hands is a huge store full of housewares and handicrafts.

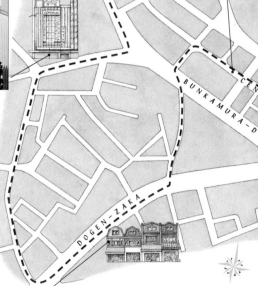

Dogen-zaka
Named after a bandit who retired here as a monk, this nighttime destination includes old houses, now art galleries.

KEY

– – – Suggested walk route

▬▬ Train line

This purple clock tower stands in front of the Shibuya Ward Office and is overlooked by Yoyogi Park and the NHK Studios.

The Tobacco and Salt Museum has excellent, well-laid-out exhibits explaining the history of tobacco and salt (both former government monopolies) in Japan.

Yoyogi Park and Olympic stadiums ↑

Tower Records has a good stock of Japanese and international music CDs at prices among the best in Tokyo.

Harajuku ↑

LOCATOR MAP
See Tokyo Street Finder Map 1

KOEN-DORI

KOEN-DORI

TEPCO Electric Energy Museum
Housed in a modern building with a distinctive dome, this fun museum is packed with inter-active exhibits illustrating the uses of electricity.

The Humax Pavilion Building is one of the more fanciful buildings in the area, resembling a cartoon rocket.

Marui Jam department store is a paradise for clothes – the place for fashionable under 25s.

Statue of Hachiko
A favorite meeting place, this 1936 statue depicts the dog who waited for his master at the station every night for more than a decade after his death. Another popular meeting point nearby is the Statue of Moyai.

Shibuya station

0 meters 100

0 yards 100

PACHINKO

One of Tokyo's most popular forms of recreation, *pachinko* is similar to pinball, but without the flippers and requiring little skill. Players buy some steel balls to feed into the *pachinko* machine, winning more steel balls; these are traded in for a prize (gambling for money is illegal). The prize in turn can be exchanged for money, usually in a small shop nearby. Shibuya and Shinjuku have hundreds of *pachinko* parlors.

A typical *pachinko* machine

The Spiral Building, Minami-Aoyama

Minami-Aoyama District ⑩

南青山地区

Map 1 C4–5, 2 D4–5. **S** *Gaienmae stn, Ginza line.* **Museum of Contemporary Art** *Tel (03) 3402-3001.* ☐ *11am–7pm Tue–Sun (to 9pm Wed).* **Nezu Institute of Fine Arts** *Tel (03) 3400-2536.* ☐ *for renovation until 2009.* **National Children's Castle** *Tel (03) 3797-5666.* ☐ *12:30–5:30pm Tue–Fri, 10am–5:30pm Sat, Sun, public hols, & school vacations.* **www. kodomono-shiro.or.jp**

Favored by artists, writers, and young entrepreneurs, this district lies between the large Aoyama Cemetery and Shibuya. Aoyama-dori, the wide street at its heart, is a center for boutiques and up-scale life. Omotesando crosses it just about in the middle.

On Gaien-Nishi-dori, a fashionable street nicknamed "Killer-dori," is the **Museum of Contemporary Art** (Watari-um). Exhibits are by international and Japanese artists, and change regularly. The bookstore stocks an excellent range of art books.

Back on Omotesando-dori, follow the road southeast away from Omotesando subway station where, on the right, the stunning **Prada Aoyama** fashion store, opened in 2003, looms into view *(see p14).* Designed by the dynamic Swiss firm Herzog and de Meuron, the striking building is a six-story chrysalis of diamond-shaped transparent glass that appear to be bubbles, moving as the building is circled. Continue in the same direction to the end of the road, and cross the street for the **Nezu Institute of Fine Arts**, which houses Japanese, Chinese, and Korean art and is situated in landscaped gardens containing traditional teahouses. A short walk from here is Kotto-dori, another fashionable street, which is full of antique shops selling scrolls, paintings, and porcelain, among many other items. This street is fast becoming one of the hottest in Tokyo, with some notable boutiques, cafés, and shops springing up. Returning to Aoyama-dori, near the Omotesando junction toward Shibuya, the next landmark is the white, geometric **Spiral Building**, which owes its name to the large, spiral ramp inside. Designed by Maki Fumihiko in 1985, and one of the most popular places in Minami-Aoyama, this building is the figurative definition of cool. There is nothing in it that cannot be described as hip and trendy (*torendi* in Japanese), and that includes most of the people seen here. Attractions inside comprise a first-floor exhibition and performance space, the Spiral Hall (on the third floor), also used for exhibitions and performances, an Italian café, a French restaurant, a stationery and housewares boutique, and a beauty salon.

Farther along, the **National Children's Castle** (*see pp10–11*) is marked by a large, moon-faced sculpture by Okamoto Taro. There are many activities for kids here, open to Japanese and non-Japanese speakers alike, including areas for free play with toys, computers, music and art classes, and even a child-friendly hotel.

Roppongi District ⑪

六本木地区

Map 2 E5. **S** *Roppongi stn, Hibiya & Toei-Oedo lines.* **Roppongi Hills** *Tel (03) 6406-6000.* **Mori Art Museum** *Tel (03) 5777-8600.* **National Art Center** *Tel (03) 6812-9900.*

Roppongi is famed for its hedonistic club scene and is particularly popular with expats. You can find just about any music you want here – jazz, blues, ska, hip-hop, classic disco, and

Nighttime scene in the district of Roppongi

Entrance to the contemporary Mori Art Museum, Roppongi

country-western. This is also the place for big-name international restaurant chains such as the Hard Rock Café, Spago's, and Tony Roma's.

Unveiled in 2003, **Roppongi Hills** aspires to be an all-purpose mini-city. The 54-story Mori Tower forms the focus of the hills. Over 200 shops, restaurants, and bars occupy the complex, which also boasts cinemas, interconnecting walkways, the Grand Hyatt Tokyo *(see p115)*, and the richly imaginative and daring exhibits of the **Mori Art Museum**. Admission to the museum includes access to the **Tokyo City View**, a 52nd-floor observation deck (open later than the museum). *Maman*, the giant, spiny, spider sculpture by Louise Bourgeois outside the main tower, is a major draw.

The new **National Art Center** is part of an effort to reinvent Roppongi as something more than just a nightlife zone. The work of renowned architect Kisho Kurokawa, the rippling façade of the building is based on computer-generated rhythmic images inspired by waves and hills. The largest exhibition space in Japan, the art center does not have a permanent collection of its own, but regularly features prominent Japanese as well as overseas exhibitions. **Almond** (*Amando* in Japanese), at the intersection of Roppongi-dori and Gaien-Higashi-dori, is the main rendezvous spot in Roppongi. The area to the south is where the action is. Clubs come in all shapes and sizes, some just wide enough for a counter and stools. Check the prices of drinks as they vary hugely. West of Almond is the **Square Building**, full of more trendy restaurants and clubs, including the intimate Birdland jazz club.

Akasaka District ⑫

赤坂地区

Map 2 C3–4, 2 F3–4. **S** *Akasaka-Mitsuke stn, Ginza & Marunouchi lines; Nagatacho stn, Yurakucho, Namboku & Hanzomon lines.*
Suntory Museum of Art *Tel (03) 3470-1073.* ○ *10am–5pm Tue–Sun (to 7pm Fri).* 🎟️ 🖼️ *Sanno Matsuri (Jun 16, Hie Jinja).*

With the Diet Building *(see p43)* and many government offices just to the east, Akasaka is a favorite place for politicians to socialize. Limousines carry dark-blue-suited men to the many exclusive establishments lining the streets here.

Opposite Akasaka-Mitsuke station is the **Suntory Museum of Art**, located in a single room on the 11th floor. It has an unrivaled collection of Edo-era screens, depicting scenes from the Edo court; one particularly fine example is *Namban* (Westerners in Japan). Traditional decorative arts are also well represented here, with ceramics, lacquerware, textiles, and tea utensils. There is also a tea ceremony room, café, and a museum shop.

About 200 m (220 yards) along Aoyama-dori from the Suntory Museum is the **Toyokawa Inari Shrine** (also called Myogon ji). With its red lanterns and flags, and dozens of statues of foxes (the messengers of Inari, a Shinto Rice deity), this is a pleasant place to linger for a while.

Back along Aoyama-dori on the left is the gleaming white ultra-modernist **Akasaka Prince Hotel** *(see p115)* designed by award-winning Japanese architect Kenze Tango. The open lobby has white marble floors and interior walls, while the exterior wall is glass. Past the Akasaka Prince Hotel to the left is the luxurious **Hotel New Otani** *(see p116)*. On the 17th floor is the revolving Blue Sky restaurant, serving Chinese food and offering stunning views across central Tokyo and the Imperial Palace. In the vast grounds and open to all is a 400-year-old Japanese garden.

South of Akasaka-Mitsuke station is the **Hie Jinja**, a shrine with a history dating back to 830. Shogun Ietsuna moved it here in the 17th century to buffer his castle; the present-day buildings are all modern. Each year in mid-June the Sanno Matsuri is celebrated here with a grand procession of 50 *Mikoshi* (portable shrines) and people in Heian-era costumes *(see pp28–30)*.

Ironware kettle in the Suntory Museum of Art

A *shinowa* circle, erected for good luck, at Hie Jinja in Akasaka

FARTHER AFIELD

Due to Tokyo's expanding in every conceivable direction, the area around the Imperial Palace is just one among several widely dispersed sights of interest. Seeking them out, though, poses few problems in a city with a superb transport system. The Japan Folk Craft Museum and the Goto Art Museum are small gems in pleasant surroundings that give an idea of Tokyo life as well as its rich heritage. Ryogoku, home to sumo wrestling, also features the interesting Edo-Tokyo Museum. The impressive

Giant lantern, Gokoku-ji temple

Tomioka Hochiman-gu shrine in downtown Fukagawa dates from the 17th century. To the northwest, Rikugi-en, near Ikebukuro, is one of the Edo period's last great stroll gardens. The mystic Sengaku-ji temple in the south, reconstructs the final scenes in the story of the 47 *ronin*, a real life tale of *samurai* loyalty and revenge. In contrast, Ikebukuro and Ebisu are modern urban centers. Daikanyama, the chic youth fashion district, and the futuristic man-made island of Odaiba, with its innovative architecture, offer a contemporary experience.

SIGHTS AT A GLANCE

Notable Districts
Ebisu District ⑪
Daikanyama District ⑫
Ikebukuro District ❶
Odaiba ⑨
Ryogoku District ❼
Shimokitazawa ⑭
Sugamo ❷
Downtown Fukagawa ❽
Zoshigaya ❻
Komagome ❸

Temples and Shrines
Gokoku-ji Temple ❺
Sengaku-ji Temple ⑩

Museums and Galleries
Japan Folk Craft Museum ⑬
Goto Art Museum ⑮

Scenic Transport Routes
Arakawa Tram Line ❹

KEY

☐ Main sightseeing area
═══ Expressway
─── Main road

0 km   1.5
0 miles   1.5

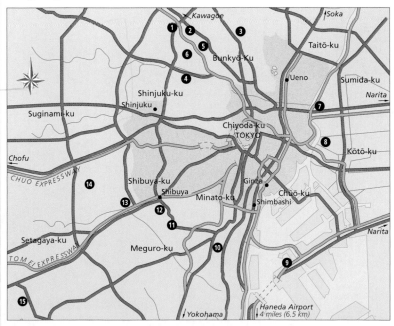

⊲ Fuji TV Building with its suspended dome of titanium, Odaiba

The striking exterior of the Metropolitan Art Space building, Ikebukuro

Ikebukuro District ❶

池袋地区

S *Ikebukuro stn, Marunouchi & Yurachuko lines.* **R** *Ikebukuro stn, Yamanote & many other lines.* **Ancient Orient Museum** *Tel (03) 3989-3491.* ⏰ *10am–5pm daily.* 🎫 **Metropolitan Art Space** *Tel (03) 5391-2111.* 🎫 *only for concerts.*

With the second-busiest train station in Japan (after Shinjuku), Ikebukuro is a designated *fuku toshin* (sub-center) of Tokyo. Devoid of the pretensions of Tokyo's other entertainment districts such as Shinjuku and Shibuya, it is a relaxed place, even when seething with people who are drawn by the area's moderately priced restaurants and bars.

A short walk east of the station lies Ikebukuro's main attraction, **Sunshine City**, a four-block complex whose core building is the iconic **Sunshine 60**, one of Asia's tallest buildings. It is built on top of what was Sugamo Prison, where seven World War II war criminals, including the prime minister, Tojo Hideki, were convicted and hanged. There is an impressive planetarium, aquarium, and 60th-floor observatory here. The often-overlooked **Ancient Orient Museum**, on the 7th floor of the Bunka

A statue in front of Ikebukuro station

Kaikan Center, is Sunshine City's high culture component featuring pre-Islamic art from the Middle East and Silk Road. Also located on Sunshine 60-dori, **Toyota Amlux**, a five-floor car showroom with a designer studio and a virtual driving simulator, is worth a quick look. Over on the west side, visitors can watch craftsmen create ceramic objects, paper, lacquer, knives, and kimonos at the **Japan Traditional Craft Center** (*see p145*). Besides its free art exhibitions on the fifth floor, the nearby **Metropolitan Art Space** is famous for its unusually long glass escalator and the world's biggest pipe organ.

Built in 1921, **Jiyu Gakuen Myonichikan** (School of Freedom) is a private school building designed by the famous architect Frank Lloyd Wright in his characteristic geometric style.

Sugamo ❷

巣鴨

S *Sugamo stn, Mita line.* **R** *Sugamo stn, Yamanote line.* **Shinsho-ji Temple** *Tel (03) 3918-4068.* ⏰ *daily.* **Kogan-ji Temple** *Tel (03) 3917-8221.* ⏰ *daily.*

Sugamo has two temples of interest. **Shinsho-ji Temple**'s courtyard is dominated by a large bronze figure. Worshipped as a protector of children and travelers, it is one of the

six roadside statues cast between 1708 and 1720. Sugamo's best-known temple **Kogan-ji** is dedicated to the thorn-removing deity "Togenuki Jizo," believed to have curative powers. Street markets outside the temple selling traditional souvenirs and Chinese cures add character to this old quarter.

Komagome ❸

駒込

S *Komagome stn, Namboku line.* **R** *Komagome stn, Yamanote line.* **Rikugi-en Garden** *Tel (03) 3941-2222.* ⏰ *9am–5pm daily.* 🎫 **Kyu Furukawa Teien** ⏰ *9am–5pm daily.*

The celebrated **Rikugi-en Garden** was constructed by Yanagisawa Yoshiyasu, grand chamberlain of the fifth shogun, in seven years, starting in 1695. Iwasaki Yataro, Mitsubishi's founder, oversaw its Meiji-era renovation. The design recreates 88 landscapes in miniature from famous *waka* (31-syllable poems), so the view changes every few steps.

Komagome's other garden of note is the **Kyu Furukawa Teien**. Its main building, a charcoal-grey stone residence designed by British architect Josiah Conder, resembles a small Scottish manor house. The mansion and its English-style rose garden sit on a ridge above steps leading down to a landscaped area, replete with a tea ceremony pavilion and a heart-shaped pond.

Manicured shrubs in the landscaped Rikugi-en garden

Minowabashi stop, a terminal of the Toden Arakawa line

Arakawa Tram Line ④

荒川都電

S *Edogawabashi stn, Yurakucho line.* **Sumida River trips** (03) 5608-8869.

As recently as 1955, 600,000 people a day were riding the dozens of tram lines that crisscrossed the city. Now the 8 miles (13 km) of the Arakawa line are all that is left. The others were eliminated as old-fashioned in the modernization for the 1964 Olympics.

The Arakawa tram line runs from Waseda in the west to Minowabashi in the east and costs ¥160 for each trip, short or long. Near the Waseda end of the line is the quiet stroll garden of **Shin Edogawa**. A short walk from Arakawa Yuenchimae stop is a modest amusement park, **Arakawa Yuen Park**; Sumida River tourboat trips leave from here. Opposite the Arakawa Nanachome stop is **Arakawa Nature Park**.

The line takes in sections of Shinjuku, Toshima, and Arakawa wards, providing convenient access to city sights within walking distance of its stations. These include the historically important **Kishimojin** (Pomegranate Temple) in Zoshigaya, and the **Kyu Furukawa Teien** *(see p72)* in Kita Ward. **Jokan-ji Temple**, the last resting place of destitute prostitutes from the old Yoshiwara pleasure quarter, is a short stroll from the line's eastern terminus at Minowabashi.

Gokoku-ji Temple ⑤

護国寺

S *Gokoku-ji stn, Yurakucho line.* **Tel** *(03) 3941-0764.*

Given Gokoku-ji's historical credentials as one of Edo's most important temples, and its survival in the face of earthquakes, fires, and air raids during World War II, the absence of visitors, especially on weekdays, is surprising.

Before entering the spacious grounds of the temple, visitors pass through the arresting **Nioman Gate**. The gate takes its name from the pair of fierce-looking, red-faced Nio statues positioned at either side of the entrance. Placed here to ward off malevolent spirits, the right-hand figure's mouth is open, while his companion's is closed. This symbolizes exhalation and inhalation, creation and dissolution; the harmony of opposites encountered throughout Japanese philosophy and arts.

Stunningly well preserved, the complex's main hall, dating from 1681, with its sweeping copper roof and massive pillars, is a treasure house of Buddhist statuary. Foremost among the deities here are Kannon, the goddess of mercy. Eight celestial

Seventeenth-century two-story pagoda, Gokoku-ji temple

maidens dance across the ceiling in paintings that float over transoms covered with colorful carvings of peonies.

Completing the ensemble of buildings that have been designated "Important Cultural Properties," are an imposing bell tower and a rare two-tiered pagoda, a popular subject for painters.

Zoshigaya ⑥

雑司ヶ谷霊園

S *Higashi-Ikebukuro stn, Yurakucho line.* *Ikebukuro stn, Yamanote line.*

To the left of Gokoku-ji temple's rear exit at Higashi-Ikebukuro, just beyond the Shuto Expressway underpass, **Zoshigaya Cemetery** is the resting place of several important literary figures, including Japanese novelists such as Natsumi Soseki and Nagai Kafu. The Greek-Irish writer, Lafcadio Hearn, whose books helped to introduce Japan to the West in the Meiji era, is also buried here. Scenic tree-endowed graveyards such as Zoshigaya can get crowded during the spring cherry-viewing season. Another little-visited spot, the **Zoshigaya Missionary Museum** built in 1907 by an American missionary John Moody McCaleb, is a well-preserved colonial house open to visitors.

Monks praying inside the well-preserved main hall, Gokoku-ji temple

Ryogoku District ❼
両国地区

Map 4 E4–5. **S** *Ryogoku stn, Toei-Oedo line.* **R** *Ryogoku stn, JR Sobu line.* **Sumo Museum** 1-3-28 Yokoami, Sumida-ku. **Tel** *(03) 3622-0366.* ◯ *10am–4:30pm Mon–Fri.* ● *public hols.* **Edo-Tokyo Museum** 1-4-1 Yokoami, Sumida-ku. **Tel** *(03) 3626-9974.* ◯ *9:30am–5:30pm Tue–Sun (7:30pm Sat).* 🖼

The interiors of Fukagawa Edo Museum

On the east bank of the Sumida River, Ryogoko was a great entertainment and commerce center in Edo's Shitamachi. These days it is a quiet place but it still has its most famous residents – sumo wrestlers. Many *beya* (sumo stables) are here, and it is not unusual to see huge young men walking the streets in *yukata* (light cotton kimonos) and *geta* (wooden sandals).

The **National Sumo Stadium** has been here since 1945; the current building dates from 1985. During a tournament *(see p18–19)* many of the wrestlers simply walk from their *beya* just down the street. Inside the stadium is a **Sumo Museum** lined with portraits of all the *yokozuna* (grand champions) dating back 200 years.

Beside the stadium is the huge **Edo-Tokyo Museum**, built to resemble an old style of elevated warehouse. One of Tokyo's most imaginative and interesting museums, its exhibition space is divided into two zones on two floors tracing life in Edo and then Tokyo, as Edo was renamed in 1868. The exhibits, some of

Kabuki actor, Edo-Tokyo Museum

which are interactive, appeal to both adults and children and have explanations in Japanese and English.

The historic route around the museum starts at a traditional arched wooden bridge, a replica of Nihonbashi *(see p42)*. There are life-sized re-constructed buildings, including the façade of a Kabuki theater. Marvelous scale-model dioramas, some of which are automated, show everything from the house of a *daimyo* (feudal lord) to a section of Shitamachi. Beside a scale model of Tokyo's first skyscraper is rubble from the 1923 earthquake. There is a rickshaw and Japan's first "light" automobile – a three-seater Subaru with a 360 cc engine. In the media section is a step-by-step example of how *ukiyo-e* woodblock prints *(see p55)* were produced. Models of the boats that once plied the Sumida River give some idea of how important the river was to Edo life. Just up from the

bridge, **Kyu Yasuda Teien**, a tiny Japanese stroll garden replete with traditional stone lanterns, an orange-colored bridge over a carp pond, azalea bushes, and topiary, is located next to the **Earthquake Memorial Park**. The park is dedicated to the victims of the Great Kanto Earthquake, which struck at precisely one minute before noon on September 1, 1923. Today, incense is burnt before the three-story pagoda and memorial hall to mark the catastrophe. The park's Yokami Gallery displays an odd collection of melted metal objects – a broken water pipe, the burnt chassis of a car, and a mass of melted nails.

Downtown Fukagawa ❽
深川

R *Monzen-Nakacho stn, Tozai, Kiyosumi-Shirakawa Oedo & Hanzomon lines.* **Fukagawa Edo Museum** **Tel** *(03) 3630-8625.* ◯ *9:30am–5pm daily.* ● *2nd & 4th Mon.* **Kiyosumi Teien** **Tel** *(03) 3641-5892.* ◯ *9am–5pm daily.*

This area is situated east of the Sumida River and squarely within what was known as Shitamachi, or the "low city" *(see p54)*. It took centuries to reclaim the land from Tokyo Bay and the estuary of the Sumida River. To get a good historical grip on the neighborhood, visit the **Fukagawa Edo Museum**. The museum recreates an old area of Fukagawa circa 1840, with 11 original buildings, homes, shops, a theater, a boathouse, a tavern, and a 33-ft (10-m)

Reconstruction of a Kabuki theater in Ryogoku's Edo-Tokyo Museum

high fire tower. The interiors of the recreated houses have an authentic atmosphere with fishing nets and workman's clothing casually hung on the walls, and empty shells strewn on the floor of a reproduced clam peddler's home.

Built within the grounds of a large estate in the area of present-day Monzen Nakacho, the **Kiyosumi Teien** is a beautifully landscaped garden in this down-to-earth district of east Tokyo. A wealthy trader, Bunzaemon Kinokuniya, built the large estate and the grounds were later taken over by the Iwasaki family, founders of the Mitsubishi group. The Kiyosumi Teien is a classic Edo-era *kaiyushiki teien*, or "pond walk around garden," with plants that bloom at different times of the year. An exquisite teahouse floats majestically above the water and 55 rare stones, brought from all over Japan by Mitsubishi steamships, are the highlight of this spacious garden.

Nearby, the **Tomioka Hachiman-gu Shrine** dates from the 17th century. The current building is a 1968 reconstruction, but its prayer and spirit halls, and towering, copper-tiled roof are very impressive. The shrine is dedicated to eight deities, including the ever-popular Benten, goddess of beauty and the arts. The famed **Flea Market**, the Fukagawa *ennichi*, is another attraction. A lively event, it is held in the shrine grounds on the first two Sundays of the month, from around 8am to sunset.

LIVING IN SMALL SPACES

Land, and therefore housing, is very expensive in Tokyo. The average home costs 7–8 times the family's yearly income, and space is at a premium. A traditional design has closets for storing rolled-up futons; in the morning the bedding is swapped for a low table at which the family sits cross-legged to eat meals. More and more families are opting for a semi-Western style with raised beds, table, and chairs, resulting in homes being even more cramped.

Crammed balconies of multi-storied apartments

Odaiba ⑨
台場

🚃 *Yurikamome monorail from Shimbashi stn; Rinkai Fukutoshin line to Tokyo Teleport.* 🚢 *from Hinode Pier 10:10am–7:10pm, every 20–25 mins.* **Museum of Maritime Sciences** *Tel (03) 5500-1111.* ◯ *10am–5pm daily (to 6pm Sat, Sun, public hols & in summer).* 📷 **National Museum of Emerging Science and Innovation** *Tel (03) 3570-9151.* ◯ *10am–5:30pm Wed–Sun.* 📷 **Oedo Onsen Monogatari** *Tel (03) 5500-1126.* ◯ *11am–9am.* 📷

The futuristic Fuji TV Building with its suspended dome

The artificial island of Odaiba across the middle of Tokyo Bay, is both a trendy entertainment zone and an ideal location for cutting edge architecture. Driverless Yurikamome line trains cross the bay, offering a majestic view of one of the island's most striking constructions, the **Fuji TV Building** *(see p83)*. **Odaiba Marine Park** and its artificial beach lies on the other side of the building. The **Rainbow Bridge** can be seen from the

Statue, Tomioka Hachiman-gu

outdoor wooden boulevards, cafés, and eateries of **Decks Tokyo Beach** *(see p83)*. Follow the elevated tracks south, where the architecturally outstanding **Museum of Maritime Science** *(see p83)* stands among the palm trees.

A short distance from the Telecom Center, the **National Museum of Emerging Science and Innovation (Miraikan)** is dedicated to Japanese hi-tech creations. Just across the road from the museum is the **Oedo Onsen Monogatari**, a traditional hot spring. A re-created Shitamachi interior takes visitors back in time.

Nearby is Tokyo Fashion Town, an enclosed complex of retail shops, boutiques, and cafés. **Palette Town**, a few blocks farther, is home to the giant ferris wheel and the **Mega Web** *(see p82)*, supposedly the world's largest automobile showroom. It also boasts the opulent **Venus Fort** *(see p82)*, a highly original fashion shopping experience. Not far away, the megalithic **Tokyo Big Sight** *(see p82)*, houses a convention center, cafés, and restaurants.

The lively flea market outside Tomioka Hachiman-gu Shrine

Sengaku-ji Temple ⑩
泉岳寺

S *Sengaku-ji stn, Toei Asakusa line.*
Museum ☐ *9am–4pm daily.* 🖼

This temple is the site of the climax of Japan's favorite tale of loyalty and revenge, re-told in the play *Chushingura* and many movies. Lord Asano was sentenced to death by *seppuku* (suicide by disembowelment) for drawing his sword when goaded by Lord Kira. Denied the right to seek revenge, 47 of Asano's retainers (*samurai*) now *ronin* (masterless *samurai*), plotted in secret. In 1703, they attacked Kira's house and beheaded him, presenting the head to Asano's grave at Sengaku-ji. They in turn were sentenced to *seppuku*, and are buried here. Inside the temple gate and up the steps on the right is the well where the retainers washed Kira's head. Farther ahead on the right are the retainers' graves, still tended with flowers. Back at the base of the steps is an interesting **museum** with artifacts from the incident and statues of some of the 47 *ronin*. Overshadowed by the *ronin* drama, the temple grounds, approached through a small gate with a traditional guard house, merit attention. The temple's original main hall dates from 1612; the current building is a faithful reconstruction. The oldest structure, the Sanmon gate dates from 1836.

Beer Museum Ebisu, with a Tasting Room for cheap draughts

Ebisu District ⑪
恵比寿地区

S *Ebisu stn, Hibiya line.* **R** *Ebisu stn, Yamanote line.* **Tokyo Metropolitan Museum of Photography** *Tel (03) 3280-0099.* ☐ *10am–6pm Tue–Sat (to 8pm Thu & Fri).* 🖼 **www.syabi.com** **Beer Museum Ebisu** *Tel (03) 5423-7255.* ☐ *10am–6pm Tue–Sun (Last adm 1 hr before closing).*

The completion in the mid-1990s of **Ebisu Garden Place**, a commercial and residential center, brought this area to life. The superb **Tokyo Metropolitan Museum of Photography**, to the right of the entrance, has a permanent collection of work by Japanese and foreign photographers, and excellent special exhibitions. In the heart of Ebisu Garden Place are a Mitsukoshi store, boutiques, two cinemas, a theater, and restaurants, including Taillevent Robuchon, a French restaurant that looks like a 19th-century chateau. The crowded central plaza is a great spot for people-watching. To the left of Mitsukoshi is the small **Beer Museum Ebisu** with exhibits and videos about beer worldwide and in Japan, and free samples.

Daikanyama District ⑫
代官山

R *Daikanyama stn, Tokyu Toyoko line.* **Hillside Gallery** *Tel (03) 3476-4868.* ☐ *10am–5pm Tue–Sun.* 🖼

An important archaeological site, where ancient pit dwellings and well-preserved burial mounds have been discovered, Daikanyama is better known these days as a classy, low-rise neighborhood. It is more popular with the smart set, who come here to explore its trendy boutiques, restaurants, patisseries, and al-fresco pavement cafés.

Some big name international fashion brands, such as Jean Paul Gaultier, have their outposts here, adding more class and distinction to an already chic district. The area, with its back lanes, shops, and home courtyards full of greenery, makes for a pleasant stroll. Interest in the area first grew when Japanese architect Fumihiki Maki began his ongoing **Hillside Terrrace**, an apartment, gallery, and shopping project along leafy Kyu Yamate-dori, in 1969. Buildings

Ebisu Garden Place skyscraper complex, lined with restaurants, shops, and museums

Exhibition of flag models by various artists, Japan Folk Craft Museum

station leads to bars and the best concentrations of live music venues in Tokyo, most hosting eager new bands.

This grungy art village, a haphazard mixture of ramshackle, Showa-era buildings, and pop art façades covered in graffiti, is unquestionably one of the city's fashion towns, though it remains light years away from the chic and sophisticated streets of Omotesando or Akasaka. Its numerous shops and stalls offer an eclectic selection.

have been added over the decades. The **Hillside Gallery** hosts interesting art exhibitions. Closer to the station **Daikan'yama Address** (see p147) and **La Fuente** complexes house boutiques, ritzy restaurants, and trendy cafés.

Japan Folk Craft Museum ⑬

日本民芸館

4-3-33 Komaba, Meguro-ku.
Tel (03) 3467-4527.
Komaba-Todaimae stn, Keio Inokashira line. 10am–5pm Tue–Sun.

Known to the Japanese as Mingeikan, this small but excellent museum was founded by art historian Yanagi Muneyoshi. The criteria for inclusion in the museum are that the object should be the work of an anonymous maker, produced for daily use, and representative of the region from which it comes. The museum building, designed by Yanagi and completed in 1931, uses black tiles and white stucco outside.

On display are items ranging from woven baskets to ax sheaths, iron kettles, pottery, and kimonos; together they present a fascinating view of rural life. There are also special themed exhibits, such as 20th-century ceramics or Japanese textiles, and a room dedicated to Korean Yi-dynasty work. A small gift shop sells fine crafts and some books.

Shimokitazawa ⑭

下北沢

Shimokitazawa stn, Inokashira & Odakyu lines. **Honda Theater** Tel (03) 3468-0030. daily (times vary according to program).

More popularly known as 'Shimokita,' the really distinguishing character of this area is its atmosphere. The seeds of the area's relaxed and well-established bohemian image were sown in the 1960s when small, fringe theaters opened here. Some of these have survived. Underground establishments, such as the famous **Honda Theater**, pack a remarkable number of people into small but convivial spaces for modern, experimental productions.

While this youthful, soulful district's north side is a colorful congestion of ethnic restaurants, cafés, fashion boutiques, and music and game stores, the south exit of the

Back carrier, Japan Folk Craft Museum

Goto Art Museum ⑮

五島美術館

3-9-25 Kaminoge, Setagaya-ku.
Tel (03) 3703-0662. Tokyu Denentoshi line from Shibuya stn to Futako-Tamagawaen, then Tokyu Oimachi line to Kaminoge. 10am–4:30pm Tue–Sun. when exhibitions change.

Set in a pleasant hillside garden, this museum showcases the private collection of the late chairman of the Tokyu Corporation, Goto Keita. Avidly interested in Zen, he was originally attracted to Buddhist calligraphy called bokuseki, particularly that of 16th-century priests. Also included are ceramics, paintings, and metalwork mirrors; items are changed several times a year. The museum's most famous works, however, are scenes from 12th-century scrolls of the Tale of Genji, painted by Fujiwara Takayoshi, which have been designated National Treasures. They are shown once a year, usually during "Golden Week" (see p160).

Women in kimonos outside a teahouse at the Goto Art Museum garden

THREE GUIDED WALKS

For all its cosmopolitan sprawl and congestion, Tokyo is a feet-friendly city. Its streets, slopes, temples, shrines, cubby-hole stores, parks and gardens, and architecturally stunning buildings are best experienced on foot. From modern, man-made, sea-facing expanses, and spacious boulevards to the narrow streets of the past, the walks in this book have been designed to maximize time and space by directing you through a concentration of sights, each route presenting different facets of the city's vibrant character. The first walk guides you from the high ground

Bust of missionary Nikolai Kassatkin

of the Yamanote hills, past Shinto and Confucian institutions to the bustling plebian districts of Ochanomizu and Jimbocho. The second walk is a step back in time to the stone courtyards of garden temples, craft shops, and the crumbling tombs of Yanaka, one of the best-preserved older quarters of Tokyo. The final walk introduces useful vantage points from which to take in the monumental scale and novelty of the artificial island of Odaiba. Food and refreshment recommendations are factored into each itinerary as enjoyable stopping off points.

KEY

····· Walk route

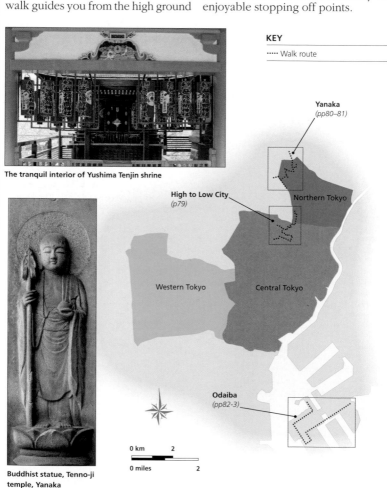

The tranquil interior of Yushima Tenjin shrine

Yanaka *(pp80–81)*

High to Low City *(p79)*

Northern Tokyo

Western Tokyo

Central Tokyo

Odaiba *(pp82-3)*

0 km   2

0 miles   2

Buddhist statue, Tenno-ji temple, Yanaka

A 45-Minute Walk from the High to Low City

The walk follows the slopes of the Yamanote, or High City, down to the flat, riverine lands of the Shitamachi, the Low City. Starting from Yushima Tenjin, the great shrine of learning, this route includes Kanda Myojin, one of the foremost places of worship in the city, and a rare Confucian temple sitting on a bluff above the Kanda River. It takes in a Russian Orthodox Cathedral, before ending at the lively streets of Ochanomizu.

Torii gate at the entrance to Kanda Myojin shrine ②

Start at Yushima Tenjin shrine ①, dedicated to a 9th-century scholar deified as Tenjin, the patron of learning. Walk down the gentle slope south of the shrine, crossing Kuramaebashi-dori. A copper-plated *torii* (gate) set at the foot of a slight incline off Hongo-dori, announces the entrance to Kanda Myojin shrine ②, the site of the Kanda Matsuri *(see p28)*, one of the city's grandest festivals. Just across the road is the Yushima Seido temple ③, dedicated to the spirit of the Chinese sage Confucius. Shady temple gardens are situated at the base of a bluff above the banks of the Kanda River ④. Walk down to the river and the stone ramparts of Hijiribashi (The Bridge of the Sages). Pause here to peer

west along the river for a good view of the 19-story Century Tower ⑤, one of Tokyo's impressive office buildings; the twin towers boast innovative air-conditioning strips, and a 19-floor atrium that allows extra light to pour in. Cross the bridge to reach the Russian Orthodox Nikolai Cathedral ⑥, with its deep green onion dome looming over

The Archeological Museum of Meiji University ⑧

the more Occidental domain of Ochanomizu. It is just a few blocks east from here to Kanda Yabu Soba *(see p132)* ⑦, a legendary buckwheat noodle restaurant just off Shoheibashi-dori. Walk directly west from here to Ochanomizu's main street, Meidai-dori. The Archeological Museum of Meiji University ⑧ appears on the right. It has one of the best collections of ancient objects and artifacts found on digs around Japan. In the same building, check out the university's Criminal Museum ⑨. Casals Hall ⑩ on the left is a smart auditorium designed by world famous

Japanese architect Arata Isozaki. Turn right at the end of Meidai-dori into Yasukuni-dori and the heart of the famous Kanda-Jimbocho book store district ⑪. The walk ends on this street near Jimbocho subway station.

TIPS FOR WALKERS

Starting point: *Yushima Tenjin shrine.*
Length: *2.5 km (1.5 miles).*
Getting there: *The start of this walk is the Yushima metro station on the Chiyoda line.*
Stopping off points: *A tea stop at the entrance to Kanda Myojin shrine; lunch at Kanda Yabu Soba, a local institution.*

0 meters 400
0 yards 400

KEY

• • • Walk route

S Subway station

R Train station

A 90-Minute Walk in Yanaka

One of the best preserved old quarters of Tokyo that has survived both the Great Kanto Earthquake of 1923 and the fire bombings of 1945 relatively unscathed, Yanaka is a rare enclave of the old city. Its famous graveyard, with mossy tombs, Buddha stones, and cherry trees, is the resting place of famous literati, actors, and former shoguns. A reclusive retreat for artists, writers, and designers, Yanaka's narrow streets preclude heavy traffic, making it ideal for walking.

The picturesque Kyoo-ji temple housing a wooden hall ④

Start this walk by turning left just after exiting JR Nishi-Nippori station's south exit. The quiet road here, sitting on a ridge known as the Suwa Plateau, is a good introduction to the old world charms of Yanaka. Follow the sloping road until a row of ginkgo trees and a well-weathered Suwa shrine ① appears on the left. Founded in 1322, the shrine is home to the deity who protects Nippori and Yanaka districts.

It is just a few steps along to Joko-ji temple ②, known as the "Snow-Viewing Temple." Once a popular spot to watch snowflakes and

Lion sculpture outside Suwa shrine ①

compose poetry, it has a rock in the temple garden where the shogun Iemitsu rested while admiring the view. Today only a mass of railway tracks and love hotels can be seen. More interesting are the well-carved stone Buddhas near the temple's entrance, and a bronze figure of Jizo, protector of children, carved in 1691 by a Buddhist priest-artist Kumu-shonin.

Walk past the small road known as Fujimi-zaka or "Fuji-Viewing Slope," a narrow road lined with old red-brick walls. Directly opposite a row of old tenements, the main attraction at Yofuku-ji temple ③ is the Nioman Gate. The two guardian statues within the gate were built at the beginning of the 18th century.

Take a left at the end of the road and Kyoo-ji temple ④ comes into view, its zelkova wood gate pitted with bullet holes from an ancient battle. Return to the main road, and continue to the Asakura Choso Museum ⑤, a sculpture gallery dedicated to the work of renowned Japanese sculptor, Fumio

Asakura. Return to the main road, turn left, and continue walking until you see a flight of stone steps descending to a narrow shopping street called the Yanaka Ginza ⑥, selling traditional crafts and foods. Follow the smell of roasting tea to Chaho Kanekichi-en, an old-fashioned teashop near the entrance to the street.

JR Nishi Nippori

Return up the stone steps, and continue past Kyoo-ji temple. Turn right up a short flight of steps to enter the Yanaka Cemetery ⑦. With its mossy tombstones, leafy walks, wrought iron gates, and worn stone lanterns, Yanaka Cemetery is almost Gothic in character. Head to Tenno-ji temple ⑧, adjoining the cemetery ground. The statue of the Great Buddha of Yanaka, a bronze figure cast in 1691 is the focal point.

Return to the road, bear left and then take the first right, reaching a T-junction at the end. It is easy to miss, but on the right corner, the Gamo residence ⑨ is a fine example of *dashigeta-zukuri*

Seventeenth-century bronze statue of Buddha, Tenno-ji temple ⑧

TIPS FOR WALKERS

Starting point: Nishi-Nippori station, south exit.
Length: 2.5 km (1.5 miles).
Getting there: Arrive via the JR Yamanote Line train or Chiyoda Line metro.
Stopping off points: A range of original tea blends at Chaho Kanekichi-en, and Kushiage Hantei, a Japanese restaurant.

(projecting girder style) design. Turn left at the T-junction, away from Nishi Nippori station. Turn right down Sansakizaka and walk to the entrance of Zensho-en temple ⑩. Meditation sessions are held here on Sunday mornings, but the main point of interest is a 20-ft (6-m) high, gold-leaf-covered statue at the rear of the main hall; this is known as the Yanaka Kannon, after the goddess of mercy. Continue down the slope for about 100 meters or so for Daien-ji temple ⑪. Two adjoining halls, one Buddhist and the other Shinto, have fine wooden carvings of dragons, nymphs, and Chinese phoenix. Across the road from Daien-ji is one of Tokyo's oldest and most exquisite paper arts shops, Isetatsu ⑫. View well-crafted fans, combs, dolls, and colorful chests of drawers. Take the lane next to the shop and walk until you reach a small road. Turn left and then bear right till the T-junction. The Daimyo Clock Museum ⑬ to your right displays a fascinating collection of timepieces made exclusively for Japan's feudal lords. Follow

The ornate exterior of Nezu shrine ⑭

the road down to busy Shinobazu-dori. Turn right and walk up to the traffic lights, then turn left for Nezu shrine ⑭. Enter through the impressive vermilion Zuishin-mon gate, then to a second portal, the Karamon Gate, with some fine lacquered partitions. You will then reach the main sanctuary, a superb Momoyama-style structure with vivid carvings. Return to Shinobazu-dori, turn right, and walk a few blocks. Cross Kototoi-dori until you see a unique three-story wooden Meiji-era building that houses the popular Hantei ⑮ *(see p135)*, an atmospheric Japanese-style restaurant. This walk ends near Nezu metro station.

0 meters 200

0 yards 200

KEY

• • • Walk route

S Subway station

R Train station

Isetatsu shop, renowned for Edo-style paper with colorful patterns ⑫

A 90-Minute Walk in Odaiba

The post-modernist buildings, art installations, and shopping malls that constitute Odaiba (see p75) seem to hail from another world. Odaiba's sheer audacity, its flamboyant marriage of design, technology, commercialism, and fun, epitomizes Japan's fascination with blending high kitsch into a concoction that is both refined and brashly artificial. A pleasure quarter for the city savvy, a walk through this island comes with restaurant and café stops to recover from the sheer over-stimulation.

The futuristic Tokyo Big Sight building, an architectural marvel ①

Start the walk at Tokyo Big Sight ①, which is accessed by overhead walkways from Kokusai-Tenjijo station, or by climbing the steps from the Suijo water bus, Tokyo Big Sight Station. One of Tokyo's prominent architectural marvels, Tokyo Big Sight combines a convention center, exhibition halls, cafés, and restaurants in a pyramidal structure that appears to be upside down. Large atriums and an eighth-floor observation gallery provide superb views of the Tokyo waterfront development and the bay.

Return to the elevated tracks of the Yurikamome monorail, following them in the direction of Aomi station and the Palette Town complex. The gigantic ferris wheel, the Stream of Starlight

TIPS FOR WALKERS

Starting point: Kokusai-Tenjijo-Seimon station on the Yurikamome line monorail.
Length: 2 km (1 mile).
Stopping off points:
Recuperate at a table with a view of the goings on at Venus Fort at Thé Chinois Madu. Daiba Little Hong Kong typifies the island's ersatz fun, and the food is good.

②, comes into sight on the right. The views from the top are worth the dizzy sensation some passengers may experience as they rise above the picturesque bay. Also in the Palette Town development, Mega Web ③, a state-of-the-art automobile showroom, is run by Toyota. Look out for Toyota City Showcase, with a driving simulator, test-drive area, and a History Garage Museum.

Cross to the next block of Palette Town and enter the unreal world of the Renaissance-themed shopping mall Venus Fort ④, a complex of retail shops, boutiques, and cafés. Lined with designer

The opulent interiors of Venus Fort shopping mall ④

boutiques such as Jean Paul Gaultier and Vanessa Bruno, windows have been eliminated for the sake of striking optical illusions, including an artificial overhead sky that morphs from cobalt blue to lush sunsets, to forked lightning. Soak in the the scenery, sitting at the authentic

DAI-SAN DAI
HISTORICAL PA

KEY

••• Walk route

🚉 Train station

🚉 Monorail

🚢 Riverboat

Daiba

SHIOKAZE
PARK

0 meters   400

0 yards   400

Fune-no-
kagakukan

⑥

Chinese-style teashop, Thé Chinois Madu.

Walk to the rear of Palette Town, turn left and move along the Central Promenade, until you reach the 88-feet (27-meter) high statue of Flame of Freedom in the form of a golden needle, the work of modern sculptor Marc Couteiler. Turn left here and walk along the West Promenade until the Nihon Kagaku Miraikan ⑤, the National Museum of Emerging Science and Innovation, appears on the right. Dedicated to displays of Japanese hi-tech designs, explore the exhibits on your own, or join a robot-conducted tour. Experimental kits, robots, and interesting space goods are on sale at the gift shop here.

A few minutes west of here, facing Fune-no-Kagakukan station, the outstanding Museum of Maritime Science ⑥, designed in the shape of a gigantic vessel, stands beside a grove of palm trees. Exhibits here trace the development of modern shipping and ocean transport. Follow the monorail north towards Daiba station. Ocean-facing Shiokaze Park, a good picnic spot with lots of trees, is on the left. Just beyond

Rainbow Bridge and the Tokyo skyline ⑪

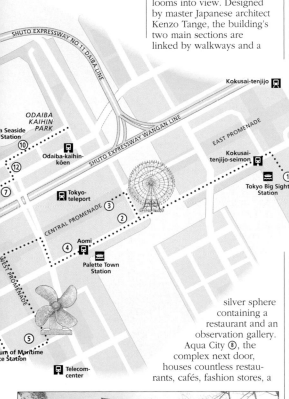

the station, the spectacular Fuji TV Building ⑦ (*see p14*) looms into view. Designed by master Japanese architect Kenzo Tange, the building's two main sections are linked by walkways and a silver sphere containing a restaurant and an observation gallery. Aqua City ⑧, the complex next door, houses countless restaurants, cafés, fashion stores, a

video arcade, and a multiplex cinema. Visitors are usually surprised when they glimpse the remarkable replica of New York City's Statue of Liberty ⑨ at the edge of the concourse. Stroll along the outdoor wooden boulevards, cafés, and eateries of Sunset Beach Restaurant Row. This forms the exterior part of Decks Tokyo Beach, a shopping and amusement complex. The Decks Tokyo Brewery, on the fifth floor, is notable for the Daiba brand micro-beer brewed on the premises. Sega Joyopolis, a virtual reality arcade, occupies the third to fifth floors. Odaiba Marine Park ⑩, a sliver of green abutting a sandy, artificial beach, lies below Decks. Visitors peer over the strip to the graceful lines of the expansive Rainbow Bridge ⑪ (*see p10*), magically illuminated at night. Duck back into the main building of Decks Tokyo Beach. Daiba Little Hong Kong ⑫ up on the sixth and seventh floors consists of several "streets" that simulate a downtown Chinese area. With speakers emitting sounds of feral cats fighting in narrow lanes and the roar of planes descending over washing lines, it is more the unsavory neighborhoods of mid-20th century Hong Kong than the modern skyscraper districts. Chinese dumplings and dim sum at Shi An Gyoza in Little Hong Kong are a treat. The walk ends here. Odaiba Kaihin-koen station is nearby.

Museum of Maritime Science, a glass-and-metal reproduction of a ship ⑥

BEYOND TOKYO

*S*ome of the country's most famous sights are just a short train trip away from Tokyo. Foremost among these are the historic temple towns of Nikko, Narita, and Kamakura, and bustling Yokohama, Japan's second largest city. Hakone is a mountainous hot spring town and on a clear day, it offers picturesque views of the soaring peak of Mount Fuji – one of the great icons of Japan.

It takes less time than one would imagine to leave behind the sprawling suburbs, dormitory towns, and industrial fringes of Tokyo to reach breathtaking natural habitats and environs. Fine hiking trails, wildlife, and flora are easily accessed at Chichibu-Tama National Park and the Fuji Five Lakes area, while the volcanic hills and gorges of Hakone and the Izu Peninsula have been hot spring destinations for foreign visitors since the 19th century.

Yokohama, a cosmopolitan city with a vibrant port area, delightful museums, and a large, atmospheric Chinatown district combines history, ethnicity, and modernity. Yokohama's neighbor, Kamakura, sitting snugly between green hills and the Pacific, is a treasurehouse of spectacular Zen temples, tranquil gardens, teahouses, and exquisite craft shops. The origins of the magnificent Tsurugaoka Hachiman-gu shrine date from the 11th century, while the Great Buddha, a splendidly realized bronze statue, has survived from when it was first cast in 1252. To the east of Tokyo, Narita-san, an important temple associated with Fudo, the god of fire, is a place of common worship throughout the year. A stone's throw from Narita Airport, a visit to this temple provides the chance to see how Japanese observe their faith, right down to having new cars blessed and protective amulets hung on them, in a ritual presided over by robed priests. Just an hour north of the capital, the elaborate shrines, grand gates, and necropolis of Nikko, where the first shogun Ieyasu is entombed, are overshadowed by towering forests of cryptomeria, creating a mood of spiritual grandeur.

A row of Buddhist statues, Nikko, Tochigi prefecture

◁ Snow-capped Mount Fuji with lush green tea fields in foreground

Exploring Beyond Tokyo

The areas beyond Tokyo offer great geographical and cultural diversity. Bayside Yokohama, a residential zone, sits just above the Miura Peninsula. Ocean-facing Kamakura is an ancient temple city. Narita-san, one of the most important temples in the Kanto area, lies on the flatlands of Chiba beyond the eastern suburbs. The thermally-rich and picturesque Izu Peninsula lies to the west. Topographic diversity continues with Hakone and Mount Fuji and the Fuji Five Lakes. At historically-rich Nikko, the low slopes of the Ashio-sanchi range span west toward Chichibu-Tama National Park. Nearby Okutama is a favorite weekend hiking area for Tokyoites.

Daibutsu, the Great Buddha of Kamakura

SEE ALSO

• *Where to Stay* p117

• *Where to Eat* p141

SIGHTS AT A GLANCE

KEY

═══ Expressway

═══ Major road

—•— Main railroad

——— Minor railroad

△ Peak

Map labels: Niigata, KANETSU EXPRESSWAY, JOETSU SHINKANSEN, Mae, Nagano, Takasaki, 18, JOSHINETSU EXPRESSWAY, Koumi, Chi, Matsumoto, Kanazawa, CHICHIBU-TAMA NATIONAL PARK ❺, Oku, 141, 20, CHUO LINE, 411, Mita, Kofu, CHUO EXPRESSWAY, 20, Mt Taka 1,965ft, Fuji-Yoshida, MOUNT FUJI AND THE FUJI FIVE LAKES ❽, 139, Mt Fuji 12,390ft, 138, Gotenba, Odawar, South Japan Alps, Fujinomiya, HAKONE ❻, TOMEI EXPRESS, 52, Fuji, A, Mishima, 136, 135, SHIZUOKA ❾, Toi, Ito, Shuzenji, IZU PENINSULA ❼, Hammatsu, Shimoda

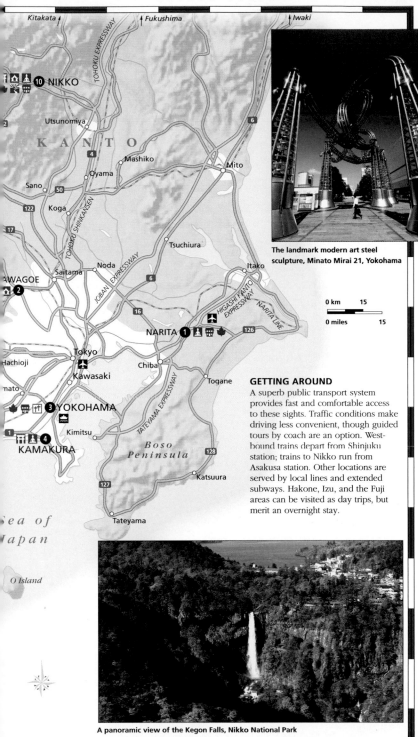

The landmark modern art steel
sculpture, Minato Mirai 21, Yokohama

| 0 km | 15 |
| 0 miles | 15 |

GETTING AROUND

A superb public transport system
provides fast and comfortable access
to these sights. Traffic conditions make
driving less convenient, though guided
tours by coach are an option. West-
bound trains depart from Shinjuku
station; trains to Nikko run from
Asakusa station. Other locations are
served by local lines and extended
subways. Hakone, Izu, and the Fuji
areas can be visited as day trips, but
merit an overnight stay.

A panoramic view of the Kegon Falls, Nikko National Park

Narita ❶

成田

Chiba prefecture. 🚶 120,000. 🚆
🚏 ℹ️ *in front of JR stn (0476) 24-3198.* **www**.*city.narita.chiba.jp/english* 🎎 *Setsubun-e (Feb 3).*

A quiet little town, Narita's main attraction is **Narita-san Shinsho-ji**, an Esoteric-Shingon-sect temple founded in 940 and dedicated to Fudo Myo-o, Deity of Immovable Wisdom. Several times daily, the priests burn wooden sticks to symbolize extinguishing of earthly passions. The streets are full of traditional shops for the 12 million temple visitors a year.

Environs
Near Narita are over 1,000 ancient burial mounds (*kofun*); the best are in **Boso Historical Park. The National Museum of Japanese History** offers a good survey of Japan.

🌸 **Boso Historical Park**
15 mins by taxi from Narita stn.
Tel *(0476) 95-3126.* ⬜ *Tue–Sun.*

🏛️ **National Museum of Japanese History**
15 mins walk from Sakura stn.
Tel *(043) 486-0123.* ⬜ *Tue–Sun.* 🖼️

Kawagoe ❷

川越

Saitama prefecture. 🚶 333,000. 🚏
ℹ️ *at JR stn (049) 222-5556.* **www**.*city.kawagoe.saitama.jp* 🎎 *Ashi-odori (Leg-dancing, Apr 14), Kawagoe Festival (3rd weekend in Oct).*

Nicknamed "Little Edo," Kawagoe preserves the atmosphere of 19th-century Edo (Tokyo) in its *kura*

Yokohama Bay Bridge

buildings. The traditional *kura* structure, with thick clay walls, double doors, and heavy shutters, was used for warehouses and shops.

About 30 *kura* remain, and are a 10-minute walk north of Hon-Kawagoe station. The **Kura-Zukuri Shiryokan**, formerly a *kura* tobacconist, is a museum. Nearby, **Toki-no-kane** wooden bell tower was built in 1624 to tell the time and warn of fires. East of the *kura* streets is **Kita-in**, a Tendai-sect temple which includes the only extant rooms from Edo Castle.

Environs
In Saitama, about 12 miles (19 km) east of Kawagoe, the **John Lennon Museum** celebrates the musician's life with photographs, videos, and music. There are also instruments and hand-written lyric sheets donated by his wife, Yoko Ono.

🏯 **Kura-Zukuri Shiryokan**
Tel *(049) 225-4287.* ⬜ *Tue–Sun.*
🔴 *4th Fri of month.* 🖼️

🏛️ **John Lennon Museum**
8 Shintoshin, Chuo-ku, Saitama.
Tel *(048) 601-0009.*
⬜ *Wed–Mon.* 🖼️

Yokohama ❸

横浜

Kanagawa prefecture.
🚶 3,600,000. 🚆 🚏 ℹ️ *Sangyo Boeki Center Bldg (045) 641-4759.*
www.*city.yokohama.jp*
🎎 *Chinese New Year (Feb), Yokohama Port Festival (May 3).*

Japan's second-largest city, Yokohama has been a center for shipping, trade, foreign contact, and modern ideas since the mid-19th century. Formerly a small fishing village on the Tokaido road, it was made a treaty port in 1859; there followed an influx of foreign traders, especially Chinese and British, making it the biggest port in Asia by the early 1900s. The 1923 Kanto Earthquake wiped out 95 percent of the city, killing 40,000 people, then World War II bombing again destroyed half the city. After the war, Yokohama became a base for US soldiers. By the 1970s, it was once again Japan's largest port. The heart of the city is compact and walkable.

Minato Mirai 21, an area of redeveloped docks, has some creative architecture (with hi-tech earthquake-proofing) and on weekends comes alive with street performers. Its focal point is the **Landmark Tower**, built in 1993 under US architect Hugh Stubbins and, at 296 m (971 ft), Japan's tallest building. Reached by the world's fastest elevator (at 750 m (2,500 ft) per minute), the 69th-floor public lounge has a spectacular 360-degree view. To the north, Kenzo

A row of *kura* buildings in Kawagoe

Tange's **Yokohama Museum of Art** houses displays of modern art and photography.

In the older, more attractive part of town, the **NYK Maritime Museum** covers the history of shipping, with detailed models. Created on rubble from the 1923 Earthquake, **Yamashita Park** is a pleasant promenade overlooking ships, including the moored liner **Hikawa Maru**, which cruised between Yokohama and Seattle in 1930–60, and the 860-m (2,800-ft) long **Yokohama Bay Bridge** (1989).

Chinatown, the largest of Japan's few Chinatowns, has around 2,500 Chinese inhabitants, and a mass of restaurants, food shops, Chinese-medicine shops, and fortune-tellers. At its heart is the Chinese **Kantei-byo Temple** (1887), dedicated to ancient Chinese hero Kuan-yu, who was worshiped as a god of war but is now popular as a god of business succes and prosperity.

Among the many 4,500 tombs in the early 20th-century **Foreigners' Cemetery**

is that of Edmund Morel, the English engineer who helped build Japan's first railroads, with a tombstone shaped like a railroad ticket. The lovely **Sankei-en Garden** belonged to silk-trader Hara Tomitaro (1868–1939). Among the ponds and flowers are 16 architectural treasures, including a three-story pagoda from Kyoto.

Landmark Tower
Tel (045) 222-5015. ⏱ *daily.*

🏛 **Yokohama Museum of Art**
Tel (045) 221-0300. ⏱ *Fri–Wed.* 📷

🏛 **NYK Maritime Museum**
Tel (045) 221-0280. ⏱ *Tue–Sun.* 📷

Hikawa Maru
Tel (045) 641-4362. ⏱ *daily.* 📷

⛩ **Foreigners' Cemetery**
Tel (045) 622-1311. ⏱ *Apr–Nov: Sat, Sun, public hols.*

🌿 **Sankei-en Garden**
10 mins by bus from Negishi stn (JR) to Honmoku Sankei-en Mae.
Tel (045) 621-0634. ⏱ *daily.* 📷

Environs
Outside the center are two entertaining venues – **Kirin Beer Village**, with tasting tours

of the automated Kirin brewery; and **Shin Yokohama Ramen Museum** *(see p141)*. The **Hodogaya Commonwealth Cemetery** (a bus ride from Yokohama, Hodogaya, or Sakuragi-cho stations) contains Allied graves from World War II (including POWs).

Kirin Beer Village
🚉 *Namamugi stn, Keihin Kyuko line.*
Tel (045) 503-8250. ⏱ *Tue–Sun.*

One of the colorful entrance gates to Yokohama's Chinatown

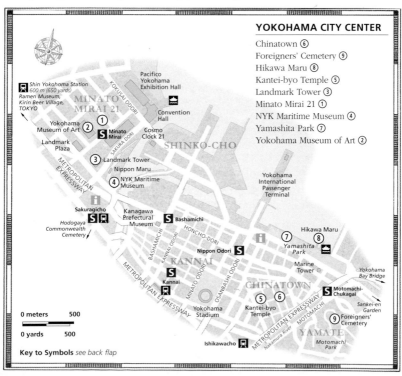

YOKOHAMA CITY CENTER

0 meters   500
0 yards   500

Key to Symbols *see back flap*

Kamakura ❹

鎌倉

An Amida Buddha, Hase-dera temple

A seaside town of temples and wooded hills, Kamakura was Japan's capital from 1185 until 1333. As a legacy, today it has 19 Shinto shrines and 65 Buddhist temples, including two of Japan's oldest Zen monasteries (in Kita Kamakura, *see p92*). Many of the temples and gardens nestle against the hills ringing the town, and are linked by three hiking trails. Favored by artists and writers, Kamakura has numerous antique and crafts shops. In cherry-blossom season and on summer weekends it can be swamped by visitors. Some parts are best explored on foot, but there are one-day bus passes, and bicycles for rent at Kamakura station.

The path down the center of Wakamiya-oji, Kamakura's main street

🔺 Hase-dera Temple

🚉 *Hase stn.* 📞 **Tel** *(0467) 22-6300.* ⏰ *daily.* 🖥 **www**.hasedera.jp
Simple and elegant, Hase-dera is home to a superb 11-faced Kannon, *bosatsu* of mercy. The Treasure House displays characteristic Muromachi-era carvings of the 33 incarnations of Kannon and a 1421 image of Daikokuten, god of wealth. Beside it is the sutra repository; rotating the sutras is said to earn as much merit as reading them. The 1264 bell is the

town's oldest. Below it is a hall dedicated to Jizo, guardian of children, surrounded by countless statues to children who have died or been aborted.

🔺 Great Buddha

🚉 *Hase stn.* 📞 **Tel** *(0467) 22-0703.* ⏰ *daily.* 🖥
The Great Buddha (Daibutsu) is Kamakura's most famous sight. Cast in 1252, the bronze statue of the Amida Buddha is

13.5 m (44 ft) tall. Having survived tidal waves, fires, earthquakes, and typhoons, it now has shock-absorbers in its base. Its proportions are distorted so that it seems balanced to those in front of it – this use of perspective may show Greek influence (via the Silk Road). The interior is open to visitors.

🏯 Hachiman-gu Shrine

🚉 *Kamakura stn.* **Tel** *(0467) 22-0315.* ⏰ *daily.* **Kamakura National Treasure House Museum Tel** *(0467) 22-0753.* ⏰ *Tue–Sun.* 🖥
Hachiman shrines are dedicated to the god of war; this one is also a guardian shrine of the Minamoto (or Genji) clan. Built in 1063 by the sea, it was moved here in 1191. The approach runs between two lotus ponds: the Genji Pond has three islands (in Japanese *san* means both three and life) while the Heike Pond, named for a rival clan, has four (*shi* means both four and death). The path leads to the Mai-den stage for dances and music. The main shrine above was

The head of the Great Buddha, or *Daibutsu*

SIGHTS AT A GLANCE

0 meters   500

0 yards   500

YOKOHA

Kita-Kamak Stat

Tok Ten

Zeni-arai Benten Shrine ⑤

Sasuke-no Inari Shrine

SHIYAKUSH

Great Buddha Hiking Trail

⑫ Great Buddha (Daibutsu)

⑪ Hase-dera Temple

Yuigahama Station 🚉

Hase Station 🚉

HIGHW

NATIONAL

Yuigahama Beach

ENOSHIMA

Key to Symbols *see back flap*

The Mai-den in front of the main shrine at Hachiman-gu shrine

reconstructed in 1828 in Edo style. To the east, the **Kamakura National Treasure House Museum** contains a wealth of temple treasures.

🔼 Myohon-ji Temple

🚉 *Kamakura stn.* **Tel** *(0467) 22-0777.* ⬜ *daily.*

On a hillside of soaring trees, this temple, with its steep, extended roof, is Kamakura's largest of the Nichiren sect. It was established in 1260, in memory of a 1203 massacre.

🔼 Hokoku-ji Temple

🚉 **Tel** *(0467) 22-0762.* ⬜ *daily.* 💮 *(for bamboo grove).*

A Rinzai Zen temple founded in 1334, Hokoku-ji's buildings are modern; its great attraction is its lovely bamboo grove. There is also a pleasant raked gravel and rock garden worth exploring.

fed lake, rocks, and sand; a Zen meditation cave is cut into the cliff. Decorative narcissi also bloom here in January, and Japanese plum trees blossom in February.

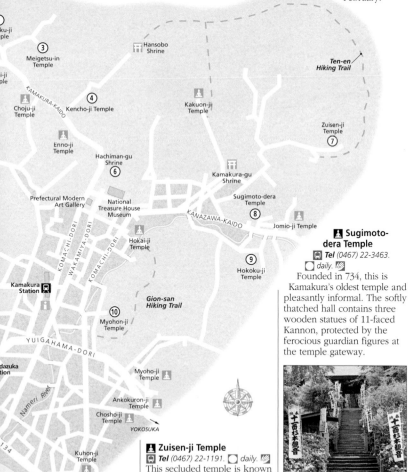

🔼 Sugimoto-dera Temple

🚉 **Tel** *(0467) 22-3463.* ⬜ *daily.* 💮

Founded in 734, this is Kamakura's oldest temple and pleasantly informal. The softly thatched hall contains three wooden statues of 11-faced Kannon, protected by the ferocious guardian figures at the temple gateway.

🔼 Zuisen-ji Temple

🚉 **Tel** *(0467) 22-1191.* ⬜ *daily.* 💮

This secluded temple is known for its naturalistic garden. Created in 1327 by the monk Muso Soseki, it features a waterfall-

Azalea-lined steps to the thatched hall at Sugimoto-dera temple

Exploring Kita Kamakura

Zen Buddhism came to Japan from China at the end of the 12th century. Its simplicity and accessibility appealed to the ethos of Kamakura samurai warriors as well as to ordinary people. Kita (north) Kamakura, a tranquil area of wooded gullies, includes three of Kamakura's so-called "five great" Zen temples – Kencho-ji, Engaku-ji, and Jochi-ji (the others are Jomyo-ji and Jufuku-ji). The area is served by its own train station, from which most sights can be reached on foot. Delicate vegetarian food *(see p120)*, which complies with Zen dietary rules, can be tried at Kita Kamakura temples and restaurants.

Statue above Kencho-ji

🏛 Engaku-ji Temple

🚉 *Kita Kamakura stn.* **Tel** *(0467) 22-0478.* ⏲ *daily.* 🎟

Deep in trees, the largest of Kamakura's "five great" Zen temples, Engaku-ji was founded by the Hojo regent Tokimune in 1282. An influential meditation center since the Meiji era, it now runs public courses.

Although much of Engaku-ji was destroyed by the 1923 Kanto Earthquake, 17 of its more than 40 subtemples remain, and careful rebuilding has made sure that it retains its characteristic Zen layout *(see opposite)*. One of its highlights, in Shozoku-in subtemple, is the Shariden. Japan's finest example of Chinese Sung-style Zen architecture, it is open only at New Year but can be seen through a gate at other times. Farther on, the Butsunichian, mausoleum of Engaku-ji's founder, serves *matcha* tea. It was the setting for Kawabata Yasunari's 1949 novel *Senbazuru* (Thousand Cranes).

Stone monuments in the peaceful cemetery at Tokei-ji temple

Bosatsu statue at Kencho-ji

🏛 Tokei-ji Temple

🚉 *Kita Kamakura stn.* **Tel** *(0467) 22-1663.* ⏲ *daily.* 🎟

This quiet little temple was set up as a convent in 1285, at a time when only men were allowed to petition for divorce. However, if a woman spent three years here she could divorce her husband. Thus Tokei-ji was nicknamed the "divorce temple." In 1873 the law was changed to allow women to initiate divorce; in 1902 Tokei-ji became a monastery. It is still refuge-like, with gardens stretching back to the wooded hillside.

🏛 Meigetsu-in Temple

🚉 *Kita Kamakura stn.* **Tel** *(0467) 24-3437.* ⏲ *daily.* 🎟

Known as the "hydrangea temple," Meigetsu-in is a small Zen temple with attractive gardens. As well as hydrangeas

(at their peak in June), there are irises; these bloom in late May, when the rear garden, usually only tantalizingly glimpsed through a round window, is opened to the public.

🏛 Kencho-ji Temple

🚉 *Kita Kamakura stn.* **Tel** *(0467) 22-0981.* ⏲ *daily.* 🎟

Kencho-ji is the foremost of Kamakura's "five great" Zen temples and the oldest Zen training monastery in Japan. Founded in 1253, the temple originally had seven main buildings and 49 subtemples; many were destroyed in fires, but ten subtemples remain. Beside the impressive Sanmon gate is the bell, cast in 1255, which has a Zen inscription by the temple's founder. The Buddha Hall contains a Jizo *bosatsu*, savior of souls of the dead, rather than the usual Buddha. Behind the hall is the Hatto, where public ceremonies are performed. The Karamon (Chinese gate) leads to the Hojo, used for services. Its rear garden is constructed around a pond supposedly in the shape of the kanji character for heart or mind. To the side of the temple a tree-lined lane leads to subtemples and up steps to Hanso-bo, the temple's shrine.

🏯 Zeni-Arai Benten Shrine

🚉 *Kamakura stn.* **Tel** *(0467) 25-1081.* ⏲ *daily.*

This popular shrine is dedicated to Benten, goddess of music, eloquence, and the arts, and one of the "seven lucky gods" of folk religion. Hidden in a niche in the cliffs, it is approached through a small tunnel and a row of *torii* (gates). These lead to a pocket of wafting incense, lucky charms, and a cave spring where visitors wash money in the hope of doubling its value.

Washing money at Zeni-Arai Benten shrine

The Layout of a Zen Buddhist Temple

Japanese Zen temple layout is typically based on Chinese Sung-dynasty temples. Essentially rectilinear and symmetrical (in contrast to native Japanese asymmetry), Zen temples have the main buildings in a

Bridge to Jochi-ji Temple

straight line one behind another, on a roughly north-south axis. The main buildings comprise the Sanmon (main gate), Butsuden (Buddha Hall), Hatto lecture hall, sometimes a meditation or study hall, and the abbot's and monks'

quarters. In practice, sub-temples often crowd around the main buildings and may obscure the basic layout. The temple compound is entered by a bridge over a pond or stream, symbolically crossing from the earthly world to that of the Buddha. Buildings are natural looking, often of unpainted wood, conducive to emptying the mind of worldly illusions, to facilitate enlightenment. The example below is based on Engaku-ji.

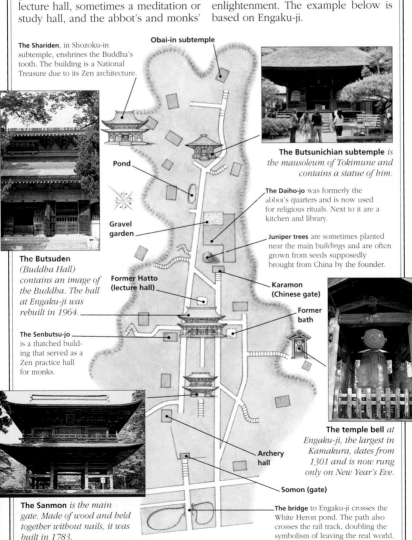

The Shariden, in Shozoku-in subtemple, enshrines the Buddha's tooth. The building is a National Treasure due to its Zen architecture.

Obai-in subtemple

Pond

Gravel garden

The Butsunichian subtemple *is the mausoleum of Tokimune and contains a statue of him.*

The Daiho-jo was formerly the abbot's quarters and is now used for religious rituals. Next to it are a kitchen and library.

Juniper trees are sometimes planted near the main buildings and are often grown from seeds supposedly brought from China by the founder.

The Butsuden *(Buddha Hall) contains an image of the Buddha. The hall at Engaku-ji was rebuilt in 1964.*

Former Hatto (lecture hall)

Karamon (Chinese gate)

Former bath

The Senbutsu-jo is a thatched building that served as a Zen practice hall for monks.

The temple bell *at Engaku-ji, the largest in Kamakura, dates from 1301 and is now rung only on New Year's Eve.*

Archery hall

Somon (gate)

The Sanmon *is the main gate. Made of wood and held together without nails, it was built in 1783.*

The bridge to Engaku-ji crosses the White Heron pond. The path also crosses the rail track, doubling the symbolism of leaving the real world.

Chichibu-Tama National Park ❺
秩父多摩国立公園

Tokyo, Saitama, Nagano, and Yamana-shi prefectures. 🚶 *71,500 (Chichibu city).* 🚉 *Seibu-Chichibu stn, Seibu-Chichibu line; Chichibu stn, Chichibu line; Okutama or Mitake stns, JR line.* ℹ️ *Chichibu stn (0494) 25-3192.* 🎎 *Yo Matsuri (Dec 2–3, Chichibu city).*

Chichibu-Tama National Park is a remote region of low mountains, rich in traditions and wildlife, stretching from the narrow valleys of Okutama in the south to the basin around Chichibu city in the north. The two parts of the park are separated by mountains, crossed only by a few hiking trails, and are reached by two separate rail networks. Within the park, railroads penetrate to a few spots, but travel is mostly by bus.

Chichibu was a prime silk-producing region until the early 20th century. Today it is known for its vibrant festivals and its pilgrim route linking 33 Kannon temples. To the north, at **Nagatoro**, the Arakawa River runs past rare crystalline schist rock formations.

In the Okutama area, **Mount Mitake** has good hiking, and an attractive mountaintop shrine village, easily reached by a funicular. Stalactite caves at **Nippara** are worth visiting.

🦇 **Nippara Caves**
NW of Okutama. *Tel (0428) 83-8491.* ⭕ *daily.* 🎫

YOSEGI-ZAIKU WOODWORK

Originating in the 9th century, this woodcraft looks like in-laid mosaic but in fact employs a very different technique. It has been a Hakone specialty for over 200 years, and today there are about 100 *yosegi-zaiku* practitioners in the area.

Strips are cut from planks of up to 40 varieties of undyed woods and glued together to form blocks of pattern, which are in turn glued into larger blocks. These are then either shaped with a lathe into bowls and boxes, or shaved into cross-sectional sheets, used to coat items such as boxes and purses. The paper-thin sheets are flexible and can be laminated. Some of the most popular creations are "magic" boxes, opened in a sequence of moves to reveal a hidden drawer.

Craftsman making a *yosegi-zaiku* box

Environs
South of Chichibu-Tama lies **Mount Takao**, (on the Keio train line to Takaosan-guchi). Its slopes have pleasant walks with sweeping views of Tokyo and Mount Fuji.

Hakone ❻
箱根

Kanagawa prefecture. 🚶 *14,000.* 🚉 ℹ️ *698 Yumoto, Hakone (0460) 85-8911.* **www**.hakone.or.jp/english/index.html 🎎 *Toriiyaki (Aug 5, Lake Ashi), Daimyo Gyoretsu (Nov 3, Hakone-Yumoto).*

Hakone is a hilly hot-spring town whose scattered attractions are both cultural and natural. Popular as a resort since the 9th century, it can be very crowded. The

Hakone area extends across the collapsed remains of a huge volcano, which was active until 3 to 4,000 years ago, leaving a legacy today of hot springs and steam vents.

Although Hakone can be visited as a long day trip from Tokyo, it is worth an overnight stay. Two- or three-day public transportation passes are available on the Odakyu line from Shinjuku, Tokyo. A convenient circuit of the main sights starts from the *onsen* (hot spring) town of **Hakone-Yumoto**, taking the Tozan switchback train up the hillside to **Hakone Open-Air Museum**, with its modern sculptures. Continue via funicular to **Hakone Art Museum**, which has an excellent Japanese ceramic collection and garden. Via the funicular and

Crossing the rocky scree and steaming vents of Owaku-dani valley in Hakone

A statue of *The Izu Dancer* by a waterfall near Kawazu, Izu Peninsula

then a ropeway over the crest of the hill is the **Owaku-dani** ("valley of great boiling"), an area of sulfurous steam vents.

The ropeway continues to **Lake Ashi**, where replicas of historical Western-style boats run to **Hakone-machi** and **Moto-Hakone**. In clear weather there are breathtaking views of Mount Fuji. At Hakone-machi is an interesting reconstruction of the **Seki-sho Barrier Gate**, a historic checkpoint that used to control the passage of people and guns on the Edo-period Tokaido road between Edo (Tokyo) and Kyoto.

Yosegi-zaiku box, Hatajuku

From Hakone-machi it is a short walk to Moto-Hakone. In a prominent position on a hilltop overlooking Lake Ashi, **Narukawa Art Museum** exhibits 1,500 artworks by modern Japanese masters, and has spectacular views of the surrounding mountains. Over a pass beyond Moto-Hakone is the **Amazake-chaya** teahouse, and **Hatajuku** village, known for *yosegi-zaiku*, a form of decorative woodwork.

🏛 **Hakone Open-Air Museum**
Tel (0460) 82-1161. ⬜ daily. 📷
🏛 **Hakone Art Museum**
Tel (0460) 82-2623. ⬜ Fri–Wed. 📷
🏯 **Seki-sho Barrier Gate**
Tel (0460) 83-6635. ⬜ daily. 📷
🏛 **Narukawa Art Museum**
Tel (0460) 83-6288. ⬜ daily. 📷

Izu Peninsula ❼
伊豆半島

Shizuoka prefecture. 🚉 🛈 *Atami, Ito, and Shuzenji stns.* 📷 *Daimonji Burning (Jul 22–3, Atagawa), Anjin Festival (Aug 8–10, Ito).*

A picturesque, hilly peninsula with a benign climate, Izu is popular for its numerous hot springs. It was a place of exile during the Middle Ages, and in the early 1600s was home to the shipwrecked Englishman Will Adams, whose story was the basis of the James Clavell novel *Shogun*. **Shimoda**, on the southern tip, became a coaling station for foreign ships in 1854, then opened to US traders. Today Shimoda has little of interest besides pretty gray-and-white walls, reinforced against typhoons with crisscross plasterwork.

Izu's east coast is quite developed, but the west has charming coves and fishing villages, such as **Toi** and **Heda**, offering delicious long-legged crabs and other seafood. The center is also relatively unspoiled, with wooded mountains and rustic hot springs, including **Shuzenji** *onsen* and a chain of villages from **Amagi Yugashima** to **Kawazu**. These latter were the setting for Kawabata Yasunari's short story *The Izu Dancer*, commemorated across Izu. Two-day transportation passes cover parts of the peninsula.

Mount Fuji and the Fuji Five Lakes ❽

See pp96–7.

Shizuoka ❾
静岡

Shizuoka & Yamanashi prefecture. 🏠 713,000. 🚉 🛈 *in JR stn* (054) 252-4247. **www**.pref.shizuoka.jp 📷 *Shizuoka Festival (1st weekend Apr).*

Settlement in this area stretches back to AD 200–300. Later a stop on the old Tokaido road, and the retirement home of Tokugawa Ieyasu *(see p101)*, Shizuoka is today a sprawling urban center, the city at greatest risk of a major earthquake in Japan. As a result it is probably the only place that is fully prepared.

The **Toro Ruins** near the port have well-explained reconstructions of ancient buildings, and an excellent interactive **museum**. The view from **Nihondaira** plateau, in the east of the city, to Mount Fuji and Izu, is superb. Nearby is **Kunozan Tosho-gu**, one of the three top Tosho-gu shrines.

🏛 **Toro Ruins**
Museum *Tel* (0542) 85-0476.
⬜ Tue–Sun. ⬛ last day of month. 📷

Environs
West of Shizuoka, **Kanaya** has one of Japan's largest tea plantations. Fields and processing plants can be visited, and the elegant **Ocha no Sato** museum portrays tea lore. Nearby, the **Oigawa steam railroad** takes you right into the untamed South Alps.

🏛 **Ocha no Sato**
Tel (0547) 46-5588.
⬜ daily. ⬛ Tue. 📷

A reconstructed dwelling at the Toro site, Shizuoka

Mount Fuji and the Fuji Five Lakes ⑧

富士山と富士五湖

Decorative drain cover in Fuji-Yoshida

At 3,776 m (12,390 ft), Mount Fuji is Japan's highest peak by far, its near-perfect cone floating lilac gray or snow-capped above hilltops and low cloud. Dormant since 1707, the volcano first erupted 8–10,000 years ago. Its upper slopes are loose volcanic ash, devoid of greenery or streams. Until 100 years ago, Mount Fuji was considered so sacred that it was climbed only by priests and pilgrims; women were not allowed until 1872. Today pilgrims are greatly out-numbered by recreational climbers. The Fuji Five Lakes area, at the foot of the mountain, is a playground for Tokyoites, with sports facilities and amusement parks.

Lake Sai
This is the least spoiled of the Fuji Five Lakes and offers beautiful views of Mount Fuji.

Lake Kawaguchi is the most accessible and commercialized lake.

KEY

🚉 Train station

🚌 Bus stop

ℹ️ Tourist information

⛩️ Shrine

▬ Expressway

═ Other road

-- Trail

Lake Motosu, the deepest lake, is depicted on the 5,000-yen note.

Lake Shojin is the smallest lake, and good for fishing.

Fugaku Wind Cave

Narusawa Ice Cave

Sea of Trees

Kawaguchi-ko

The Sea of Trees (Aokigahara Jukai) is a primeval forest famed for being easy to get lost in.

Kawaguchi-ko trail is 5–6 hours up from the 5th stage, and 3 hours down. Another trail, the Yoshida, shares most of its route with this one.

5th stage

5th stage

TIPS FOR WALKERS

Planning: *The mountain is open for climbing only in July and August. Trails and huts can be very crowded on weekends.*
Stages: *The trails are divided into 10 stages. Climbers usually start at the 5th stage. To see the sunrise and avoid the midday sun, it is usual to climb by night or start in the afternoon, sleep in a hut at the 7th or 8th stage, and rise very early to finish the climb.*
Conditions: *The climb is hard work as the steep volcanic cinder shifts underfoot like sand. Above the 8th stage, altitude sickness occasionally strikes: if you have a serious head-ache or nausea, descend at once. The summit is much colder than the base.*
What to take: *Sun-protection cream, hat, sweater, raincoat, hiking shoes, flashlight, and emergency drink supplies; a walking stick is useful.*

The top is not a single summit, but a crater rim. A circuit of the rim takes about an hour.

Fujinomiya trail is 5 hours up from the 5th stage, and 3 hours 30 minutes down.

Approaching the Crater Rim
At the top, climbers and pilgrims can visit the Sengen shrine, 24-hour noodle stalls, a post office, and an office for souvenir stamps.

Sengen Jinja
Many Sengen shrines, including this main one at Fuji-Yoshida, can be found around Fuji. The inner sanctum of Sengen shrines is on the crater rim at the summit. They are dedicated to the deity of the mountain.

VISITORS' CHECKLIST

Shizuoka & Yamanashi prefecture. Fuji-Yoshida, Kawaguchi-ko, Gotenba, Mishima (Tokaido Shinkansen), or Fujinomiya. summer only, from all stns to the nearest 5th stage, also direct from Tokyo (Shinjuku stn W side or Hamamatsu-cho) to Kawaguchi-ko, Gotenba, and Lake Yamanaka. Fuji-Yoshida (0555) 22-7000. www.fujiyoshida.net Fuji-Yoshida Fire Festival (Aug 26 & 27).

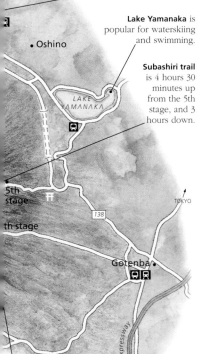

OTSUKI AND TOKYO

Expressway

Fuji-Yoshida, the traditional pilgrim base, has old inns, and waterfalls for cleansing and praying before the climb.

• Oshino

Lake Yamanaka is popular for waterskiing and swimming.

LAKE YAMANAKA

Subashiri trail is 4 hours 30 minutes up from the 5th stage, and 3 hours down.

5th stage

138

th stage

TOKYO

Gotenba

Tomei Expressway

MISHIMA

Gotenba trail is 8 hours up from the 5th stage, and 3 hours down.

0 kilometers 5
0 miles 5

MOUNT FUJI IN ART

Mount Fuji's graceful, almost symmetrical form, its changing appearance at different seasons and times of day, and its dominance over the landscape have made it both a symbol of Japan and a popular subject for artists. The mountain features in various series of 19th-century woodblock prints: Katsushika Hokusai (1790–1849) and Ando Hiroshige (1797–1858) both published series called *Thirty-Six Views of Mount Fuji*, and Hiroshige also depicted Fuji in his *Fifty-Three Stages of the Tokaido* published in 1833–4. It often appears in the background of prints of downtown Edo (Tokyo), from where it is sometimes visible between high-rises even today. In other arts, Mount Fuji is echoed in decorative motifs, for instance on kimonos, in wood carvings, and even in the shape of window frames.

One of Hiroshige's *Thirty-Six Views of Mount Fuji*

Beneath the Wave off Kanagawa from Hokusai's *Thirty-Six Views of Mount Fuji*

Nikko ⑩

日光

Over 1,200 years ago, the formidable Buddhist priest Shodo Shonin, on his way to Mount Nantai, crossed the Daiya River and founded the first temple at Nikko. Centuries later, Nikko was a renowned Buddhist-Shinto religious center, and the warlord Tokugawa Ieyasu *(see p101)* chose it for the site of his mausoleum. When his grandson Iemitsu had Ieyasu's shrine-mausoleum Tosho-gu built in 1634, he wanted to impress upon any rivals the wealth and might of the Tokugawa clan. Since then, Nikko, written with characters that mean sunlight, has become a Japanese byword for splendor.

Bato Kannon, with a horse on the headdress, at Rinno-ji Temple

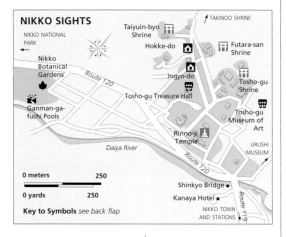

NIKKO SIGHTS

NIKKO NATIONAL PARK ←

Nikko Botanical Gardens

Route 120

Ganman-ga-fuchi Pools

Daiya River

Taiyuin-byo Shrine

Hokke-do

Jogyo-do

Tosho-gu Treasure Hall

Rinno-ji Temple

TAKINOO SHRINE

Futara-san Shrine

Tosho-gu Shrine

Tosho-gu Museum of Art

URUSHI MUSEUM

Route 120

Shinkyo Bridge ●

Kanaya Hotel ●

NIKKO TOWN AND STATIONS

0 meters   250
0 yards   250
Key to Symbols see back flap

Route 119

Exploring Nikko Town

Of the two stations in Nikko, the JR station, the oldest in eastern Japan, is a classic. The graceful wooden edifice, built in 1915, was designed by American architect Frank Lloyd Wright. Buses to many of Nikko's sights run from

here. The 1-km (about half-a-mile) long avenue from the train stations to the Tosho-gu precincts is lined with shops, restaurants, and inns. A good shop for Nikko wood carvings and *geta* (wooden sandals) is Tezuka, on the left halfway up the street. An

architectural treat is the venerable 19th-century Kanaya Hotel *(see p117)*, situated on a rise to the left, just before the Daiya River.

Shinkyo Bridge

◻ daily.

This red-lacquered wooden bridge, just to the left of the road bridge, arches over the Daiya River where, legend has it, Shodo Shonin crossed the river on the backs of two huge serpents. The original, built in 1636 for the exclusive use of the shogun and imperial messengers, was destroyed by flood. The current bridge dates from 1907.

Rinno-ji Temple

◻ daily.

The first temple founded at Nikko, by Shodo Shonin in 766, this was originally called Shihonryu-ji. When it became a Tendai-sect temple in the 17th century, it was renamed Rinno-ji. Its **Sanbutsu-do** (Three Buddha Hall) is the largest hall at Nikko. The three gilt images, of Amida Buddha, Senju (thousand-armed) Kannon, and Bato (horse-headed) Kannon, enshrined in the hall correspond to the three mountain deities enshrined at Futara-san Shrine. Beyond the hall, the nine-ringed bronze pillar, **Sorinto**, contains

The Shinkyo Bridge spanning the Daiya River

1,000 volumes of *sutras* (Buddhist scriptures) and is a symbol of world peace. The **Treasure Hall** (Homotsuden) has a large and fascinating array of temple treasures, mainly dating from the Edo period. Behind it is the **Shoyoen**, a lovely landscaped Edo-style 19th-century stroll garden for all seasons. Its path meanders around a large pond, over stone bridges, and past mossy stone lanterns.

The Sanbutsu-do hall at Rinno-ji

Tosho-gu Shrine
See pp100–101.

Tosho-gu Treasure Hall and Museum of Art
Tel (0288) 54-2558 (Treasure Hall); (0288) 54-0560 (Museum of Art). ◯ *daily.*
In the Treasure Hall are shrine treasures along with armor and swords used by the Tokugawa shoguns. In the Museum of Art is an outstanding collection of early 20th-century painted doors and panels by Yokoyama Taikan and others.

Hokke-do and Jogyo-do
These two halls belong to Rinno-ji and house Buddhist relics. Linked by a corridor, they are often referred to as the twin halls.

Futara-san Shrine
◯ *daily.*
Founded by Shodo Shonin in 782, this shrine is dedicated to the gods of Mounts Nantai

(male), Nyotai (female), and Taro, their child. It is actually the main shrine of three; the other two are at Lake Chuzenji and on the summit of Mount Nantai. The bronze *torii* (gate) here is an Important Cultural Property. More interesting is the tall bronze lantern, which was said to take the shape of a monster at night. The gashes in the lantern are from the sword of a samurai.

Takinoo Shrine
Tel (0288) 21-0765.
◯ *daily.*
A quiet 30-minute uphill walk through the woods via a stone path to the left of Futara-san Shrine, this peaceful, rustic shrine, thought to be dedicated to a female deity, draws women and those looking for love. Toss a stone through the hole in the top of the *torii* (gate) and into the shrine grounds and your wish, they say, will come true.

Shrine interior at Futara-san

VISITORS' CHECKLIST

Tochigi prefecture. 94,500. JR and Tobu-Nikko lines. at Tobu Nikko stn (0288) 54-2496. Tosho-gu Grand Festival (May 17–18); Tosho-gu Fall Festival (Oct 17). www.city.nikko.lg.jp/fl/index.html

Taiyuin-byo Shrine
See pp102–3.

Ganman-ga-fuchi Pools
to Nishisando bus stop.
Lava flows from an old eruption of Mount Nantai, combines with the limpid waters of the Daiya River to make these unusual scenic pools, a sacred spot to followers of Buddhism. About 70 stone statues of Jizo, the *bodhisattva* of children, line the path by the river. They are known as phantom statues because their numbers always appear to change.

Nikko Botanical Gardens
to Rengeishi bus stop. *Tel (0288) 54-0206.* ◯ *Tue–Sun.* ◯ *Dec 1–Apr 14.*
Some 3,000 varieties of plants and flowers from Japan and around the world can be seen at these gardens, a branch of the Koishikawa Botanical Gardens of the University of Tokyo. Flora from Nikko National Park are showcased. April to July, when skunk cabbages and irises bloom, is a lovely time to visit.

Urushi Museum
to Marumi bus stop. *Tel (0288) 53-6807.* ◯ *Mar 20–Nov 20: Sat, Sun, Mon.*
This small museum, which opened in 1998 in wooded Ogurayama Park, showcases the lacquer arts of Nikko and Japan – *urushi* is Japanese for lacquer. Used in Japan for over 5,000 years, lacquer has reached the height of refinement only in the past 1,000 years. The museum collection also includes examples of lacquerware from China, India, and Egypt.

Painted sliding doors at the Tosho-gu Museum of Art

Nikko: Tosho-gu Shrine

Tokugawa Iemitsu set out to dazzle with this shrine-mausoleum for his grandfather Ieyasu. For two years some 15,000 artisans from all over Japan worked, building, carving, gilting, painting, and lacquering, to create this flowery, gorgeous Momoyama-style complex. Almost anything that can be decorated is. Although designated a shrine in the Meiji period, it retains many of its Buddhist elements, including its unusual pagoda, sutra library, and Niomon gate. The famed *sugi-namiki* (Japanese cedar avenue) leading to the shrine was planted by a 17th-century lord, in lieu of a more opulent offering.

Sleeping Cat Carving
Over an entrance in the east corridor, this tiny, exquisite carving of a sleeping cat is attributed to Hidari Jingoro (Hidari the Left-handed).

Bell towe

Honden (inner sanctuary)

Haiden (sanctuary)

The Karamon gate is the smallest at Tosho-gu.

The Honji-do's ceiling is painted with the "crying dragon," which echoes resoundingly if you clap your hands beneath it.

Drum tower

The Rinzo contains a sutra library of Buddhist scriptures in a revolving structure.

★ **Yomeimon Gate**
Lavishly decorated with beasts and flowers, this gate has one of its 12 columns carved upside-down, a deliberate imperfection to avoid angering jealous spirits. Statues of imperial ministers occupy the niches.

STAR SIGHTS

- ★ Yomeimon Gate
- ★ Pagoda
- ★ Sacred Stable

Sacred Fountain
The granite basin (1618), for ritual purification, is covered with an ornate Chinese-style roof.

TOKUGAWA IEYASU

Ieyasu (1543–1616) was a wily strategist and master politician who founded the dynasty that would rule Japan for over 250 years. Born the son of a minor lord, he spent his life accumulating power, not becoming shogun until 1603, when he was 60. He built his capital at the swampy village of Edo (now Tokyo), and his rule saw the start of the blooming of Edo culture. He ensured that, after his death,

Ieyasu's treasure tower, containing his ashes

he would be enshrined as a god and *gongen* (incarnation of the Buddha). His posthumous name was Tosho-Daigongen (the great incarnation illuminating the East).

VISITORS' CHECKLIST

Tel (0288) 54-0560. 🖼 ▢ *8am–4pm daily; 5pm Nov–Mar.*

★ Pagoda
Donated by a daimyo (feudal lord) in 1650, this five-story pagoda was rebuilt in 1818 after a fire. Each story represents an element – earth, water, fire, wind, and heaven – in ascending order.

To Ieyasu's tomb and treasure tower

The three sacred storehouses are built according to a traditional design.

The Niomon (or Omotemon) gate is guarded by two fearsome Nio figures, one with an open mouth to pronounce the first letter of the Sanskrit alphabet (ah), the other with a closed mouth for the last letter (un).

Ticket office

Granite *torii* (gate)

Entrance

★ Sacred Stable
A carving of the three wise monkeys decorates this unpainted wooden building. A horse given by the New Zealand government is stabled here for several hours a day.

Nikko: Taiyuin-byo Shrine

Completed in 1653, Taiyuin-byo Shrine is the mausoleum of Tokugawa Iemitsu (1603–51), the grandson of Ieyasu *(see p101)* and powerful third shogun, who closed Japan to foreign commerce and isolated it from the world for over 200 years. Tayuin is his posthumous Buddhist name. If Tosho-gu is splendid, Taiyuin-byo is sublime. Set in a grove of Japanese cedars, it has a number of ornate gates ascending to the Haiden (sanctuary) and Honden (inner sanctuary). The shogun's ashes are entombed beyond the sixth and final gate.

The Honden (usually closed to the public) holds a gilded Buddhist altar with a wooden statue of Iemitsu.

The Ai No Ma is a richly decorated connecting chamber.

Kokamon Gate
This striking Ming-dynasty Chinese-style massive gate is beside the picturesque path to Iemitsu's tomb.

★ **Haiden**
Decorated with lovely carvings of dragons, the Haiden (Hall of Worship) also has some famous 17th-century lion paintings by Kano School painters.

The Karamon gate is adorned with delicate carvings, such as a pair of cranes.

The drum tower leads to Honji-do hall, with a painting of a dragon on its huge ceiling.

STAR SIGHTS
★ Haiden
★ Nitenmon Gate

Niomon Gate
This marks the main entrance to the shrine. A single Nio warrior god stands guard on each side.

Entrance

VISITORS' CHECKLIST

Tel (0288) 53-1567. 🗺 ◯ 8am–4pm daily; 5pm Nov–Mar.

Bell Tower
This structure forms a pair with the drum tower. No longer used, but the drum signifies positive/birth, while the bell negative/death.

Yashamon Gate
The third gate is beautifully gilded and contains four statues of Yasha, a fierce guardian spirit. It is also known as Botanmon, or peony gate, after its detailed peony carvings.

★ **Nitenmon Gate**
Four guardian statues occupy the niches here. At the front are the gods Komoku and Jikoku, while at the back are the green god of wind and the red god of thunder.

Granite Fountain
On the ceiling above the basin is a dragon painting by Kano Yasunobu, which is sometimes reflected in the water below.

Stone lanterns were donated over the years by *daimyo* (feudal lords).

TRAVELERS'
NEEDS

WHERE TO STAY

The choice of accommodations can be truly overwhelming in Tokyo, ranging from five-star skyscraper hotels, well-known foreign brand-name chains, and cozy boutique hotels to *ryokan* (*see p108*), traditional Japanese inns. At higher-end *ryokan*, where you sleep on *futons* (mattresses), soak in aromatic cedar tubs, and enjoy *kaiseki* (*see p120*) dinners served in private rooms, even a short stay can be a memorable experience. But one thing

Sign for the Palace Hotel, Central Tokyo (*see p112*)

that all opulent establishments, business hotels, and modest, family-run *minshuku* (*see p109*) have in common is a concern for comfort combined with a long tradition of hospitality. Most accommodations are located in the central areas of the city, usually near the main line and metro stations, but if you can forego exquisite service, designer interiors, and spectacular night views, there are cheaper options available on the fringes of the central districts.

HELPFUL ORGANIZATIONS

Designed for overseas visitors, the **Welcome Inn Reservation Center** (WIRC) arranges free bookings through their website for approved traditional inns (*ryokan*), government-run lodges, business hotels, and pensions. JNTO offices (*see p163*) stock the *Directory of Welcome Inns*. There are WIRC counters in the arrivals lobby of Narita airport, and at Tokyo's TIC (*see p173*).

Many of the traditional inns approved by the WIRC also belong to the **Japanese Inn Group**, which covers about 80 moderately rated *ryokan* that are geared to receiving mainly foreign visitors.

The **Japan City Hotel Association** has online information about member hotels and advance bookings for accommodations in Tokyo

Fifty-two story Park Tower, Park Hyatt Tokyo (*see p116*)

The understated porch of Hotel Seiyo Ginza (*see p111*)

and the areas beyond the capital city. The **Japan Economy Hotel** (JEH) **Group** offers clean, modern rooms at reasonable rates.

BOOKING AND PAYING

Booking accommodations in advance is advisable, especially at times of major public holidays (*see p31*). Reservations made directly need to be confirmed by letter, fax, or email. Rates quoted are often per person, not per room.

Most hotels accept the best-known international credit cards. The bill is usually payable on departure, but business hotels and some others may request advance payment.

There is a basic 5 percent consumption tax on all rooms, rising in the case of higher-end hotels (usually over ¥15,000). A small hotel tax is added in Tokyo hotels for rooms priced above ¥10,000 per person.

DELUXE HOTELS

Top American chains such as the Hilton, Sheraton, Hyatt, Westin, and Four Seasons are well established in Tokyo.

Among Japanese-owned hotels, there is a vast range – staid conservatism; over-the-top opulence; discreet exclusivity; chic minimalism; and quaint eccentricity. Increasingly common are "intelligent" hotels, which monitor temperature, have electronic cards in place of room keys, computerized toilets, a voicemail message system, and fast, reliable broadband telecommunication networks

Deluxe hotels often feature popular restaurants and bars, many with spectacular views.

PENSIONS

Western-style pensions have become popular in recent years. Located mostly in resort areas, they are rustic and

◁ **Resplendent azalea bushes at Nezu Shrine, Yanaka**

relaxed in style and offer good hearty meals. Generally managed by married couples, they fall somewhere between a *minshuku* and the more service-oriented pamperings of a small hotel.

BUSINESS HOTELS

The majority of mid-range hotels in Tokyo fall into the category of business hotels. Many are located within easy reach of stations on the Yamanote line. As the name suggests, business hotels (*bijinesu hoteru*) cater to budget-conscious business travelers. Anyone can stay, and being generally located in city centers around train stations, they are convenient. Do not expect English to be spoken.

Rooms are Western-style, functional, small, and spotlessly clean. Slippers and a cotton robe are generally supplied. There is no room service, but vending machines offer the ubiquitous "health drinks," beer, and sake. There is usually at least one restaurant with a good choice of traditional Japanese or Western-style breakfasts.

CAPSULE HOTELS

Unique to Japan, these custom-built hotels feature encapsulated beds in and out of which guests must slide, since there is no room to sit up, let alone stand up. Rattan blinds or curtains can be pulled across for a degree of

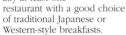
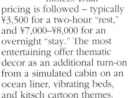

Sign showing rates for a Tokyo love hotel

privacy. Usually constructed in two tiers, they cater mainly to "*salarymen*" who are too tired or inebriated to make the last train home. Most are clustered around major train stations or nightlife areas. Facilities include a personal TV, radio, alarm call system, and airconditioning. Smoking is not allowed. Vending machines may be nearby. Baths and sometimes saunas are included in the price.

The size of such hotels varies widely, ranging from 50 capsules to over 600. Some still cater only to men, but women are increasingly encouraged to stay. Expect to pay between ¥3,500–¥5,000 in cash.

LOVE HOTELS

Love Hotels are designed for dating couples and married partners living in extended families, who may feel that they need some privacy. They are mainly found in entertainment areas and along expressways and highways, much like motels. Dual pricing is followed – typically ¥3,500 for a two-hour "rest," and ¥7,000–¥8,000 for an overnight "stay." The most entertaining offer thematic decor as an additional turn-on from a simulated cabin on an ocean liner, vibrating beds, and kitsch cartoon themes.

Entrances to love hotels are screened off by a wall that has a sign listing the room rates – credit cards are not accepted. Privacy is ensured

Sparse interior of a Central Tokyo youth hostel

by a rather anonymous method of payment – couples choose their room from a photo board, and then pay a cashier who sits behind a screen. Guests then receive their change and a key.

Rooms are reasonably spacious, clean, and with a private bath.

YOUTH HOSTELS

Cheap, clean, and open to people of all ages, youth hostel services have been improving in Tokyo in recent years. Membership is usually not required. The cheapest option for travelers, rates run between ¥2,500–¥4,000. Payment is in cash only. All meals come at an additional cost.

DIRECTORY

Japan Economy Hotel Group
www.kid97.co.jp/~jeh-group/jeh-group.html

Japan City Hotel Association
www.jcha.or.jp/english/

Japanese Inn Group
Tel (06) 6444-6740.
Fax (06) 6444-6750.
www.jpinn.com

Welcome Inn Reservation Center
www.itcj.or.jp

For JNTO offices and website see p163.

Typical capsule hotel, with two tiers of encapsulated beds

Traditional Accommodations

A *ryokan* is a unique fusion of private and communal styles of living. Such Japanese traditions as removing shoes at the right point are important, no matter what the cost of the room, and the most expensive of these traditional inns may demand a high level of etiquette. A family-run *minshuku* – a type of guesthouse – is an even more intimate way to experience the Japanese lifestyle. There are also options that are *ryokan* at heart, but with Western-style touches such as private bathrooms.

Sawanoya *ryokan*, in a quiet neighborhood near Ueno Park

WHAT IS A RYOKAN?

A *ryokan* is a traditional inn, usually associated with older towns, mountain, and hot spring areas. While top-end Tokyo *ryokan* can be relied on to have many of the traditional graces found in their rural counterparts, mid-range *ryokan*, with modern touches and conveniences, can be a little different. Some are set in Edo-period buildings – confections of wood, glass, bamboo, paper screens, and *tatami* matting.

Certain important Japanese customs apply – the biggest difference and greatest surprise for many foreigners is that bathing facilities are traditionally communal, not private. The bathing facilities may be quite elaborate, and when part of an exclusive hot spring resort the establishment is called an *onsen*.

Most *ryokan* place emphasis on the quality of their meals, and the room price often includes breakfast and dinner (as specified in the listings). This can be ideal in quiet areas where few restaurants are open in the evening, but a constraint elsewhere. Another possible problem, mainly for elderly foreigners, is the Japanese tradition of living at floor level, using legless chairs and beds.

Note that many *ryokan* impose a curfew around 11pm, so check before you step out, or make special arrangements about keys in advance if you plan to stay out late.

ARRIVING AT A RYOKAN

Guests generally check into a *ryokan* in the mid- to late afternoon, to allow plenty of time for bathing and dinner. At larger *ryokan*, there may be a doorman to smooth the way, but in smaller establishments, guests should slide open the front door and politely call *"gomen kudasai"* to announce arrival.

Do not step up into the lobby proper until the *okamisan* (female owner or manager) appears. This is the signal to remove outdoor shoes and step up into a pair of waiting house slippers (*see p165*). Then, before entering the guestroom, remove the house slippers and leave them outside the door.

TYPICAL ROOMS

Guestrooms are floored in *tatami* mats. In one corner of the room is an alcove, called *tokonoma*, which may contain a hanging scroll, flowers, or other artifacts. The *tokonoma* is to be respected – no suitcases, ashtrays, or drinks should be left here. There will also be a low table surrounded by cushions (*zabuton*) or folding chairs. On the table top will be a tray, bearing a tea set and possibly *wagashi* sweets (*see p130*).

Your futon mattress and bedding will be stowed in cupboards when you first enter the room. These will usually be laid out discreetly for you in the evening while you are out of the room.

Ordinarily a room will be further supplied with a TV, airconditioner, and/or heater. There is usually a telephone, although it may not have an international connection. You should also find a small towel in a box or basket, which you can take to the communal bathroom to use as a washcloth. A personal outdoor bath (*rotenburo*) counts as a luxury. A screened-off veranda, with Western-style table and armchairs, is more commonplace. There may be other Western-style touches.

Handle everything in the room with care, and walk only in bare feet or socks on the fragile *tatami*.

Room with *tatami* mats, low table, and *zabuton*, and additional Western-style daybed

Small communal bath and separate low shower for cleansing

WEARING YUKATA

Somewhere in the room will be traditional robes for you to wear, called *yukata*. Most people change into *yukata* for the duration of their stay, since the loose cotton kimonos symbolize relaxation and leisure time. In resort towns and hot springs, they are even worn outside on the streets, together with the high wooden sandals called *geta*. A loose jacket may also be provided. It is best to follow the example of others as to exactly where and when to wear the robes.

Fold *yukata* left-side over right. Right-side over left symbolizes death in Buddhism and can cause upset. Use the *obi* sash provided to secure the gown.

BATHING ARRANGEMENTS

Within the *ryokan* will be at least one communal bath and a toilet block with either Western-style cubicles, Japanese squat toilets, or a choice of the two styles.

In smaller *ryokan* with only one bath, bathing times may differ for men and women. In larger establishments bathing is segregated, with one entrance for men, and another for women (*for symbols see p167*). Mixed-sex bathing used to be the norm but is very rare these days. The size of the bath and bathroom naturally dictate how many people can bathe at any one time. Check with the *okamisan* if you are unsure about the house rules, which vary between establishments.

In the bathroom there will be an area for undressing; a low shower or tap area; and the large bath itself. The golden rule to observe is that you must perform ablutions with the shower first and not enter the hot bath until you are clean. The bath itself is intended only for therapeutic relaxation. The same bathwater is used by other guests, thus it is considered extremely bad manners to contaminate the water either with an unwashed body or soap and shampoo.

People wearing *yukata*, the design of which is specific to each *ryokan*

EATING ARRANGEMENTS

Meals are sometimes served in a dining room, but more often in the room by a maid or the *okamisan*. The more exclusive the establishment, the more likely meals will be served in private.

Meal times are usually set quite early in the evening. Depending on the situation, the *okamisan* may stay for a while, explaining the dishes, demonstrating how they should be eaten, and to chat. Or she may leave discreetly, returning only to clear the table.

STAYING IN A MINSHUKU

These family-run enterprises open the family home to travelers as and when demand requires. With rates from ¥5,000–¥9,000, this is an economical option as well as a good opportunity to see how regular working people live. The atmosphere is more homely; guests are treated as part of the family at mealtimes and bathtime, and should fold up and stow away their own bedding.

STAYING IN LODGES

People's lodges, or **Kokumin-Shukusha**, are moderate-rated accommodations within the national parks. Rooms, baths, and toilets are Japanese style. Meals based on local produce are often fresh and of good quality. Room rates are often less than ¥6,000 per person, per night and ¥8,000 per person with two meals.

OTHER OPTIONS

There are several other affordable lodging options in Tokyo. Staying at a *shukubo* (on the grounds of a temple) is mostly confined to areas beyond Tokyo. The TIC (*see p162*) can provide information on other suitable accommodations in the city such as *onsen* (hot spring resorts), and converted farmhouses.

DIRECTORY

Japan Ryokan Association
Tel (03) 3231-5310.
Fax (03) 3548-8080.
www.ryokan.or.jp

Japan Minshuku Center
Tel (03) 044-271-8967.
www.minshuku.jp
@ abc@minshuku.jp

Kokumin-Shukusha Association
Tel (03) 3581-5310.
Fax (03) 3581-5315.

Choosing a Hotel

The hotels in this guide have been selected across a wide range for their good value, facilities, and location. These listings highlight some of the factors that may influence your choice. Hotels are listed by area, beginning with Central Tokyo. For the location of each hotel in Tokyo refer to the Street Finder, pages 180–89.

PRICE GUIDE
Price categories per night for two people sharing a room, including tax and service charges.
Ⓨ Under ¥8,000
ⓎⓎ ¥8,000–¥15,000
ⓎⓎⓎ ¥15,000–¥25,000
ⓎⓎⓎⓎ ¥25,000–¥35,000
ⓎⓎⓎⓎⓎ Over ¥35,000

CENTRAL TOKYO

Sakura Hotel
Ⓨ
2-21-4 Kanda-Jimbocho, Chiyoda-ku **Tel** *(03) 3261-3939* **Fax** *(03) 3264-2777* **Rooms** *43*   **Map** *3 A5*

Ideally located in the center of the Kanda-Jimbocho book quarter *(see p44)*, this small hotel is geared towards accommodating foreign guests. Popular with backpackers, the rooms are basic but cozy, and the English-speaking staff helpful. Internet access and a 24-hour café are a bonus. **www.sakura-hotel.co.jp**

Hotel Alcyone
ⓎⓎ
4-14-3 Ginza, Chuo-ku **Tel** *(03) 3531-3621* **Fax** *(03) 3541-3263* **Rooms** *74*   **Map** *5 C3*

A short walk from the Kabuki-za Theater *(see p154)*, this hotel was converted from a former *ryokan (see p108)*. The friendly staff at this snug hotel, some of whom speak English, have kept the Japanese tradition of hospitality alive. The hotel is very close to upmarket Ginza shops and restaurants. **www.hotel-alcyone.co.jp**

Hotel New Kanda
ⓎⓎ
2-10-6 Kanda Awajicho, Chiyoda-ku **Tel** *(03) 3258-3911* **Rooms** *123*   **Map** *3 C4*

Within short walking distance of JR Ochanomizu station, this reasonably priced and comfortable upscale business hotel offers all the basic amenities along with the additional benefits of Internet access arranged at check-in. It also houses a handy Family Mart convenience store and a restaurant downstairs. **www.hotelnewkanda.com**

New Central Hotel
ⓎⓎ
2-7-2 Kanda-Tacho, Chiyoda-ku **Tel** *(03) 3256-2171* **Fax** *(03) 3256-3219* **Rooms** *301*   **Map** *3 C5*

This 12-story Western-style hotel offers easy access to JR Kanda station and the nearby Akihabara electronics district *(see p45)*. The double rooms are the best value at this reasonably-priced accommodation. The highlight is the 24-hour Japanese communal bath. The men's bath is roomier than the bamboo-floored women's bath. **www.pelican.co.jp**

Ryokan Ryumeikan Honten
ⓎⓎ
3-4-3 Kanda-Surugadai, Chiyoda-ku **Tel** *(03) 3251-1135* **Fax** *(03) 3251-0270* **Rooms** *12*   **Map** *3 B4*

This modern, Japanese-style *ryokan* just south of the picturesque Nikolai Cathedral *(see p79)* is surrounded by skyscrapers and commercial banks. Relatively spacious and clean, the *ryokan* is curiously located in part of an office block. It has friendly and helpful staff. **www.ryumeikan.co.jp/honten_eng.htm**

Tokyo Green Hotel Ochanomizu
ⓎⓎ
2-6 Kanda-Awajicho, Chiyoda-ku **Tel** *(03) 3255-4161* **Fax** *(03) 3255-4962* **Rooms** *207*   **Map** *3 C4*

One of the best options in the Kanda area, the room rates at Tokyo Green belie the tastefully-screened rooms and varnished wood finishing. Close to Ochanomizu and the Kanda bookstore area, this comfortable and spotless hotel is a quiet retreat. The staff is bilingual. **www.greenhotel.co.jp**

Akihabara Washington Hotel
ⓎⓎⓎ
1-8-3 Kanda-Sakumacho, Chiyoda-ku **Tel** *(03) 3255-3311* **Fax** *(03) 3263-2222* **Rooms** *311*   **Map** *3 C4*

This hotel is a great option for those who would like to reside within strolling distance of the electronic hum of the Akihabara district. Architecturally attractive, this business hotel between the Kanda River and Akihabara station has well-equipped rooms and reliable facilities, and makes for a pleasant stay. **www.akihabara-wh.com**

Diamond Hotel
ⓎⓎⓎ
1-10-3 Kojimachi, Chiyoda-ku **Tel** *(03) 3263-2211* **Fax** *(03) 3263-2222* **Rooms** *157*   **Map** *2 F1*

Located in a pleasantly quiet setting, this moderately-priced hotel is close to the Hanzomon metro line, the British Embassy, and a few minutes walk from the Imperial Palace. It is both comfortable and reasonably priced. The multilingual staff is helpful. **www.diamond-hotel.co.jp**

Ginza Capital Hotel
ⓎⓎⓎ
2-1-4 Tsukiji, Chuo-ku **Tel** *(03) 3543-8211* **Rooms** *574*   **Map** *5 C3*

This well-equipped business hotel in central Tokyo is ideally located for both business travel and sightseeing in the city. The annex has a women-only floor. Non-smoking rooms are also available in the main building. The hotel also organizes sightseeing bus tours daily. **www.ginza-capital.co.jp**

Key to Symbols *see back cover flap*

Ginza Mercure

2-9-4 Ginza, Chuo-ku **Tel** *(03) 4335-1111* **Fax** *(03) 4335-1222* **Rooms** *208*　　**Map** *5 2C*

This trendy, boutique hotel is just a stroll away from the popular shopping area of the Ginza. Sound-insulated rooms, stylish decor, and an elegant French restaurant make it popular with business people and shopaholics. Half the rooms are non-smoking. The staff is multi-lingual. **www.mercureginza.com**

Ginza Nikko Hotel

8-4-21 Ginza, Chuo-ku **Tel** *(03) 3571-4911* **Fax** *(03) 3571-8379* **Rooms** *112*　　**Map** *5 B3*

An old establishment that has been around for 45 years, this remodelled, reliable, mid-range hotel affiliated with JAL (Japan Air Lines), is in a convenient location near Ginza's main department stores, bars, and restaurants. Tsukiji Fish Market *(see p40)* makes for a pleasant stroll from this well-appointed hotel. **www.agoda.com**

Ginza Renaissance Tobu Hotel

6-14-10 Ginza, Chuo-ku **Tel** *(03) 3546-0111* **Fax** *(03) 3546-8990* **Rooms** *206*　　**Map** *5 B3*

This top-of-the-range business hotel close to the Kabuki-za Theater is now a popular wedding reception venue. The decent sized, well-furnished rooms are comfortable and equipped with cable TV, minibar, voicemail, and Internet access. The staff is multi-lingual. **www.tobuhotel.co.jp/ginza**

Hill Top Hotel

1-1 Kanda-Surugadai, Chiyoda-ku **Tel** *(03) 3293-2311* **Fax** *(03) 3233-4567* **Rooms** *75*　　**Map** *3 B4*

This small, Art Deco period hotel, a favorite of writers such as Mishima Yukio, is located close to Meii University, the musical instrument store area of Ochanomizu, and the book store mecca of Kanda-Jimbocho *(see p44)*. Oxygen and negative ions are pumped into the rooms to promote a sense of well-being. **www.yamanoue-hotel.co.jp**

Hotel Yaesu Ryumeikan

1-3-22 Yaesu, Chuo-ku **Tel** *(03) 3271-0971* **Fax** *(03) 3271-0977* **Rooms** *30*　　**Map** *5 C1*

Set in a terrific location close to the Yaesu exit of Tokyo Station *(see p42)*, this hotel has slightly tatty, Japanese-style rooms. There is a Japanese breakfast on offer – including fish, rice, pickles, and miso soup, which is included in the room rate. **www.ryumeikan.co.jp.yaesu_e.htm**

Kudan Kaikan

1-6-5 Kudan-minami, Chiyoda-ku **Tel** *(03) 3261-5521* **Fax** *(03) 3221-7238* **Rooms** *162*　　**Map** *3 A5*

An old stone and brick construction that dates from 1934, this cozy, mid-range hotel, is just a one-minute walk from Kudanshita station, and the nearby martial arts Nihon Budokan Hall *(see pg152)*. The hotel has a famous summer rooftop beer garden. **www.kudankaikan.or.jp**

Mitsui Urban Hotel Ginza

8-6-15 Ginza, Chuo-ku **Tel** *(03) 3572-4131* **Fax** *(03) 3572-4254* **Rooms** *235*　　**Map** *5 B3*

This smart, efficiently-run business hotel in the backstreets of Ginza has well-furnished rooms equipped with plasma-screen TVs and broadband access. This is a good location for trips to both Ginza and Shimbashi. Two floors of restaurants cater to all tastes. **www.mitsuikanko.co.jp**

Royal Park Hotel

2-1 Nihonbashi, Kakigara-cho, Chuo-ku **Tel** *(03) 3667-1111* **Fax** *(03) 3667-1115* **Rooms** *450*　　**Map** *6 E1*

In the heart of the business and commercial center, next to the Tokyo City Air Terminal, this well-decked hotel has excellent transportation links. Special features include high-quality Oriental and Western furnishings, a beautiful Japanese garden, and the 19th-floor cocktail bar, Orpheus. **www.royalparkhotels.co.jp**

Yaesu Fujiya Hotel

2-9-1 Yaesu, Chuo-ku **Tel** *(03) 3273-2111* **Fax** *(03) 3273-2180* **Rooms** *377*　　**Map** *5 C2*

Part of the well-established Fujiya hotel chain, this medium-range business hotel has good service and larger- than-average rooms. Renovated recently, the rooms are bright and comfortable. The location near Tokyo Station and Yurakucho is an added advantage. **www.yaesufujiya.com/english**

Ginza Dai-ichi Hotel

8-13-1 Ginza, Chuo-ku **Tel** *(03) 3542-5311* **Fax** *(03) 3542-3030* **Rooms** *801*　　**Map** *5 B3*

Part of a huge chain that extends beyond Japan, there are plenty of Western-style facilities and services here, including a good selection of eateries and bars, spa, and sauna facilities, which make for a good stay. The efficient staff is multilingual. **www.daiichihotels.com**

Marunouchi Hotel

Oazu Bldg, 1-6-3 Marunouchi, Chiyoda-ku **Tel** *(03) 3215-2151* **Fax** *(03) 3217-1155* **Rooms** *205*　　**Map** *5 B1*

This comfortable, tastefully decorated hotel is housed in the new Oazu Building facing Tokyo Station. The decor and other features have charming retro touches that add interest to the rooms. The higher floors and bars offer great views over the nearby Imperial Palace and business districts. **www.marunouchi-hotel.co.jp**

Hotel Seiyo Ginza

1-11-2 Ginza, Chuo-ku **Tel** *(03) 3535-1111* **Fax** *(03) 3535-1110* **Rooms** *77*　　**Map** *5 C2*

This discreet and tasteful five-star luxury hotel is within walking distance of the entertainment and shopping centers of the commercial Marunouchi district. Uniquely, each room has its own valet. Noted for its superb Italian restaurant, the hotel also offers *kaiseki ryori (see p120)* menus, Japan's haute cuisine. **www.seiyo-ginza.com**

Imperial Hotel

1-1-1 Uchisawaicho, Chiyoda-ku **Tel** *(03) 3504-1111* **Fax** *(03) 3581-9146* **Rooms** *1058*   **Map** *5 B2*

A deluxe hotel right by Hibiya station and near Hibiya Park *(see p43)*. The current building replaces architect Frank Lloyd Wright's masterpiece, and offers top-notch facilities and services but without a personal touch. Large rooms in the newest Imperial floor have large-screen plasma TVs. **www.imperialhotel.co.jp**

Palace Hotel

1-1-1 Marunouchi, Chiyoda-ku **Tel** *(03) 3211-5211* **Fax** *(03) 3211-6987* **Rooms** *389*   **Map** *5 B1*

This well-established hotel has spacious guest rooms and a tranquil ambience. Though the interiors are a little dark, guests are treated to sweeping views of the Imperial Palace, moats, and the Otemon Gate *(see p43)*. For a prime location, this luxury hotel offers good service and value. **www.palacehotel.co.jp**

Peninsular Hotel Tokyo

1-8-1 Yurakucho, Chiyoda-ku **Tel** *(03) 6270-2888* **Fax** *(03) 6270-2000* **Rooms** *314*   **Map** *5 B2*

Keeping up the high standards of its Hong Kong original, this is a new addition to the city of Tokyo. Superbly located between the palace grounds and the shopping center of Ginza, the middle and upper rooms of this 24-story tower afford superb views. **www.peninsula.com/tokyo**

NORTHERN TOKYO

Capsule Hotel Riverside

2-20-4 Kaminarimon, Taito-ku **Tel** *(03) 3844-1155* **Fax** *(03) 3841-6566* **Rooms** *160*   **Map** *4 F3*

This cheap capsule hotel by Asakusa station, Azuma Bridge, and the famous Kamiya Bar *(see p157)* is one of the few capsule set-ups to accept women, with almost 20 female-only units. Asakusa's nightlife is rather limited, so the hotel almost always has vacancies. **www.asakusa-capsule.jp/english**

Hotel New Koyo

2-26-13 Nihonzutsumi **Tel** *(03) 3878-0343* **Fax** *(03) 3873-1358* **Rooms** *76*   **Map** *4 F1*

Popular with backpackers, this may be the cheapest hotel in Tokyo. Located in the day-laborer district of Sanya, Tokyo's Skid Row, the rooms are miniscule but spotlessly clean. The management is helpful, and there is even free Internet access. **www.newkoyo.com**

Kikuya Ryokan

2-18-9 Nishi-Asakusa, Taito-ku **Tel** *(03) 3841-4051* *(03) 3841-6404* **Rooms** *6*   **Map** *4 E3*

This slightly shabby concrete building, in a backstreet near Tawaramachi station, is more comfortable than initial impressions would suggest. With Senso-ji Temple *(see pp56–7)* just a stroll away and lots of "Shitamachi" atmosphere in the area, this is a good choice. Western-style breakfast is available. **r@mb.infoweb.ne.jp**

Ryokan Katsutaro Annex

3-8-4 Yanaka, Taito-ku **Tel** *(03) 3828-2500* *(03) 3821-5400* **Rooms** *11*   **Map** *3 B1*

Just around the corner from the lively Yanaka Ginza street and shops, this hotel has a stylish, modern exterior and crisp and clean Japanese-style *tatami* rooms, each with an attached bathroom. Coffee and free Internet access are available in the lobby. **www.katsutaro.com**

Sakura Ryokan

2-6-2 Iriya, Taito-ku **Tel** *(03) 3876-8118* **Fax**   **Rooms** *18*   **Map** *4 D2*

This hotel is close to both the sights of Asakusa and Ueno *(see pp48–9)*; a good location in an area famous for its July morning glory fair. A friendly, English-speaking management runs this cozy place. Half the rooms are Japanese-style, the rest Western. Only some rooms have en-suite bathrooms. **www.sakura-ryokan.com/index-en.html**

Sawanoya Ryokan

2-3-11 Yanaka, Taito-ku **Tel** *(03) 3822-2251* **Fax** *(03) 3822-2252* **Rooms** *12*   **Map** *3 B2*

The Sawanoya has become quite an institution among backpackers and budget travelers over the years. The inn's husband and wife owners are a charming couple, happy to dispense information about this historical locality. Free coffee, tea, and Internet access. **www.sawanoya.com**

Suzuki Ryokan

7-15-23 Yanaka, Taito-ku **Tel** *(03) 3821-4944* **Rooms** *11*   **Map** *3 C1*

Ideal for exploring the old-world charm of Yanaka, this modest *ryokan* is on the edge of the area's atmospheric graveyard. Run by elderly ladies, the warm welcome more than makes up for the creaky wooden floors and their inability to converse in English. **www.itcj.jp**

Taito Ryokan

2-1-4 Nishi-Asakusa, Taito-ku **Tel** *(03) 3843-2822* **Rooms** *9*   **Map** *4 E3*

Ruinous looking from the outside, the interiors are full of 1940s Asakusa charm. Though there is not enough privacy and the single shower is shared, the friendly, English-speaking staff and affordable rates more than make up for these drawbacks. This old, wooden building is strictly non-smoking. **www.libertyhouse.gr.jp**

Hotel Edoya

3-20-3 Yushima, Bunkyo-ku **Tel** *(03) 3833-8751* **Fax** *(03) 3833-8759* **Rooms** *49*   **Map** *3 C3*

A very smart looking hotel in the *ryokan* style, it is a short distance from both the Yushima and Ueno areas. Most of the rooms are Japanese-style and come with individual cedar bathtubs – quite a treat. There is also an outdoor bath on the roof, open to both men and women. **www.hoteledoya.com/**

Ryokan Shigetsu

1-31-1 Asakusa, Taito-ku **Tel** *(03) 3843-2345* **Fax** *(03) 3843-2348* **Rooms** *24*   **Map** *4 E3*

This *ryokan* is a perfect ensemble of Japanese traditional design, with sliding doors, paper screens, and *tatami* mats, all lovingly maintained. Close to Asakusa Park, one of the attractions here is the Japanese-style communal bath on the top floor, affording leisurely views across the older part of town. **www.shigetsu.com**

Suigetsu Hotel/Ohgaiso

3-3-21 Ikenohata, Taito-ku **Tel** *(03) 3822-4611* **Fax** *(03) 3823-4340* **Rooms** *124*   **Map** *3 C2*

A comfortable, medium-size hotel within walking distance of Nezu station on the Chiyoda metro line. The baths use water from a private hot-spring well, a rarity in the modern city of Tokyo. There are two buildings arranged around a tranquil Japanese garden, one a traditional *ryokan*. **www.ohgai.co.jp\e\index.html**

Sukeroku No Yado Sadachiyo

2-20-1 Asakusa, Taito-ku **Tel** *(03) 3842-6431* **Fax** *(03) 3842-6433* **Rooms** *20*   **Map** *4 E2*

The old world of Edo is successfully re-created in this atmospheric *ryokan* with sumptuously decorated Japanese-style rooms. The traditional bath is made from aromatic cypress. Another highlight are the full-course Japanese meals, exquisitely laid out and served. **www.sadachiyo.co.jp**

Ueno First City Hotel

1-14-8 Ueno, Taito-ku **Tel** *(03) 3831-8215* **Fax** *(03) 3837-8469* **Rooms** *77*   **Map** *3 C3*

This comfortable and efficient business hotel, closer to Yushima metro than Ueno, has both Western and Japanese *tatami* rooms, with en suite bathrooms. The small number of rooms and quiet location make this a cozy and comfortable place to stay. **www.uenocity-hotel.com**

Asakusa View Hotel

3-17-1 Nishi-Asakusa, Taito-ku **Tel** *(03) 3847-1111* **Fax** *(03) 3842-2117* **Rooms** *337*   **Map** *4 E2*

In a perfect location for exploring the Asakusa district, this hotel has spacious rooms that look out over the Sumida River and the rooftops of the Senso-ji Temple. There are nine restaurants and bars in this hotel. The Karuta Japanese restaurant has a great sushi corner, and tables with lovely garden views. **www.viewhotels.co.jp/asakusa/english**

Hotel Parkside

2-11-18 Ueno, Taito-ku **Tel** *(03) 3836-5711* **Fax** *(03) 3831-6641* **Rooms** *128*   **Map** *3 C3*

This hotel provides good value for this area, especially given the great views over the lotus pond in Ueno Park *(see pp48–9)*. Select rooms on the middle to upper floors for best views. Double rooms have been renovated. Both Japanese- and Western-style rooms are available. **www.parkside.co.jp**

Hotel Sofitel Tokyo

2-1-48 Ikenohata, Taito-ku **Tel** *(03) 5685-7111* **Fax** *(03) 5685-6171* **Rooms** *83*   **Map** *3 C3*

Soaring above the edges of Ueno Park's Shinobazu pond, some have likened the Sofitel's structure to a concrete pagoda. The hotel rooms offer superb views over the water and Benten shrine. The French-and English-speaking staff are helpful, and the rooms comfortable. A French restaurant and bar round out the *savoir vivre* theme. **www.sofiteltokyo.com**

WESTERN TOKYO

Capsule Hotel Fontaine Akasaka

4-3-5 Akasaka, Minato-ku **Tel** *(03) 3583-6554* **Fax** *(03) 3584-3163* **Rooms** *294*   **Map** *2 E3*

This is one of the few upscale capsule hotels in Tokyo where women are accepted, though only on weekends and national holidays. The luxurious Fontaine Akasaka also features comfortable seating areas, sauna facilities, and baths. Coin lockers are available but may not be large enough for a big suitcase.

Central Land Shibuya

1-12-2 Dogenzaka, Shibuya-ku **Tel** *(03) 3464-1777* **Fax** *(03) 3464-7771* **Rooms** *158*   **Map** *1 A5*

If you miss the last train, this hotel might be a final resort or a good place to experience capsule life for a night. Units have a small wall bracket TV, and just enough space to stretch out. Other facilities include coin lockers, vending machines, a restaurant, communal bathing, and showers. At present this is for men only. **www.capsule-land.com**

Akasaka Yoko Hotel

6-14-12 Akasaka, Minato-ku **Tel** *(03) 3586-4050* **Fax** *(03) 3586-5944* **Rooms** *245*   **Map** *2 E4*

This plain, brown, nine-story business hotel with good facilities and helpful staff has some real advantages when it comes to location. Equidistant from Nogi and Hie shrines, the quiet location is within an easy walk of Roppongi's daytime culture venues, international restaurants, and nightlife entertainment. **www.yokohotel.co.jp/english**

Asia Center of Japan Hotel

8-10-32 Akasaka, Minato-ku **Tel** *(03) 3402-6111* **Fax** *(03) 3402-0738* **Rooms** *173*   **Map** *2 E4*

A good value, basic hotel in a location that is good for visiting both Aoyama and Roppongi, this hotel is especially popular with foreign visitors for long stays. The budget priced rooms book up quickly. All rooms are well equipped but it is advisable to book a stay in the newer wing where the rooms are a little larger. **www.asiacenter.or.jp**

Children's Castle Hotel

5-53-1 Jingumae, Shibuya-ku **Tel** *(03) 3797-5677* **Fax** *(03) 3406-7805* **Rooms** *27*   **Map** *1 B5*

Ideal for a family stay, the Castle offers terrific recreational facilities for children. It is also popular with couples and business people. Large windows with good views make up for the slightly small rooms. Note that there is an 11pm curfew. **www.kodomono-shiro.or.jp.english/hotel**

Hotel Excellent

1-9-5 Ebisu-Nishi, Shibuya-ku **Tel** *(03) 5458-0087* **Fax** *(03) 5488-8787* **Rooms** *127*

A moderately priced business hotel in a laidback area just a minute from JR Ebisu station. The facilities are minimal, with no restaurant or provision for breakfast, but the area has plenty of other eating options. The rooms are clean and pleasant, and free Internet access is available.

Hotel Sunlite Shinjuku

5-15-8 Shinnjuku, Shinjuku-ku **Tel** *(03) 3356-0391* **Fax** *(03) 3356-1223* **Rooms** *197*   **Map** *1 C1*

A budget alternative to Shinjuku's high-end accommodation, this comfortable, well-managed business hotel on the east side of the station is ideally located for the shops and Kabukicho nightlife *(see p60)*. The simple rooms are well-maintained and comfortable. **www.sunlite.co.jp/top-e.htm**

Hotel Sunroute Akasaka

3-21-7 Akasaka, Minato-ku **Tel** *(03) 3589-3610* **Fax** **Rooms** *237*   **Map** *1 B2*

Part of the Sunroute Hotel Chain, this establishment is located near Akasaka-mitsuke metro station and is a quick taxi ride or 15-minute walk to Roppongi. The hotel has cheerful, well-equipped rooms with Internet access. The Excelsior Café makes up for the absence of a restaurant. **www.sunroute.jp**

Sansuiso Ryokan

2-9-5 Higashi-Gotanda **Tel** *(03) 3441-7475* **Fax** *(03) 3449-1944* **Rooms** *9*

This basic but friendly *ryokan* is just a short distance from JR Gotanda station. The relaxed and cozy atmosphere with affordable prices makes this place a favorite with long-staying foreigners. The Japanese-style rooms come with private or shared facilities. The doors close at midnight.

Shibuya City Hotel

1-1 Maruyamacho, Shibuya-ku **Tel** *(03) 5489-1010* **Fax** *(03) 5489-1030* **Rooms** *57*   **Map** *1 A5*

This friendly, well-serviced boutique hotel is great value. Just a seven-minute walk from JR Shibuya station, and across the road from the Bunkamura, the location is ideal for Shibuya shopping, arts, and nightlife. The nine-story building has unusually spacious rooms at affordable rates. A friendly and attentive staff.

Akasaka Tokyu Hotel

2-14-3 Nagatacho, Chiyoda-ku **Tel** *(03) 3580-2311* **Rooms** *531*   **Map** *2 F3*

Located in an area full of luxury hotels, close to Akasaka and Roppongi, with impeccable service and first rate facilities, this hotel is a very good deal. Good shops, restaurants and bars, and a mall in the vicinity add to the experience. Select rooms away from the main road which are quieter. **www.tokyuhotel.co.jp**

Arca Torre

6-1-23 Roppongi, Minato-ku **Tel** *(03) 3404-5111* **Fax** *(03) 3404-5115* **Rooms** *77*   **Map** *2 5E*

Noises rising from the street is the price you pay for this terrific location right in the heart of the upscale Roppongi entertainment district, located between Roppongi Hills and the new Tokyo Midtown. Rooms are functional, but even standard singles are furnished with semi-double beds. **www.arktower.co.jp**

Creston Hotel

10-8 Kamiyamacho, Shibuya-ku **Tel** *(03) 3481-5800* **Fax** *(03) 3481-5515* **Rooms** *43*   **Map** *1 A5*

Tucked down a quiet backstreet near to NHK and a stroll from the Bunkamura, the Creston is an ideal spot for a bit of peace and quiet, although it has a reputation as a hidden getaway for visiting rock stars. Located right in the center of Shibuya *(see pp66–7)*. The staff is bilingual. **www.crestonhotel.co.jp**

Excel Hotel Tokyu

1-12-2 Dogenzaka, Shibuya-ku **Tel** *(03) 5457-0109* **Fax** **Rooms** *407*   **Map** *1 B5*

Given its location right next to JR Shibuya station, this is a good deal. Part of the Mark City shopping complex, rooms are surprisingly quiet, but once you step out of the hotel you are in the heart of Shibuya street life. Comfortable, well-equipped rooms; two floors are set aside for women. **www.tokyuhotels.co.jp**

Haneda Excel Hotel Tokyu

3-4-2 Haneda Airport, Ota-ku **Tel** *(03) 5756-6000* **Fax** *(03) 5756-6001* **Rooms** *387*

If you have an early morning domestic flight, this hotel is a good option as it is on the same floor as the check-in and departure areas of Haneda airport. With a superior business hotel ambience, the desk is open 24-hours. The staff is bilingual and helpful. **www.tokyuhotels.co.jp**

Key to Price Guide *see p110* **Key to Symbols** *see back cover flap*

Hotel Ibis

▨ ▯▯ ▤ ▯ ¥¥¥

7-14-4 Roppongi, Minato-ku **Tel** *(03) 3403-4411* **Fax** *(03) 3479-0609* **Rooms** *182* **Map** *2 E5*

This stylish hotel in the midst of the Roppongi nightlife scene offers smallish but comfortable rooms. The friendly staff will point you in the direction of the karaoke rooms and the Sabatini restaurant, which claims to re-create the mood of a Roman market. **www.ibis-hotel.com**

Keio Plaza Hotel

▨ ▯▯ ▤ ▯ ▯ ¥¥¥

2-2-1 Nishi-Shinjuku, Shinjuku-ku **Tel** *(03) 3344-0111* **Fax** *(03) 3345-8269* **Rooms** *1450* **Map** *1 A5*

This colossal hotel in the middle of Shinjuku's skyscraper district is an ideal location for exploring the area. Fine restaurants, a tea ceremony room, beauty salon, sauna, shops, and the outdoor, heated Sky Pool ensure a high level of comfort and leisure. **www.keioplaza.co.jp**

Shiba Park Hotel

▨ ▯▯ ▤ ▯ ¥¥¥

1-5-10 Shiba-Koen, Minato-ku **Tel** *(03) 3433-4141* **Fax** *(03) 3433-4142* **Rooms** *318* **Map** *5 A4*

Set in a quiet, leafy location just a minute or two from the Onarimon subway and the superb Sanmon gate leading to Zojo-ji temple *(see p41)*, this hotel has tastefully decorated rooms. There is a main building and an annexe across the road. The rooms are clean and well equipped, and the bilingual staff very helpful. **www.shibaparkhotel.com**

Shibuya Tobu Hotel

▨ ▯▯ ▤ ▯ ¥¥¥

3-1 Udagawacho, Shibuya-ku **Tel** *(03) 3476-0111* **Rooms** *197* **Map** *1 B5*

A business hotel with more space and style than usual. The singles have wide, comfortable, double beds and do not cost much more than standard twins. Although all rooms are double-glazed, try to get a room facing away from the traffic of Koen-dori. There are several restaurants here serving different cuisines. **www.tobuhotel.co.jp/shibuya**

Shibuya Tokyu Inn

▨ ▯▯ ▯ ▤ ▯ ¥¥¥

1-24-10 Shibuya, Shibuya-ku **Tel** *(03) 3498-0109* **Fax** *(03) 3498-0189* **Rooms** *223* **Map** *1 B5*

A stylish hotel close enough to JR Shibuya station and metro lines for convenience, but far away enough to get a good night's sleep. Double-paned windows block out the street noise. The rooms are spacious, comfortable, and have the latest facilities, including Internet access. **www.tokyuhotels.co.jp**

The President Hotel

▨ ▯▯ ▤ ▯ ¥¥¥

2-2-3 Minami-Aoyama, Minato-ku **Tel** *(03) 3497-0111* **Fax** *(03) 3401-4816* **Rooms** *210* **Map** *2 D4*

A well-located establishment with a pleasant European atmosphere, this is good value for such a high-end, centrally located district without many hotel options. Only a short walk from Aoyama-itchome, the hotel's decent-sized rooms, large windows, and friendly staff make for a pleasant stay. **www.president-hotel.co.jp**

Arimax Hotel

▨ ▯▯ ▤ ▯ ¥¥¥¥

11-15 Kamiyama-cho, Shibuya-ku **Tel** *(03) 5454-1122* **Fax** *(03) 3460-6513* **Rooms** *23* **Map** *1 A5*

A graceful, European anomaly in trendy Shibuya, this small hotel's mellow mood and Neo-Classical decor is pure escapism. The rooms are luxurious. JR Shibuya station is a slow 10-minute walk away. The hotel's French restaurant, Polyantha, is well known among more affluent Tokyoites. **www.arimaxhotelshibuya.co.jp**

Cerulean Tower Tokyu Hotel

▨ ▯▯ ▤ ▯ ¥¥¥¥

26-1, Sakuragaoka-cho, Shibuya-ku **Tel** *(03) 3476-3000* **Fax** *(03) 3476-3001* **Rooms** *414*

This high-end hotel occupies the 13th–37th floors of the tower, offering spectacular views even from the bathrooms. Zen-like interiors, *kaiseki* restaurants, a Noh theater, and high-speed Internet connections create a modern, highly cultural ambience. **www.ceruleantower-hotel.com**

Tokyo Prince Hotel

▨ ▯▯ ▤ ▯ ▯ ▯ ¥¥¥¥

3-3-1 Shibakoen, Minato-ku **Tel** *(03) 3432-1111* **Rooms** *484* **Map** *5 A4*

A large hotel complex surrounded by landscaped gardens and tranquility, it is a short stroll to Zojo-ji temple and the landmark Tokyo Tower *(see p41)*. The rooms are luxurious, with attractive, comfortable furnishings and Internet access. **www.princehotels.co.jp**

Akasaka Prince Hotel

▨ ▯▯ ▤ ▯ ▯ ▯ ¥¥¥¥¥

1-2, Kioi-cho, Chiyoda-ku **Tel** *(03) 3234-1111* **Fax** *(03) 3262-5163* **Rooms** *761* **Map** *2 F3*

One of the premier ultra-modernist hotels of this famous Japanese chain, this hotel is in a building designed by Japanese architect Kenzo Tange. Some find the marble, gleaming white, and steel off-putting and sterile, while others appreciate its simplicity. Offers great views across the city. **www.princehotels.co.jp**

ANA Hotel Tokyo

▨ ▯▯ ▤ ▯ ▯ ▯ ¥¥¥¥¥

1-12-23 Akasaka, Minato-ku **Tel** *(03) 3505-1111* **Fax** *(03) 3505-1155* **Rooms** *901* **Map** *2 F4*

The flagship hotel of the well-respected ANA airline chain lies within the huge Ark Hills complex in Roppongi, which includes restaurants, shops, cafés, and the Japan Foundation Library. All rooms come with views of either Mount Fuji *(see pp96–7)* or the Imperial Palace. **www.anahoteltokyo.jp/e/**

Grand Hyatt Tokyo

▨ ▯▯ ▤ ▯ ▯ ▯ ¥¥¥¥¥

6-10-3 Roppongi, Minato-ku **Tel** *(03) 4333-1234* **Fax** *(03) 4333-8123* **Rooms** *389* **Map** *2 E4*

A spectacular, contemporary design fuses with natural elements, such as stone and hard wood trimmings, in the bedrooms and bathrooms to create a warm, refined mood in the grandest of Tokyo's Hyatt properties. Spa services, a tasty pastry boutique, and a shopping mall add to the interest. **www.grandhyatttokyo.com**

Hilton Tokyo

6-6-2 Nishi-Shinjuku, Shinjuku-ku **Tel** *(03) 3344-5111* **Fax** *(03) 3342-6094* **Rooms** *806*   **Map** *1 A1*

This branch of the luxury chain has just completed extensive renovations to its guestrooms and lobby to bring it up to speed with a highly competitive hotel market. There are tennis courts, a gym, an indoor heated pool for the energetic, shops, restaurants, and bars. **www.hilton.com**

Hotel Okura

2-10-4 Toranomon, Minato-ku **Tel** *(03) 3582-0111* **Fax** *(03) 3582-3707* **Rooms** *857*   **Map** *2 F4*

This is a popular hotel among the international business community, visiting VIPs, and the discerning and wealthy. The timeless Japanese decor, tearoom, and immaculate gardens create a restful mood. The service is attentive. **www.travelweb.com/okura/tokyo**

New Takanawa Prince Hotel

3-13-1 Takanawa, Minato-ku **Tel** *(03) 3442-1111* **Fax** *(03) 3444-1234* **Rooms** *946*

This hotel offers spacious, luxurious rooms with all the modern fixtures and fittings, and views out over manicured landscape gardens. Although there is not a lot to do at night in the immediate area, JR Shinagawa station is only a five-minute walk away. **www.princehotels.co.jp**

Park Hyatt Tokyo

3-7-1-2 Nishi-Shinjuku, Shinjuku-ku **Tel** *(03) 5322-1234* **Fax** *(03) 5322-1288* **Rooms** *178*   **Map** *1 A2*

This is the hotel where the film *Lost in Translation* was shot. It occupies the top 14 floors of this 52-story skyscraper. Well-appointed rooms are finished in natural woods, marble, and fine fabrics, making for a very refined ambience. Sunday brunches at the Park Tower's New York Grill restaurant are legendary. **http://tokyo.park.hyatt.com**

Sheraton Miyako Hotel Tokyo

1-1-50 Shirokanedai, Minato-ku **Tel** *(03) 3447-3111* **Fax** *(03) 3447-3133* **Rooms** *500*

Located in a very green and expensive district, this offshoot of the chain's famous Kyoto prototype was designed by the renowned architect Minoru Yamasaki. This is a modern hotel but with carefully executed Japanese aesthetics. Stay here to enjoy lovely gardens and dine at Zen-like restaurants. **www.miyako-hotel-tokyo.co.jp**

Westin Hotel Tokyo

1-4-1 Mita, Meguro-ku **Tel** *(03) 5423-7000* **Fax** *(03) 5423-7600* **Rooms** *444*

A grand, European-style hotel, the Westin is part of the Ebisu Garden Place complex *(see p76)*. The lobby has black marble floors and columns, and flower displays. There are large rooms with faux antique furnishings. Access is by the skywalk that runs from Ebisu station. **www.westin-tokyo.co.jp/en/**

Hotel New Otani

4-1 Kioi-cho, Chiyoda-ku **Tel** *(03) 3265-1111* **Fax** *(03) 3237-3408* **Rooms** *1600*   **Map** *2 E3*

This gigantic luxury hotel has hundreds of rooms, labyrinthine corridors, upscale restaurants, boutiques, and gift shops. Former guests include diplomats, noted business leaders, and rock stars. Rooms have been recently renovated. **www.newotani.co.jp/en/tokyo/index.html**

FARTHER AFIELD

IKEBUKURO Kimi Ryokan

2-36-8 Ikebukuro, Toshima-ku **Tel** *(03) 3971-3766* **Fax** *(03) 3987-1326* **Rooms** *50*

A very basic *ryokan* with a relaxed atmosphere, the Kimi Ryokan offers great value – an established favorite with long-term foreign visitors. Toilets and showers are shared. The pleasant rooms, traditional bath, and large communal lounge make for a comfortable experience. **www.kimi-ryokan.jp**

ODAIBA Hotel Nikko Tokyo

1-9-1 Daiba, Minato-ku **Tel** *(03) 5500-5500* **Fax** *(03) 5500-2525* **Rooms** *453*

Occupying one of the finest waterfront settings in Tokyo, this hotel is surrounded by picturesque gardens and parks. It is a short stroll away from Palette Town and Aqua City *(see pp82–3)*. Popular with young couples, the service is impeccable and the setting romantic. **www.hnt.co.jp**

ODAIBA Le Meridien Grand Pacific

2-6-1 Daiiba, Minato-ku **Tel** *(03) 5500-6711* **Fax** *(03) 5500-4507* **Rooms** *884*

Another towering, luxurious hotel opposite Odaiba station. Although some may think the location is too far out, for others it is a quiet option. Guests can enjoy super bayside views from well-appointed rooms and the hotel's 30th-floor Sky Lounge. The service is impeccable. **www.htl-pacific.co.jp**

SHIODOME Conrad Hotel

1-9-1 Higashi-Shimbashi, Minato-ku **Tel** *(03) 6388-8000* **Fax** *(03) 6388-8001* **Rooms** *290*

The most prestigious accommodation in Shiodome, the views of the serene Hama Detached Palace Garden *(see pp40–41)* from the tastefully understated rooms are superb. Guests should indulge in the cedarwood spas, aroma-therapy, and other leisure options on offer in this 37-story wonder. **www.conradtokyo.co.jp**

Key to Price Guide *see p110* **Key to Symbols** *see back cover flap*

BEYOND TOKYO

CHICHIBU-TAMA NATIONAL PARK Komadori Sanso Shukubo   🍴📋   ¥¥
155 Mitake-san, Ome-shi **Tel** *(0428) 78-8472* **Rooms** *10*

Dating from 1776, this old pilgrim's mountain lodge on Mount Mitake has all the comforts of a modern *ryokan*. Close to Mitake Shrine *(see p94)*, all the rooms with traditional *tatami* flooring have wonderful views of the mountainside and there are two shared cypress bathtubs. **www.komodori.com**

FUJI FIVE LAKES Fujitomita Inn   🍴📋📋📋🔥   ¥¥
3235, Shibokusa, Oshino-mura, Minanitsura-gun, Yamanashi **Tel** *(0555) 84-3359* **Rooms** *10*

This inn enjoys clear views of breathtaking Mount Fuji *(see pp96–7)* from all its guest rooms and surrounding gardens. The outside pool, set in a garden, and the natural hot spring add to the leisure options at this relaxing inn. The helpful staff speaks English. **www.tim.hi-ho.ne.jp/innfuji/**

FUJI-HAKONE Fuji-Hakone Guest House   📋🔥   ¥
912 Sengokuhara, Hakone-machi, Ashigarashimo-gun **Tel** *(0460) 4-6577* **Rooms** *8*

A cozy guesthouse with 24-hour indoor and outdoor hot springs in a lovely setting in the middle of Hakone National Park *(see p94)*. It provides simple but comfortable Japanese rooms, shared baths, and toilets. Located a minute's walk from Senkyoro-mae bus stop No. 4 from Odawara station. **www.fujihakone.com**

IZU PENINSULA Osawa Onsen   🍴📋🔥   ¥¥¥
153 Osawa, Matsuzaki Onsen, Matsuzaki-cho **Tel** *(0558) 43-0121* **Fax** *(0558) 43-0123* **Rooms** *25*

A 370-year-old former samurai villa in a sleepy village, with beautifully decorated rooms, inner and outer gardens, and cedar *onsen* baths. Western- and Japanese-style bedding is available. The highly rated dinners are served in private rooms. **www.osawaonsen.co.jp/**

IZU PENINSULA Shimoda Tokyu Hotel   📶🍴📋📋🔥📺📋🔥   ¥¥¥
5-12-1 Shhimmoda-shi, Shimoda **Tel** *(0558) 22-2411* **Rooms** *115*

Built on a cliff 1 mile (2 km) south of Shimoda, this hotel has the full range of hot springs, a sauna, and a swimming pool. Sea views and gardens sloping to the cliff's edge add to the appeal. A minibus picks guests up from Shimoda station. **www.tokyuhotels.co.jp**

KAMAKURA Kamakura Kagetsuen Youth Hostel   🍴📋   ¥
27-9 Sakanoshita, Kamakura-shi **Tel** *(0467) 25-1238* **Fax** *(0467) 25-1236* **Rooms** *24*

Nicely situated between the beach, temples, and the Great Buddha, this friendly hostel is just a 5-minute walk from Hase station. Rooms are Western and Japanese style. Though dinner is not provided, there are facilities to store and heat food. Non-youth hostel members have to pay an extra ¥1000. **www.jyh.or.jp/english/index.html**

KAMAKURA Kamakura Prince Hotel   🍴📋📺📋📋   ¥¥¥
1-2-18 Shichirigahama-Higashi, Kamakura-shi **Tel** *(0467) 32-1111* **Fax** *(0467) 32-9290* **Rooms** *98*

Bright, sea-facing rooms located on a beach in the Shonan area of Sugami Bay create a relaxed resort feel. The curving two-story building, outside pool, and modern Japanese garden blend to form an appealing and original design. **www.princehotels.co.jp**

NIKKO Turtle Inn Nikko   📋   ¥
2-16 Takumi-cho, Nikko **Tel** *(0288) 53-3168* **Fax** *(0288) 53-3883* **Rooms** *10*

This 'petit inn' is just a 10-minute stroll from the Toshogu Shrine World Heritage sites. The friendly, English-speaking owners will fill you in on local attractions. Fans of Mashiko-yaki, a well-known Japanese pottery center, will appreciate the tableware here, fired in nearby kilns. **www.turtle-nikko.com/turtle/index_en.html**

NIKKO Nikko Kanaya Hotel   📶🍴📋🔥   ¥¥
1300, Kami-Hatsuishi-machi, Nikko **Tel** *(0288) 54-0001* **Fax** *(0288) 53-2487* **Rooms** *70*

A classic resort hotel dating from 1873, the Kanaya combines effortless, old-fashioned elegance with superb service. The rooms dating from the Meiji-era to the mid-1950s are equipped with modern amenities. Make reservations during the peak holiday season. **www.kanayahotel.co.jp/nkh/index-e.html**

YOKOHAMA Hotel New Grand   📶🍴📋📺📋📋   ¥¥¥¥
10 Yamashita-cho, Yokohama **Tel** *(045) 681-1841* **Fax** *(045) 681-1895* **Rooms** *264*

This is where General MacArthur had his digs for a short time during the US Occupation of 1945. A luxury European-style hotel, the original building dates from 1927; the tower is an addition from the 1990s. There is a choice of three restaurants. **www.hotel-newgrand.co.jp/english/**

YOKOHAMA Yokohama Royal Park Hotel   📶🍴📋📺📋📋   ¥¥¥¥
2-2-1 Minato-ku, Nishi-ku, Yokohama **Tel** *(045) 221-1111* **Fax** *(045) 224-5143* **Rooms** *603*

A super-luxury hotel within walking distance of the showpiece Minato Mirai port complex. The real appeal here are the unmatched room views of the waterfront and Mount Fuji. Rooms are located on the 52nd–67th floors of the hugely impressive Landmark Tower, the tallest building in Japan. **www.yrph.com/index.e.html**

WHERE TO EAT

Tokyo is one of the major gourmet cities of the world known not only for its staple sushi and other Japanese delicacies, but also the remarkable variety of foreign cuisines. Humble taverns or grills that have been in business for centuries nestle side by side with gleaming highrise malls lined with delis and markets serving foods from around the world. The quality of meals at high-end restaurants is matched by their prices, but

A typical selection of Japanese food in a *bento* box

eating out does not have to be exorbitant. There are numerous mid- or low-end diners; noodle shops abound, as do fast-food restaurants (both Western and local); and if pressed for time and money, you can pick up snacks in supermarkets, convenience stores, and mid-range restaurants clustered around train stations. Best of all, wherever you go, standards of service and cleanliness are invariably high. It is hard to get a poor meal in Tokyo.

Savoring a sushi meal at a restaurant in Jingumae

MEALS AND MEAL TIMES

Most *ryokan (see p108)* and some hotels serve traditional breakfasts from 7–9am. If your hotel does not serve it, you will easily find a nearby café serving coffee and croissants or Danish pastries. When Japanese eat breakfast out, they usually do so in coffee shops that serve sets called *moningu* (morning), consisting of coffee, toast, a hard-boiled egg, and a small salad. However, breakfast is not a major meal in modern Tokyo.

Tokyo tends to eat lunch early. Typically, lunch runs from 11:30am to 2:30pm, and dinner starts at 5:30 or 6pm. Some upscale restaurants stop serving at 9 or 10pm, while most stay open to around 11 or 11:30pm (later still in areas such as Roppongi) to cater to after-hours office crowd.

RESERVATIONS AND DRESS CODE

Reservations are advisable at top restaurants in Tokyo and essential at the most exclusive Japanese dining places. Elsewhere, you can usually find a table without a reservation, especially if you arrive early in the evening.

Jeans and casual shirts are acceptable in most places, provided they are not torn or dirty. Women may find long, loose clothing advantageous when dining at a place with *zashiki* (low platform) seating. Also be sure to wear clean socks or stockings without holes if seating on *tatami* mats is involved, as you will have to take off your shoes. Avoid wearing strong perfumes or colognes if dining at a *kaiseki* restaurant or participating in a tea ceremony.

SET MENUS (TEISHOKU)

Most restaurants in Tokyo offer fixed-price menus, and these can be especially good value at lunchtime. Usually there will be a number of menu choices. These set menus are called *teishoku*. Some budget restaurants have window displays with realistic-looking plastic models of their dishes, or menus with photographs. Point to an item if you do not know its name. At many noodle restaurants and basic diners, it may be necessary to buy a ticket at the entrance before you place an order.

PRICES AND PAYING

Tokyo has restaurants to suit all budgets. You can slurp a hearty bowl of noodles for less than ¥500, or spend your entire budget for a week on a single night out on the town. Many upscale restaurants that might charge ¥10,000 or ¥20,000 per head at dinner often have economical lunch menus for ¥3,000 to ¥5,000.

The consumption tax (5%) is included in the quoted price, but many Western restaurants add a service charge. At some traditional Japanese eateries, an obligatory starter (*otoshi*) is served to all customers in lieu of a table charge.

At coffee shops and some restaurants, the bill is placed on your table. Just take it to the cashier to pay. At most bars and restaurants you will

Realistic-looking plastic "food" display in restaurant window

be asked to pay your bill at your table. The amount, written on a slip of paper, will generally be presented to you on a small tray. You place your payment (cash or card) on this tray, and your change will be returned on the same tray. Tipping is not expected, and may be refused.

ENTERING A RESTAURANT OR BAR

Traditional restaurants often have half-curtains hanging outside the door. This indicates that they are open for business. Duck past the curtain, slide open the door, and pause at the threshold. If you do not have a reservation, it is common practice to indicate how many people there are in your group by raising the appropriate number of fingers. In some restaurants, you may be asked to remove your shoes on entering. Slippers will, however, be provided for walking around on the wooden floor areas.

Many Japanese restaurants in Tokyo offer Western-style tables and chairs, plus counter seating looking into the open kitchen. They may also have traditional seating, known as *zashiki* with low tables. This involves sitting on thin cushions (*zabuton*) on *tatami* mats. Shoes and slippers are never worn on *tatami* mats. Women are expected to sit with their legs underneath them, *seiza*-style or to the side, mermaid-style; men usually sit cross-legged. It is ill-mannered to stretch your legs out under a low table. Special chairs with backs but no legs are often provided, or there may be leg-wells set under the tables, a plus for most visitors.

The counter is often the preferred place to sit, especially in sushi and tempura restaurants, as it gives prime views of the chefs skillfully preparing the food. Increasingly, smoking is discouraged at seats close to the kitchen.

Lunchbox counter in shopping mall

FOOD CUSTOMS, ETIQUETTE & TABOOS

Most restaurants offer guests *oshibori*, small damp towels, often hot, after they are seated for a meal. These are used to wipe hands (not the face and neck), and then left on the table top for dabbing fingers and spills, rather than being placed in the lap. Never blow your nose into the *oshibori* or even a handkerchief in public.

Japanese say, *"itadakimass"* ("I humbly receive") before eating; on leaving, it is customary to say *"gochisosama desh'ta"* ("it was a feast"). Calling *"sumimasen"* (excuse me!) is the standard method of attracting the waiter's attention.

Japanese drinking etiquette requires that you pour for the other person and vice versa. When on the receiving end, you pick up your glass, supporting the bottom with the other hand. When a toast (*kanpai*) is made, beer and whisky glasses should be clinked; with sake, cups are raised in a salute.

Japanese meals comprise numerous courses, each

served in separate bowls or plates. In formal situations, each person will have his own individual vessels; more informally, you serve yourself from shared bowls in the middle of the table. Instead of eating directly from communal bowls, first transfer a few bite-sized portions onto a small plate in front of you, using the serving chopsticks, if provided.

It is quite acceptable to pick up small bowls (such as rice bowls) and hold them half way to the mouth. Soup is slurped directly from the bowl, but any solid morsels should be picked out with chopsticks (*hashi*). If a morsel proves too difficult to handle, you can hold a chopstick in each hand and make a sawing motion to cut it.

Do not use chopsticks to spear food, or to push it straight from the bowl into the mouth (as commonly done in China). Gesturing and pointing with your chopsticks are also definite no-nos.

When not using them, lay your chopsticks on your chopstick-rest (*hashi-oki*) if provided, or place them across the lowest dish, keeping them uncrossed and parallel with your side of the table.

Chopsticks should never be stuck upright into bowls of rice or other food; and food should never be passed from one set of chopsticks to another. These are associated with funerary customs and are taboo at the dinner table.

Sitting *seiza*-style on *zabuton* cushions

Types of Restaurants and Bars

Tokyo has restaurants to suit every taste and budget, from hole-in-the-wall noodle stands to havens of refinement serving formal *kaiseki* banquets, not to mention the fine French, Italian, and Chinese cuisine. Most Japanese restaurants tend to specialize in specific genres, such as sushi, sukiyaki, tempura, or even individual ingredients such as tofu or *fugu* (blowfish).

Re-created traditional warehouse *(kura)*, Gonpachi restaurant, Ginza

KAISEKI RYORI

Japan's traditional "haute cuisine," *kaiseki ryori* is derived from the food served to accompany tea ceremonies, developed in Kyoto some 500 years ago. A typical banquet comprises numerous small courses, each exquisitely arranged, served in a prescribed order, and with careful reference to the season. Typically, *kaiseki* meals are served with great formality in elegant restaurants (sometimes known as *ryoriya*) or at *ryotei*, discreet establishments with courtyard gardens and spare but elegant private rooms.

KYO-RYORI AND KAPPO

Traditional cuisine prepared in the Kyoto style is often known as *Kyo-ryori*. Although the procession of dishes follows the established *kaiseki* pattern, the atmosphere is less formal. Meals feature typical Kyoto ingredients such as *fu* (wheat gluten) and *yuba* (soy-milk skin). Smaller places, with often no more than a single counter and where you do not have to order full-course meals, are often called *kappo*.

SHOJIN RYORI

The tradition of vegetarian cuisine known as *shojin ryori* developed along with Zen Buddhism in the 12th century. Meals can range from elaborate banquets similar to *kaiseki* (and just as expensive) but without using any fish, meat, or eggs to modern versions served in contemporary settings. Although Kyoto is better known for its *shojin ryori*, there are several fine specialist restaurants in Tokyo, as well as around the Zen temples in Kamakura.

IZAKAYA AND DINING BARS

Izakaya are down-to-earth places where you eat as you drink (rather than vice versa), ordering a few dishes at a time. At their most basic, these are budget taverns, identified by raucous, smoke-filled interiors, and battered red lanterns by the front door. Others are more refined, and may serve food of considerable quality. Many have large platters of pre-cooked items on their counter tops to pick from. A similar genre, now common in Tokyo, is the "dining bar." The approach is similar to an *izakaya* but with plenty of French and Italian influences.

SUSHI RESTAURANTS

Restaurants specializing in sushi *(see pp128-9)* vary greatly in style, from low-priced *kaiten-zushi* shops, where the sushi comes to you on a conveyor belt, to astronomically expensive places where everything, from the fish to the ginger, is of optimum freshness and quality. As a general rule, if there are no prices listed anywhere, it will be expensive.

While sitting at the counter, diners normally order servings of *nigiri-zushi* (hand-pressed sushi). If seated at a table or a *zashiki* (low platform), diners tend to have combos of *nigiri-zushi*, served on a platter or slab of polished wood.

Counter seating looking into the open kitchen, sushi restaurant, Ginza

Specialty *dengaku* restaurant

SPECIALTY RESTAURANTS

Tempura, sukiyaki, teppanyaki, and *tonkatsu* are generally served at restaurants that focus on each particular genre. Other areas of specialization worth investigating include *yakitori* (charcoal-grilled skewers of chicken), *unagi* (eel, grilled to delectable perfection), *nabe* (winter hotpots cooked at the table), and *dengaku* (bamboo shoots stuffed with miso and grilled). *Fugu* restaurants serve up the delight of the adventurous gourmet, the poisonous blowfish.

VEGETARIAN FOOD

Although traditional Japanese cuisine includes plenty of vegetables and high-protein soyfoods such as tofu and natto (fermented soybeans), it is not a vegetarian's paradise, as most dishes are cooked in fish-based *dashi* stock. However, *shojin ryori* restaurants use kelp and mushroom stock instead. Tokyo has a growing number of macrobiotic and natural foods eateries. Indian restaurants also offer good vegetarian options.

NOODLE RESTAURANTS

Japanese noodles come in two forms – brown buckwheat *soba*, a favorite in Tokyo since Edo times, and white *udon*, made from wheat flour. These are served cold with a dip or in a hot, savory soup. *Ramen* is a Japanese variant on Chinese noodles, usually served with a meaty broth. Late-night *ramen* counters are cheap, ubiquitous, and enduringly popular.

A cozy noodle bar with compact outdoor seating, Shinjuku

OTHER ASIAN RESTAURANTS

Chinese and Korean food is hugely popular in Tokyo. Yakiniku (Korean-style barbecue with plenty of red meat) diners are found throughout the city, with the most authentic found in Korea Town, north of Shinjuku. Good Thai, Vietnamese, and Mongolian restaurants are also available throughout the city.

WESTERN RESTAURANTS

Yoshoku are Western meal restaurants that feature such standards as *omu-raisu* (omelet rice), hamburger steak, and *hayashi* rice. Tokyo boasts French and Italian cuisine to rival the finest in Europe and North America. There are also numerous budget bistros and trattorias of remarkable authenticity. Spanish food is catching on fast, while German, Belgian, and Portuguese restaurants can be easily found. The British Isles are well-represented by many pubs of varying quality. However servings, especially of wine, tend to be skimpy.

FOOD HALLS AND MARKET STALLS

The food halls, located in the basements of most upmarket department stores are an essential stop for anyone with an interest in food. Colorful delicatessen-type stalls display a huge range of food both cooked and packaged. On the same floor, there may be small counter-style restaurants serving sushi, tempura, or a variety of noodles. Most department stores have restaurants on the top floor that serve substantial meals. You may also be offered free samples, with no obligation to buy.

Food markets have artful displays and stalls offering snacks and presentation boxes of sweets, tea, rice crackers, and fruit.

FAST FOOD AND CONVENIENCE STORES

There are a number of fast food chains, serving burgers, fried chicken, and the like. Many have familiar names (McDonald's, Kentucky), albeit with Japanese variations. Local clones such as Mosburger offer innovative twists, such as serving burgers between rice patties, with shreds of cooked burdock.

Convenience stores offer a good selection of *bento* boxes (*see p127*), onigiri (rice balls), and snacks.

THE TANUKI

In Japanese folklore badgers are celebrated as lovable buffoons or drunken rascals. This is one of the reasons why the ceramic likeness of the *tanuki* is often found at the entrance of *izakaya* and other drinking places.

Reading the Menu

General vocabulary likely to be useful when eating out is given in the *Phrase Book* on pages 204–8. Individual ingredients are also listed there. A selection of some of the most popular dishes and styles of cooking are listed in this glossary, including Japanese script to help you read menus in Japanese. Further details about some of the dishes follow on pages 124–9.

DONBURI: RICE-BOWL DISHES

Katsudon
カツどん
Rice bowl topped with a breaded, deep-fried pork cutlet and semi-cooked egg.

Nikudon
肉どん
Rice bowl with beef, tofu, and gelatinous noodles.

Oyakodon
親子どん
Rice bowl with chicken, onions, and runny, semi-cooked egg.

Tamagodon
卵どん
Rice bowl topped with a semi-cooked egg.

Tendon
天どん
Rice bowl that has one or two shrimp tempura and sauce.

Unadon
鰻どん
Rice bowl with grilled eel.

OTHER RICE DISHES

Kamameshi
釜飯／かまめし
Rice and tidbits steamed in a clay or metal pot with a wooden lid. Served in the container it was steamed in.

Kare raisu
カレーライス
"Curry rice", Can be *ebi-kare* (shrimp curry), *katsu-kare* (with deep-fried pork cutlet), etc.

Makunouchi bento
幕の内弁当
Classic *bento* (see p127).

Ocha-zuke
お茶漬け
Rice in a bowl with a piece of grilled salmon, pickled plum, etc., over which tea is poured.

Omu-raisu
オムライス
Thin omelet wrapped around rice mixed with tomato sauce and chicken or pork bits.

Onigiri
おにぎり
Two or three triangular chunks of rice wrapped with strips of dried seaweed *(nori)*.

Unaju
鰻重
Grilled eel served over rice in a lacquered, lidded box.

Yaki-onigiri
焼おにぎり
Variation of *onigiri*, without seaweed, grilled over a flame.

Onigiri and yaki-onigiri

Zosui
雑炊
Rice soup made with the leftover stock of a one-pot *(nabemono)* meal.

NOODLE DISHES

Kitsune soba/udon
きつねそば／うどん
Soba or *udon* noodles in flavored *dashi* broth with pieces of fried tofu.

Nabe yaki udon
鍋焼うどん
Udon noodles simmered in a lidded ceramic pot *(donabe)* with a flavored *dashi* broth, perhaps with shrimp tempura, shiitake mushroom, and egg. Popular in winter.

Ramen
ラーメン
Chinese noodles in pork broth. Usually there are some thin slices of roast pork on top, along with sliced leeks, spinach, and a slice of fish-paste roll.

Reimen (Hiyashi chuka)
冷麺（冷やし中華）
Chinese noodles topped with strips of ham or roast pork, cucumbers, and cabbage. Dressed with a vinegar and sesame oil sauce. Popular summer dish.

Somen
そうめん
Very thin white noodles, usually served in ice water. A summer dish.

Tamago-toji soba/udon
卵とじそば／うどん
Soba or *udon* in a flavored *dashi* broth into which an egg has been dropped and stirred to cook gently.

Tempura soba/udon
天ぷらそば／うどん
Soba or *udon* in a flavored *dashi* broth with one or two pieces of shrimp tempura.

Yakisoba
焼そば
Soft Chinese noodles sautéed on a griddle with vegetables and some form of meat or fish.

Zarusoba
ざるそば
Soba noodles served cold on a bamboo rack.Variation: *ten-zarusoba* has shrimp and vegetable tempura next to noodles.

RICE CRACKERS AND NIBBLES

Crackers *(senbei* or *osenbei)* are sold in supermarkets. Beautifully made and presented, they are also sold at station gift counters and stalls at the popular tourist attractions.

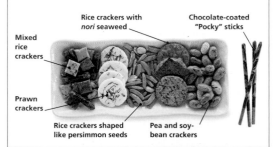

Rice crackers with *nori* seaweed

Chocolate-coated "Pocky" sticks

Mixed rice crackers

Prawn crackers

Rice crackers shaped like persimmon seeds

Pea and soy-bean crackers

DISHES PREPARED AT THE TABLE

Mizutaki/Chirinabe
水焚き／ちり鍋
Nabemono (one-pot meal) of vegetables, tofu, and chicken (*mizutaki*) or fish (*chirinabe*).

Okonomiyaki
お好み焼
Thick pancake-shaped mix of cabbage, egg, shrimp, squid, or pork cooked on a griddle.

Shabu-shabu
しゃぶしゃぶ
Nabemono (hot pot) with thinly sliced beef and vegetables cooked in a brass pan.

Table condiments: seven-spice *shichimi* powder, jar of soy sauce, and *ichimi* ground chili pepper

Sukiyaki
すき焼き
High-quality pan-cooked beef or chicken and vegetables.

Teppanyaki
鉄板焼
Meat and/or shrimp or squid and vegetables grilled on a griddle in front of the diner.

Udon-suki
うどんすき
Udon noodles, chicken, and sometimes clams or shrimp simmered in a soup.

SUSHI

Chirashi-zushi
ちらし寿司／鮨
"Scattered" sushi *(see p128)*.

Nigiri-zushi
握り寿司／鮨
"Fingers" of sushi *(see p128)*.

Maki-zushi
巻寿司／鮨
"Rolled" sushi *(see p129)*.

SET MEAL

Teishoku
定食
A set meal *(see p118)*, with rice, soup, some vegetables, salad, a main meat dish, and pickles.

MENU CATEGORIES

Aemono
和え物
Dressed salad dishes.

Agemono
揚げ物
Deep-fried foods.

Nimono
煮物
Simmered foods.

Sashimi (Otsukuri)
刺身（お造り）
Raw fish *(see p129)*.

Sunomono
酢の物
Vinegared dishes.

Yakimono
焼き物
Grilled foods.

À LA CARTE

Agedashi-dofu
揚げだし豆腐
Deep-fried tofu (bean curd) in a stock.

Chikuzen-ni
筑前煮
Vegetables and bits of chicken simmered together.

Eda mame
枝豆
Soybeans steamed in the pod. Popular summer snack.

Hiya-yakko/Yudofu
冷やっこ／湯豆腐
Cold/simmered tofu.

Kinpira
きんぴら
Sautéed burdock and carrot strips seasoned with sauces.

Natto
納豆
Fermented soybeans.

Niku-jaga
肉じゃが
Beef or pork simmered with potatoes and other ingredients.

Oden
おでん
Hot pot with white radish, boiled egg, and fish cake in soy broth.

Ohitashi
おひたし
Boiled spinach or other green leafy vegetable with sauce.

Shio-yaki
塩焼
Fish sprinkled with salt and grilled over a flame or charcoal.

Tamago-yaki
卵焼
Rolled omelet.

Tonkatsu
豚カツ／トンカツ
Breaded, fried pork cutlet.

Grilled eel *(unagi)* basted in a sweet sauce, a *yakimono* dish

Tori no kara-age
鶏の空揚げ
Fried chicken pieces.

Tsukemono no moriawase
漬物の盛り合わせ
Combination of pickles.

Yakitori
焼鶏／やきとり
Marinated chicken grilled on skewers.

Yakiniku
焼肉
Korean-style beef barbecue.

CHINESE-STYLE DISHES

Gyoza
餃子／ギョウザ
Fried dumplings.

Harumaki
春巻
Spring roll.

Shumai
焼売／シュウマイ
Small, pork dumplings crimped at the top and steamed.

Yakimeshi/chahan
焼めし／チャーハン
Fried rice.

IZAKAYA SNACKS

Cucumber and sea-weed

Dried squid

Onion and bonito

At *izakaya (see p120)* establishments, which are tavern-like places serving food rather than restaurants, dishes such as dried strips of squid and pickles complement the beer, *shochu* and other drinks *(see pp130–31)*.

The Flavors of Japan

More so than in most developed countries, where the produce of the entire world is available in supermarkets all year round, Japan is a country in which local and seasonal produce is still highly valued. The traditional cuisine of Tokyo reflects its waterfront location and its easy access to the fertile plains inland. Tokyo is also the focus of the nation's food distribution network, especially through the busy stalls of its central wholesale market in Tsukiji *(see p40)*. The city also boasts numerous restaurants serving the specialties of other regions of Japan. Its modern cuisine reflects influences from all around the world.

Ramen noodles

Chef at work, using chopsticks to arrange exquisite dishes

EDO CUISINE

In the early 16th century Tokyo, then known as Edo, became the capital of Japan when the powerful Tokugawa family moved there. With them arrived thousands of rich landowning samurai and wealthy merchants. This led to the development of Edo cuisine, a fusion of dishes from diverse parts of the country, that is today the most commonly recognized form of Japanese food.

The story of the ascendancy of Edo cuisine is also that of the decline in dominance of typically delicate flavors from Western Japan. *Soba* (buckwheat noodles) has been a popular food among Edo residents since the late 17th century and is renowned as one of the true tastes of Edo cuisine. As more people from the north of Japan moved to Edo, *udon* noodles, which were popular in the south, were replaced by *soba* noodles. *Soba* is most commonly eaten in the same simple way that it was eaten in the past: in a *zaru* (a small bamboo sieve). The weaker soy sauce of Western Japan also became less

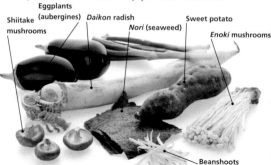
Shiitake mushrooms   **Eggplants (aubergines)**   *Daikon* **radish**   *Nori* **(seaweed)**   **Sweet potato**   *Enoki* **mushrooms**   **Beanshoots**
Selection of vegetables that feature in Japanese cuisine

TRADITIONAL JAPANESE SPECIALTIES

A typical banquet, such as might be served at a *ryotei* (upscale restaurant), may have up to 20 courses. Much is made of seasonal ingredients, with decorative flourishes also chosen to reflect the time of year. *Kaiseki* is a traditional style of cuisine in which a dozen or more dishes are served to each person, categorized according to cooking method, not ingredients. Sake *(see p131)* is the usual accompaniment. Vegetarian cusine, called *shojin ryori*, uses protein-rich tofu rather than meat or fish. It was developed by Zen Buddhists and is now found in many restaurants located in or near the precincts of Zen temples. The Japanese have also elevated tea snacks to an art form – delicate and pretty *wagashi* are usually made from sweet bean paste.

Bonito tuna flakes

Unadon, *featuring grilled eel over a bed of rice, is popular as it is thought to have great health benefits.*

Tuna being laid out for sale at Tokyo's Tsukiji Fish Market *(see p40)*

Chilly Hokkaido in Northern Japan boasts warming hotpots. Osaka and Hiroshima in Western Japan vie over their respective recipes for *okonomiyaki* pancakes *(see p135)*. On the island of Shikoku, Kochi is famous for *katsuo* (bonito fish); on the island of Kyushu, Kumamoto is renowned for horsemeat sashimi, while Kagoshima washes its seafood down with copious shochu liquor *(see p131)*. The southern islands of Okinawa boast a pork-rich cuisine.

favored when people in Edo adopted a stronger tasting sauce. Even grilled eel, which is thought to be a typical part of Edo cuisine, was originally a dish from Kyoto, but it is the Edo method of cooking the eel and preparing the sauce that we know today. Other foods which feature strongly in Edo cuisine are sushi, tempura, and oden *(see p123)*.

REGIONAL CUISINE

As the nation's capital, Tokyo has continued to draw its population from all corners of the country. This has had a significant impact on the way the city eats. There are numerous restaurants serving regional cuisines, and it is quite possible to sample the specialties of every corner of Japan without leaving the city. The cuisine of Kyoto is esteemed for its refinement and exquisite arrangements, especially *kaiseki* and temple cuisine *(see p120)*, featuring tofu and other products based on soybeans. Areas along the Japan Sea are renowned for their seafood.

Omoide Yokacho, a lane of restaurants in Shinjuku, Tokyo

KOBE BEEF

One significant contribution that the Japanese have given to meat connoisseurs across the world is Kobe beef. The black *wagyu* cows of Hyogo prefecture, of which Kobe is the capital, are bred and reared using strictly guarded and time-honoured traditions to make some of the highest quality beef in the world. Although similar cows are raised in America and Australia, the meat is not considered to be genuine if it is not from Hyogo, which makes authentic Kobe beef an expensive delicacy. Kobe beef is an extremely tender meat, and it is identifiable by the striations of fat that run through it. It is used in a range of Japanese dishes – it can be eaten raw as sashimi, cooked as teppanyaki or, as is popular nowadays, served simply as a big hearty steak or even a luxurious burger.

Tempura, *originally a Portuguese dish, is lightly battered deep-fried vegetables or seafood.*

Okonomiyaki *is a thick, pancake-shaped mix of egg and other ingredients, cooked on a griddle.*

Yakiudon *are thick noodles fried with seafood, seaweed, shiitake mushrooms, tuna flakes, and beansprouts.*

The Japanese Meal

Along with the indispensable rice and miso soup (made from fermented soy bean paste), a Japanese meal always consists of a variety of smaller dishes which are designed to complement each other. Plain ingredients are often given strong flavors, such as a bowl of rice topped off with an *umeboshi* (sour plum) or pickled ginger, or tofu that has been marinated in a strong, vinegary sauce. Two liquid ingredients central to most Japanese dishes are *dashi*, a light stock made from giant kelp *(konbu)* and dried bonito shavings, and Japanese soy sauce *(shoyu)*.

Firm tofu

Japanese family enjoying breakfast together

THE JAPANESE BREAKFAST

One of the many attractions of staying in the home of a Japanese family, or in a traditional Japanese hotel, is sampling the Japanese breakfast. Like most other Japanese meals, it consists of different dishes served separately. At its heart is a bowl of rice and some miso soup. It is polite for the rice to be placed to the left and the soup to the right of the sitter. Not only is it common for there to be variations in miso soup from region to region, individual families tend to have their own idiosyncratic method of producing this most Japanese of soups. The basic rice and soup are accompanied by a range of side dishes, of which the most common is a portion of grilled fish, usually salted salmon or mackerel. Other dishes may include dried seaweed, omelet, and a small portion of pickles.

Natto is a dish made out of fermented soy beans and it is a much-loved breakfast dish among health-conscious Japanese. Usually eaten with rice, it is famous not only for being extremely healthy, but also for the obnoxious smell that it gives off.

Miso soup · Nori (seaweed) · Grilled salmon · Pickled eggplant (aubergine) · Shiso ume (pickled plums) · Rice · Pickled radish · Tofu

Some of the ingredients for a typical Japanese breakfast

PREPARATION AND PORTIONS

A fastidiousness about detail characterizes both the preparation and presentation of Japanese food. Good presentation is vital to a Japanese restaurant's success, but it is not only the highly expensive, multi-course *kaiseki* meals that display this quality; even the cheapest food has a touch of the meticulous about it. This attention to culinary aesthetics naturally favors portions that are small and served individually to maximize the impact that they have on both taste and sight. Vegetables are cooked to remain crisp and retain their colors and, even when fried, food is not allowed to become greasy – the oil is heated high enough to seal the food instantly. The serving of small portions also has health benefits, and it should come as no surprise that obesity is much less of a problem here than in Western developed countries. Nowhere else in the world is healthy eating so attractive, varied, or delicious.

Small portions of a number of complementary dishes

The Bento Box

A *bento* is a take-home meal in a compartmentalized box – office workers buy them for lunch, schoolchildren eat from them at their desk, and business travelers have them with a beer on the bullet train. In its neat, individual compartments there will invariably be a large portion of rice, a main serving of meat or fish, pieces of omelet, some vegetables, and a selection of pickles. But part of the charm of the *bento* is that anything goes. It is not uncommon to open a *bento* and find a small octopus or a tiny whole fish gazing up at you, or even something that completely defies identification.

Slivers of pickled ginger

Pickled daikon radish

Tempura

Tamagoyake (omelet)

Sake (salmon)   *Hijiki* (seaweed)

Rice with black sesame   *Shiso ume* (pickled plums)   *Onishime* (simmered vegetables)

Typical selection of food to be found in a *bento* box

IN THE BENTO BOX

Agedofu Fried tofu.

Chikuwa Tubular steamed fishcakes.

Furikake Variety of condiments to add extra flavor, including *nori* (seaweed) flakes and toasted sesame seeds.

Jako Miniature whole dried fish.

Kabocha Squash, often served simmered.

Konnyaku Gelatinous paste made from Devil's Tongue (similar to sweet potato).

Korokke Croquettes filled with potato and meat.

Kurage Jellyfish.

Maguro sashimi Tuna sashimi.

Negi Salad onion, used for flavoring and garnish.

Onigiri Triangles of rice with various fillings.

Saba sashimi Mackerel sashimi.

Takenoko Bamboo shoots.

Tonkatsu Deep-fried breaded pork.

Tsukemono Pickled vegetables.

Umeboshi Pickled apricot.

Unagi Grilled eel in black bean sauce.

Yakiniku Miniature meatballs.

Japanese student eating lunch from a *bento* box

Sushi and Sashimi

Newcomers to Japan are most often both fascinated and intimidated by these native dishes. The term "sushi" applies to a variety of dishes (usually written with the suffix "-*zushi*") in which cold, lightly sweetened, and vinegared sushi rice is topped or wrapped up with raw fish or other items such as pickles, cooked fish, and meat. Sliced fillets of raw fish served without rice are called sashimi. Even those visitors used to Japanese restaurants abroad may be surprised at how ubiquitous such foods are in Japan. Fresh fish is always used, and the vinegar in sushi rice is a preservative.

Shiso leaf, garnish for sashimi

Sushi bar counter and sushi chefs with years of training

Nigiri-zushi
Here, thin slices of raw fish are laid over molded fingers of sushi rice with a thin layer of wasabi *(green horseradish) in between. Using chopsticks or fingers, pick up a piece, dip the fish lightly in soy sauce, and consume in one mouthful.*

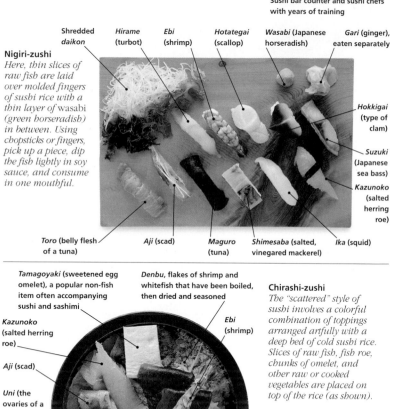

Shredded daikon · Hirame (turbot) · Ebi (shrimp) · Hotategai (scallop) · Wasabi (Japanese horseradish) · Gari (ginger), eaten separately

Hokkigai (type of clam)
Suzuki (Japanese sea bass)
Kazunoko (salted herring roe)

Toro (belly flesh of a tuna) · Aji (scad) · Maguro (tuna) · Shimesaba (salted, vinegared mackerel) · Ika (squid)

Tamagoyaki (sweetened egg omelet), a popular non-fish item often accompanying sushi and sashimi

Denbu, flakes of shrimp and whitefish that have been boiled, then dried and seasoned

Chirashi-zushi
The "scattered" style of sushi involves a colorful combination of toppings arranged artfully with a deep bed of cold sushi rice. Slices of raw fish, fish roe, chunks of omelet, and other raw or cooked vegetables are placed on top of the rice (as shown).

Kazunoko (salted herring roe)
Aji (scad)
Ebi (shrimp)
Uni (the ovaries of a sea urchin), a highly prized delicacy in Japan
Ikura (salmon roe)
Gari (ginger)
Slice of kamaboko, a type of steamed fish-paste roll with pink-dyed rim
Thin slice of ika (squid)

Maki-zushi
"Rolled" sushi is becoming increasingly familiar outside Japan – the California roll, for instance, is a version using avocado and other non-Japanese ingredients. For maki-zushi the sushi rice is combined with slivers of fish, pickles, or other morsels, and rolled up in a sheet of toasted seaweed (nori).

Temaki-zushi *is rolled by hand into a large cone shape.*

Kappa (cucumber)

Umejiso-maki (pickled plum and *shiso* herb)

Negitoro-maki (scallions and tuna)

Takuan (pickled radish)

Natto-maki (fermented soy beans)

Ebi (shrimp)

Tamago (egg)

Kampyo (gourd)

Oshinko-maki (pickled daikon)

Futo-maki, *or thick-rolled sushi, has three or more ingredients.*

Kampyo-maki (gourd)

Kappa-maki (cucumber)

Ebi (shrimp) tempura

Tail end of *ebi*

Tekka-maki (tuna)

Ura-maki, *or reverse rolls, are made so that the sushi rice, rather than the nori, forms the outside of the cylinder.*

Hoso-maki, *or thin-rolled sushi, has one central ingredient at its core. It is rolled into a cylindrical shape with the help of a bamboo mat.*

Hotategai (scallop) arranged in the shell

Thick slices of raw *maguro* (tuna)

Tarako, cod roe rolled up in squid and strips of seaweed

Red seaweed garnish

Sashimi
Sliced fillets of the freshest uncooked fish may be served as a single course. Sashimi is delicate and creamy, and the only accompaniments should be soy sauce, wasabi, daikon, and maybe a shiso leaf.

Hotate (scallop) arranged with thin strips of *nori* (seaweed)

Hokkigai, out of its shell

Tako (octopus)

Aji (scad), topped with finely sliced scallions

Wasabi (green horseradish) molded into the shape of a shiso leaf

---

POPULAR FISH IN JAPAN

Fish display at Kochi street market

Of the 3,000 or so varieties of fish eaten in Japan, the most common, available year-round, are *maguro* (tuna), *tai* (sea bream), *haze* (gobies), *buri* (yellowtail), *saba* (mackerel), crustaceans such as *ebi* (shrimp) and *kani* (crab), and fish that are usually salted such as *sake* (salmon) and *tara* (cod). Spring is the start of the season for the river fish *ayu* (sweetfish), traditionally caught by trained cormorants. *Bonito* is available in spring and summer, *unagi* (eel) in midsummer, *sanma* (saury) in the fall. Winter is the time for *dojo* (loach), *anko* (monkfish), and *fugu* (poisonous globefish), prized for its delicate flavor but also feared for deadly toxins in its liver and ovaries.

What to Drink in Tokyo

Tea ceremony

Green tea and sake (rice wine) are the traditional drinks of Japan. Both have ancient histories, and the appreciation of each has been elevated to connoisseurship. The tea ceremony is the ultimate expression of tea appreciation, a social ritual imbued with Buddhist ideals. Sake has long associations with Shinto – the fox god Inari presides over sake – and many Shinto festivals still involve the drink as a central theme. Other Japanese drinks include *shochu* spirit and "health" drinks.

Picking green tea in May, when leaves are at their most tender

TYPES OF TEA

Green tea leaves are divided into three main grades – *gyokuro*, which are the most tender, protected leaves that come out in May; *sencha*, which are tender leaves picked in May or June; and *bancha*, which are large leaves left until August. Leaves are sterilized with steam and then dried. *Bancha* is often roasted or mixed with other ingredients such as brown rice to form robust teas. Other teas are available; of foreign ones the Japanese especially enjoy imported fine English teas.

Basic green tea *is sold loose or in tea bags.*

Mugicha *is a tea brewed from roasted barley.*

Hojicha *is roasted* bancha, *a coarse tea.*

Genmaicha *is brown rice (genmai) and* bancha.

Sencha *is a popular medium-to-high grade of tea.*

Gyokuro *is a delicate, high grade of tea.*

Powdered matcha *is used at the tea ceremony.*

SOFT DRINKS

With names that conjure up disturbing images for English-speaking foreigners, Calpis and Pocari Sweat are among the most popular Japanese brands of canned soft drinks. Some are marketed as energy and vitamin boosters. Vending machines *(see p143)* stock them alongside canned green tea and coffee, and a wide range of fruit juices.

Chawan, a wide-brimmed cup without handles

Kyusu (teapot)

Wagashi (sweets)

Tea leaves, *usually loose, are placed in a teapot.* Bancha *is brewed with boiling water, but* sencha *and* gyokuro *should be brewed with boiled water that has been allowed to cool slightly first. The brewing tea should then stand for about a minute.*

SAKE (RICE WINE)

Sake is made from rice and water, which are fermented together then pasteurized to create a superb alcoholic "wine." Many connoisseurs judge sake on the five qualities of sweetness, sourness, pungency, bitterness, and astringency. Sake can be drunk warm, but the finer types should be lightly chilled to retain the subtle flavors. Unlike grape wine, sake is rarely expected to improve in the bottle. Store it in a cool, dry place for no more than a few months.

Everyday *hon-jozo* type by Gekkeikan

Fine *ginjo* type by Nihonsakari

Finer *dai-ginjo* by Tsukasa Botan

Taruzake (cask sake) *is matured in wooden casks made of cypress. Casks are often presented to Shinto shrines as offerings. The brewer's logo is displayed prominently.*

The finest grade of sake, dai-ginjo, *is made from the hardest core of the rice – more than 50 percent of each grain is shaved away. For the* ginjo *type about 40 percent is shaved; for hon-jozo, the average sake, about 30 percent. Some are brewed with added alcohol; those without are called* junmai, *"pure rice."*

A classic serving set *consists of a ceramic bottle* (tokkuri) *and matching cups* (sakazuki). *The bottle can be placed in hot water to warm the sake to about 50°C (122°F).*

Sake breweries *traditionally hang a ball of cedar leaves* (sakabayashi) *and sometimes a sacred rope* (shimenawa) *over their entrance.*

OTHER ALCOHOLIC DRINKS

Japan has several beers that have become well known around the world. Suntory whisky is also sold abroad, popular with those who prefer a milder whisky. Less well known abroad, *shochu* is a name for a group of Japanese spirits made from barley or other grains, or potatoes.

The alcohol content of *shochu* varies from 40 to 90 proof. The distilled spirit is often mixed with hot water or used as a base for cocktails, but it is also drunk neat, either heated or on the rocks. It is also used to make bottled fruit liqueurs such as *umeshu*, which uses whole Japanese apricots.

Suntory whisky   Sapporo beer   Asahi beer   Barley *shochu*   Rice *shochu*

Choosing a Restaurant

The restaurants in this guide have been selected across a wide range for their exceptional food, good value, and interesting location. Restaurants are listed by area, and within these by price, both for central Tokyo and surrounding areas. For the location of each restaurant in Tokyo refer to the Street Finder, pages 180–89.

CENTRAL TOKYO

Kanda Yabu Soba
2-10 Kanda-Awajicho, Minato-ku **Tel** (03) 3251-0287

Map 3 C4

A squat building set in its own quiet garden, this restaurant is refined yet informal. For locals, it is just the neighborhood noodle joint, albeit one with a century of history. House specials include *kamo-nanban* (hot noodles in soup with slices of duck meat) and tempura *seiro* (cold noodles with deep-fried prawns).

Meal Muji
2F, Infos Yurakucho, 3-8-3 Marunouchi, Chiyoda-ku **Tel** (03) 5208-8241

Map 5 B2

A casual, self-service, Western-style caféteria in the spacious, light-filled mezzanine of Muji's flagship Ginza store. Its wholesome and inexpensive menu draws lots of students and families. The almost-Scandinavian simplicity of the Muji decor comes as a welcome contrast to the rest of Ginza.

Phuket Aroyna Tabeta
3-7-11 Marunouchi, Chiyoda-ku **Tel** (03) 5219-6099

Map 5 B2

In the shadow of the Tokyo International Forum building *(see p43)*, this cozy little diner under the train tracks provides an extensive array of full-flavored Thai street food. The Thai cooks pull no punches with their seasonings. The set meals, available at any time of the day, are good value for money.

Yakitori Bars
Under the JR tracks in Yurakucho to the east of Harumi-dori

Map 5 B2

Cramped, smoky, and always convivial, these grills under the railroad arches are a throwback to what Tokyo used to be like before it was cleaned up. Huddle with the afterhours salarymen for *yakitori* (skewers of grilled chicken) and grilled organ meats at the stalls. Wash it down with sake or beer. Open from late afternoon till around midnight.

Bangkok Kitchen
Ginza Corridor, 8-2-saki Ginza, Chuo-ku **Tel** (03) 5537-3886

Map 5 B3

High quality Thai cuisine much as you would find in the heart of contemporary Bangkok, transported to Ginza with very little lost in translation. They use all the right spices and herbs in their fiery curries, soups, and yam salads. The lighting is rather too bright. The service is fast and always with a smile.

Coca Restaurant
2-1-11 Yurakucho, Chiyoda-ku **Tel** (03) 3507-5489

Map 5 B2

The most accessible of all the Coca outlets in the city, this branch is geared just as much to dining solo. The specialty here is Thai-suki, an exotic Southeast-Asian take on Japanese *shabu-shabu (see p123)*. Diners can watch their food cook in front of them in a bubbling casserole. Dips are rich and spicy.

Daiwa-zushi
Bldg No 6 Chuo Shijo, 5-2-1 Tsukiji, Chuo-ku **Tel** (03) 3547-6807

Map 5 C3

Of the many hole-in-the-wall counters inside Tsukiji Market *(see p40)*, Daiwa-zushi has the longest queue, no matter what time in the morning you arrive. The seating is cramped but the set meal is the ultimate sushi breakfast. A daytime eatery, it closes soon after midday.

Dhaba India
2-7-9 Yaesu, Chuo-ku **Tel** (03) 3272-7160

Map 5 C2

Nowhere in Tokyo serves up spicy South Indian cuisine better than this Indian restaurant. Top-value *thali* (platter) meals; curries rich in coconut, tamarind, and chili; *sambhar* (lentil purée) and *rasam* (peppery soup) on the side; and the finest *dosas* (savory pancakes) in the city straight from the griddle. There are plenty of vegetarian options.

Edogin
4-5-1 Ginza, Chuo-ku **Tel** (03) 3543-4401

Map 5 C3

This large, no-frills sushi emporium close to Tsukiji Market is known for the generous cuts of seafood that dwarf the rice underneath. Needless to say the fish is super-fresh – indeed it may be netted from the giant tank in the center of the room, prepared, and dispatched to your table still visibly twitching.

Key to Symbols *see back cover flap*

Kanda Shinpachi
¥¥

5F Shin-Marunouchi Bldg, 1-5-1 Marunouchi, Chiyoda-ku **Tel** *(03) 3287-3688* **Map** *5 B1*

Featuring fresh seafood shipped straight from Japanese seaports and a cellar with at least 50 kinds of premium sake, Kanda Shinpachi offers a superior take on traditional Tokyo *izakaya (see p120)* values. It is a small place, with many loyal customers, so reservations are at a premium.

Khyber
🆅 🍴 ¥¥

1-14-6 Ginza, Chuo-ku **Tel** *(03) 5159-7610* **Map** *5 C2*

Tokyo's first tandoor specialist positions itself several notches above the standard curry houses. The chefs (all from the Subcontinent) do not stint on the spices as they turn out delectable seekh kebabs (skewered meat), tandoori-cooked vegetables, spicy fish *tikkas* (cutlets), and several chicken dishes to accompany great oven breads.

Pero
🔲 🔳 🔲 🍴 ¥¥

6-3-12 Ginza, Chuo-ku **Tel** *(03) 5537-6091* **Map** *5 B2*

The look is that of an archetypal Spanish tapas bar, with Iberico hams hanging from the ceiling, excellent tapas, and a good range of sherries and Riojas – all to a flamenco backbeat. Dining at the rooftop lounge is preferable during the heat of the summer.

Saikabo
🔲 ¥¥

4F Coredo Nihonbashi Bldg, 1-4-1 Nihonbashi, Chuo-ku **Tel** *(03) 5204-0108* **Map** *5 C1*

Set in an attractive modern setting, this restaurant serves Korean cuisine such as *pulgogi* (grilled) beef, *chige* (spicy seafood and tofu) stews, and excellent *chijimi* (seafood) pancakes. In deference to local palates, none of the preparations are too spicy, but if you like your chili they provide plenty of their trademark *kimchi* (fermented vegetables).

Shin-Hinomoto
🔲 🍴 ¥¥

2-4-4 Yurakucho, Chiyoda-ku **Tel** *(03) 3214-8021* **Map** *5 B2*

The cramped seating, boisterous laughter, and cigarette smoke here make for a convivial dining experience. This old-school *izakaya (see p120)* under the railroad tracks in Yurakucho is typical in every way except one – the master of the house is British. This accounts for the English menu and the non-Japanese faces among the customers.

Soba Sasuga
🆅 ¥¥

B1 Riken Bldg, 1-19-12 Ginza, Chuo-ku **Tel** *(03) 3567-0012* **Map** *5 C2*

Soba noodles *(see p122)*, hand-chopped with craftsmen's expertise, are the specialty of this stylish basement eatery. At lunchtime that is about all they serve. In the evening, however, it transforms into a sophisticated *izakaya*, serving both sake and wine, with a delicate range of side dishes.

Sushi-zanmai
♿ 🔳 🔲 🍴 ¥¥

4-11-9 Tsukiji, Chuo-ku **Tel** *(03) 3541-1117* **Map** *5 C3*

Bright and brash, Sushi-zanmai is not a place for a leisurely sushi dinner. But it is accessible, affordable, and, unlike the other market shops, open around the clock. Just ask for one of the set meals, or point at whatever you fancy. There is unlimited green tea to wash it all down.

Azumitei
🔲 🍴 ¥¥¥

2F Ginza Inz 1 Bldg, 3-1 Ginza Nishi, Chuo-ku **Tel** *(03) 5524-7890* **Map** *5 B2*

Azumitei serves meals of *sukiyaki* and *shabu-shabu (see p123)* from Japanese *wagyu* beef. However, it is the interior that makes it special – tables are set in private bowers formed from huge sake barrels, linked by flagstone paths. This is not what you expect to find inside a mundane mall underneath an expressway.

Bird Land
🍴 ¥¥¥

B1F Tsukamoto Sozan Bldg, 4-2-15 Ginza, Chuo-ku **Tel** *(03) 5250-1081* **Map** *5 B2*

Yakitori (see p123), usually considered a fast food option, is raised to the level of high craftsmanship at this unpretentious but ever-popular grill. The premium free-range chicken is served in many ways, both raw and cooked. Start with liver pâté and do not miss the *sansho-yaki* grilled chicken. It all goes just as well with wine as with sake.

Botan
🔲 ¥¥¥

1-15 Kanda-Sudacho, Chiyoda-ku **Tel** *(03) 3251-0577* **Map** *3 C5*

This charming, old-world restaurant serves only one item – chicken *sukiyaki (see p123)*, cooked in a sweet-savory sauce over charcoal braziers. Install yourself at a low table (*tatami* rooms only) and choose what to drink; the kimono-clad waitresses take care of everything.

Isegen
🔲 ¥¥¥

1-11-1 Kanda-Sudacho, Chiyoda-ku **Tel** *(03) 3251-1229* **Map** *3 C4*

Isegen's specialty is *anko nabe*, cuts of monkfish cooked in bubbling hotpots at the table in traditional Edo style. It is not refined dining but is warming and hearty, and the venerable timber building is wonderful. Be aware that *anko* is only in season April to September, and you cannot reserve a table. Get there early or be ready to wait.

Maimon
🔳 🔲 🔲 🍴 ¥¥¥

Ginza Corridor, 8-3-Saki Ginza, Chuo-ku **Tel** *(03) 3569-7733* **Map** *5 B3*

The oyster bar is the first thing you see as you enter this gleaming designer restaurant. Run by the same group that operates the uber-chic Japanese Megu restaurant in New York, the menu features a range of grilled tidbits and more elaborate fusion dishes.

Ohmatsuya

†●↑ ⊕⊕⊕

2F Ail d'Or Bldg, 6-5-8 Ginza, Chuo-ku **Tel** *(03) 3571-7053*

Map *5 B3*

The interior of this restaurant looks quaintly rustic, but the quality of meals and service are as refined as one would expect from a Ginza address. Ohmatsuya serves the food and sake of the mountainous Yamagata prefecture. Each table has its own grill, where guests cook their seafood, river fish, or prime Yonezawa beef.

Rangetsu

☲†●↑ ⊕⊕⊕

3-5-8 Ginza, Chuo-ku **Tel** *(03) 3567-1021*

Map *5 B2*

A Ginza institution, Rangetsu has been offering its distinctive Japanese cuisine for over half a century. Full-course *kaiseki* meals are served by demure waitresses in kimonos. Highlights include *sukiyaki* and *shabu-shabu* prepared from top-grade, finely marbled beef from Japanese cattle. Other appetizing seafood dishes are also served.

Salt

☲Ⅴ†●↑ ⊕⊕⊕⊕

6F Shin-Marunouchi Bldg, 1-5-1 Marunouchi, Chiyoda-ku **Tel** *(03) 5288-7828*

Map *5 B1*

A perfect place for business lunches or romantic dinners, where celebrity chef Luke Mangan brings his innovative Australian cooking to Tokyo. Lots of eclectic flourishes – including green-tea-smoked scampi, quail tempura, lamb in *ras el hanout* spices – and a good cellar of Australian wines are also on offer.

Shunju Tsugihagi

☲Ⅴ†●↑ ⊕⊕⊕

Nihon Seimei Bldg B1F, 1-1-1 Yurakucho, Chiyoda-ku **Tel** *(03) 3595-0511*

Map *5 B2*

Shunju Tsugihagi epitomizes modern Japanese dining, blending flavors and inspiration from Europe and Asia, both in its food and decor. It is a rambling warren of interconnected alcoves, each with its own design motifs. Whether you want sushi, grilled meat, or home-made tofu, this eclecticism works brilliantly.

Viron

♿🖼Ⓨ☲†●↑ ⊕⊕⊕

1F Tokyo Bldg, 2-7-3 Marunouchi, Chiyoda-ku **Tel** *(03) 5220-7288*

Map *5 B2*

The interior of Viron is a faithful replica of a Parisian brasserie and so is the cuisine. Cassoulet, choucroute, confit of goose, or *pot au feu* – it is all hearty bourgeois cuisine, but cooked with a precision and quality only found in Japan. Those in a hurry can stand at the zinc bar or order a sandwich from the bakery.

Daigo

☲Ⅴ ⊕⊕⊕⊕

2F Forest Tower, 2-3-1, Atago, Minato-ku **Tel** *(03) 3431-0811*

Map *5 A4*

Tokyo's preeminent *shojin ryori (see p120)* restaurant is as refined as any *kaiseiki* establishment. There is no menu – diners need to specify a price range when they reserve a place. Dining is in private rooms, served by matrons in kimonos who bring in a succession of courses as simple, beautiful, and uplifting as Zen brush paintings.

Kanetanaka-an

♿Ⓨ☲†●↑ ⊕⊕⊕⊕

2F Kanetanaka Bldg, 7-6-16 Ginza, Chuo-ku **Tel** *(03) 3289-8822*

Map *5 B3*

One of Tokyo's most exclusive *ryotei*, Kanetanaka-an caters to politicians and captains of industry. This Ginza branch is not as well regarded, but the *kaiseki* banquets are just as refined. A limited number of simpler *kaiseki bento (see p127)* lunches are also offered each day on a first-come first-served basis.

Les Saisons

♿Ⓨ☲†●↑ ⊕⊕⊕⊕

2F Imperial Hotel, 1-1-1 Uchisaiwai-cho, Chiyoda-ku **Tel** *(03) 3539-8087*

Map *5 B2*

Les Saisons's reputation for high-end dining has been bolstered by the arrival of reputed chef Thierry Voisin. His culinary flair and superb cooking technique is complemented by the seamless service and luxurious decor. This is heavyweight haute cuisine that can match the best in France.

Ten-Ichi

☲Ⅴ†●↑ ⊕⊕⊕⊕

6-6-5 Ginza, Chuo-ku **Tel** *(03) 3571-1949*

Map *5 B3*

One of the finest tempura (vegetables and seafood) restaurants in the city, Ten-Ichi's flagship outlet in Ginza has a plush traditional feel and offers impeccable service. A popular restaurant, it plays host to visiting celebrities and politicians. Full-course banquets showcase the full gamut of delicacies, along with a range of side dishes.

NORTHERN TOKYO

Hatsuogawa

🖼 ⊕

2-8-4 Kaminarimon, Taito-ku **Tel** *(03) 3844-2723*

Map *4 E3*

Broiled *unagi* (eel) is considered one of the specialties of old Tokyo. Entering this atmospheric little diner with its bric-a-brac-cluttered interior is like stepping back in time. The *unagi* is served as *kabayaki* (on rice) or *unaju* (separately) – either way it comes slathered in soy sauce and is delectable.

Nezu-no-Jinpachi

🖼†●↑ ⊕

2-26-4 Nezu, Bunkyo-ku **Tel** *(03) 5685-1387*

Map *3 C3*

It is easy to miss the entrance to this modest *izakaya (see p120)* in the alleys of Nezu. If there is no room at the small counter, guests will be shown to the *tatami* room at the back, which has the intimate feel of someone's living room. The menu includes various home-made snacks to go with sake or beer.

Key to Price Guide *see p132* **Key to Symbols** *see back cover flap*

Otafuku
🍴 Ⓨ
1-6-2 Senzoku, Taito-ku **Tel** *(03) 3871-2521*
Map 4 E2

Oden – chunks of fish, vegetables, and eggs, slow-simmered in a savory broth – has been the *raison d'etre* of this neighborhood diner for over 100 years. This is nibbling food to accompany a flagon or two of warmed sake, of which Otafuku boasts a good selection.

Sometaro
🎌🍴 Ⓨ
2-2-2 Nishi-Asakusa, Taito-ku **Tel** *(03) 3844-9502*
Map 4 E3

Round off a day exploring the Asakusa backstreets with a light meal of *okonomiyaki* pancakes, which guests prepare on a hot plate set into the table. This can be hot work in mid-summer. Sitting in this vine-covered shack, one feels a century away from the glitter of downtown Tokyo.

Hantei
♿🍷🎌🍴 ⓎⓎ
2-12-15 Nezu, Bunkyo-ku **Tel** *(03) 3828-1440*
Map 3 B2

This handsome Taisho-era wooden townhouse serves only one thing – *kushiage*. Morsels of fish, meat, and vegetables are skewered, breaded, and deep-fried, then eaten with a savory dip. There is no need to order (just specify beer or sake). The staff bring course after course till they are told to stop. Reach early as they do not take reservations.

Ikenohata Yabu Soba
🎌Ⓥ🍴 ⓎⓎ
3-44-7 Yushima, Bunkyo-ku **Tel** *(03) 3831-8977*
Map 3 C3

This branch may not be as atmospheric as its namesake in Kanda (the parent restaurant), but the noodles – cold in summer and warm in winter – are predictably satisfying at this simple *soba* restaurant to the south of Ueno Park *(see pp48–9)*. A good range of side dishes are also on offer.

Mugitoro
Ⓥ🍴 ⓎⓎ
2-2-4 Kaminarimon, Taito-ku **Tel** *(03) 3842-1066*
Map 4 F3

Close to the ferry jetty in Asakusa, this is a popular lunch spot for Japanese travelers. It serves a wide range of simple, satisfying meals, many featuring its trademark rice cooked with barley, served with bowls of grated yam. There are plenty of other options too, ranging from simple lunches to full evening meals.

Sasanoyuki
🎌24 ⓎⓎ
2-15-10 Negishi, Taito-ku **Tel** *(03) 3873-1145*
Map 4 D1

A humble place in a nondescript part of town, Sasanoyuki "Snow on Bamboo" specializes in tofu cuisine, preparing the humble bean curd in numerous guises. Aficionados come from far and wide for its multi-course meals. However, few of the dishes are strictly vegetarian.

Vin Chou
🎌 ⓎⓎ
2-2-13 Nishi-Asakusa, Taito-ku **Tel** *(03) 3845-4430*
Map 4 E3

Part bistro, part *izakaya*, Vin Chou proves that imported French fowl (duck, guinea fowl, and quail) is just as delicious as local chicken when given the *yakitori* treatment; and that it all goes just as well with wine as with sake or shochu. The home-made sausages are not to be missed, nor is the crème brulée.

Yoshiba
🎌 ⓎⓎ
2-14-5 Yokoami, Sumida-ku **Tel** *(03) 3623-4480*
Map 4 E4

A converted sumo stable is the perfect place to sample *chanko-nabe*, the substantial hotpots of meat, fish, and vegetables reputed to give the giant wrestlers their strength and girth. Diners sit at tables around the periphery of the clay practice ring, while their meal cooks in front of them. This is simple but warming winter fare.

Bon
🎌Ⓥ🍴 ⓎⓎⓎ
1-2-11 Ryusen, Taito-ku **Tel** *(03) 3872-0375*
Map 4 C1

Housed in a charming old Japanese house, this restaurant serves traditional vegetarian temple cuisine executed with understated simplicity and a devotion to seasonal flavors. The multi-course set meals are a succession of miniature edible landscapes. The utensils are of hand-crafted lacquer, wood, and ceramic. Reservations are required.

Kuremutsu
ⓎⓎⓎ
2-2-13 Asakusa, Taito-ku **Tel** *(03) 3842-0906*
Map 4 F2

With its low gables, antique furnishings, and polished wooden floors, Kuremutsu looks centuries older than the famous Asakusa temple nearby. Grilled seafood is the specialty here, along with tidbits to accompany the sake. The prices are higher than elsewhere, because of the location and ambience.

Nakase
♿🍷🎌🍴 ⓎⓎⓎ
1-39-13 Asakasa, Taito-ku **Tel** *(03) 3841-4015*
Map 4 E2

An Asakusa institution for over a century, Nakase fries its tempura in sesame oil, giving it a rich, aromatic flavor. The multi-course dinners are substantial meals. For lunch, the most popular choice is *tendon* – a bowl of white rice topped with a single large patty of shrimp and vegetables.

Nezu Club
Ⓥ ⓎⓎⓎ
2-30-2 Nezu, Bunkyo-ku **Tel** *(03) 3828-4004*
Map 3 B2

Tucked away in the backstreets of old-time Nezu, this is the perfect place to round off a day wandering around the historic neighborhood. Chef Etsuko Yamada prepares simple, creative meals with the elegance of *kaiseki* and the hands-on personal touch of home cooking.

WESTERN TOKYO

Angkor Wat

📋 🍴   ¥

1-38-13 Yoyogi, Shibuya-ku **Tel** *(03) 3370-3019*   **Map** *1 B2*

This is the place to savor authentic Cambodian home cooking with the complete flavors of a Phnom Penh street stall. The house specialties reflect Thai, Chinese, and Vietnamese influences – spicy salads, chicken curries, vegetable spring rolls, and robust noodle dishes. If you are not sure what to order, just ask the cheerful waitresses.

Heirokuzushi

📋 🖢 🍴   ¥

5-8-5 Jingumae, Shibuya-ku **Tel** *(03) 3498-3968*   **Map** *1 C4*

This perennially popular *kaitenzushi* (conveyor belt sushi) restaurant in a prime location on Omotesando is one of the best and most established. Just grab whatever you want as the array of dishes go past. Each portion comes in a color-coded tray – pink is cheapest and gold the most expensive.

Nataraj

🖢 V 🍴   ¥

B1F Sanwa-Aoyama Bldg, 2-22-19 Minami-Aoyama, Minato-ku **Tel** *(03) 5474-0510*   **Map** *1 D4*

A welcome change of pace and cultures in the heart of busy Tokyo, this tranquil basement restaurant serves a full range of classy vegetarian Indian cuisine. Spice levels are restrained in deference both to local palates and the yogic teachings of its founder.

Natural Harmony Angolo

📋 🖢 V 🍴   ¥

3-38-12 Jingumae, Shibuya-ku **Tel** *(03) 3405-8393*   **Map** *1 C4*

No artificial additives, no smoking, no cellphones – good, honest home cooking using organic produce characterizes this restaurant. The cuisine is mostly Japanese, but with a few Western dishes. While the food is not purely vegetarian, there are plenty of meat- and fish-free options.

Yakitori Yokocho

📋 🕘   ¥

1 Nishi-Shinjuku, Shinjuku-ku **Tel** *n/a*   **Map** *1 B1*

"Yakitori Alley" is a warren of hole-in-the-wall bars and eateries that occupy an entire block by the northeast exit of Shinjuku station. Not all of them are salubrious, but most are welcoming. Unchanged for 50 years now, this is one of the last vestiges of blue-collar city life.

Bosphorus Hassan

V 🍴   ¥¥

2F Dai-Ichi Tamaya Bldg, 3-6-11 Shinjuku, Shinjuku-ku **Tel** *(03) 3354-7947*   **Map** *1 B1*

One of the first and still among the best of Tokyo's Turkish restaurants, Bosphorus Hassan offers an extensive range of meze, flavorful kebabs, and plenty of Anatolian beer, wine, and raki. A couple of times a week, the restaurant hosts belly dancing performances.

Buta-gumi

🖢   ¥¥

2-24-9 Nishi-Azabu, Minato-ku **Tel** *(03) 5466-6775*   **Map** *2 D5*

This small, free-standing house has been beautifully converted to create Tokyo's finest *tonkatsu* (deep-fried, breaded pork cutlet) restaurant. Only premium pork, from contract farmers around Japan (plus Iberico black hogs) are used here. The cutlets are delectable and the presentation impeccable, with absolutely no use of cooking oil.

Chinese Café Eight

📋 🕘   ¥¥

2F Court Annex, 3-2-13 Nishi-Azabu, Minato-ku **Tel** *(03) 5414-5708*   **Map** *2 E5*

Located opposite the Grand Hyatt Tokyo (see p115), this Chinese restaurant is one of Tokyo's best bargains. House specialties include Jiaozi dumplings, stir-fried dishes, and a whole Peking duck large enough for three or four people. The café stays open round the clock.

Fujimamas

🏧 🕘 Y 🖢 V 🍴   ¥¥

6-3-2 Jingumae, Shibuya-ku **Tel** *(03) 5485-2262*   **Map** *1 B4*

A converted, timber-frame *tatami* shop is the venue for this one-of-a-kind fusion restaurant, popular with both visitors and expats. The staff hails from around the world and so does the cuisine. There is a small terrace, several *tatami* rooms, a bar, and central dining area that stays busy till the early hours.

Genpin-fugu

¥¥

4-12-12 Roppongi, Minato-ku **Tel** *(03) 5775-5029*   **Map** *2 E5*

The spotlit giant fish displayed on the roof of this restaurant tells what is in store here – *fugu* (puffer fish). Its flesh is potentially lethal, but the licensed chefs carefully remove all the toxins. Not that flavorful when eaten as sashimi, it goes nicely in *nabe* hotpots (fugu-chili). Visit the aquariums filled with live fish on the second floor.

Gonpachi

🏧 🕘 Y V 🍴   ¥¥

1-13-11 Nishi-Azabu, Minato-ku **Tel** *(03) 5771-0170*   **Map** *2 D5*

Located inside a grand Edo-style building, the fabulous faux-medieval dining room at Gonpachi serves cheerful *izakaya* cuisine – *yakitori* chicken, *soba* noodles, simple seafood, tofu, and vegetables accompanied by beer, sake, or shochu. The rooftop sushi restaurant is more exclusive.

Key to Price Guide *see p132* **Key to Symbols** *see back cover flap*

Jap Cho Ok

🔲 Ⓥ ⑪⦿🅘   ⓎⓎ

4-1-15 Minami-Aoyama, Minato-ku **Tel** *(03) 5410-3408*   **Map** *2 D4*

The striking interior of this casual but sophisticated restaurant evokes the calm of a mountain monastery. Jap Cho Ok (House of Weeds) proves that there is more to Korean cuisine than just barbecue beef and kimchi, including a variety of seafood and vegetarian dishes.

Kitchen Shunju

🔁 Ⓥ ⑪⦿🅘   ⓎⓎ

8F My City, 3-38-1 Shinjuku, Shinjuku-ku **Tel** *(03) 5369-0377*   **Map** *1 B2*

A pleasant, informal eatery in the Shunkan restaurant section of the My City mall, Kitchen Shunju offers appetizing, modern Japanese cuisine, using fresh seasonal ingredients and plenty of influences from Asia and the West. There are various seating options including private alcoves and open dining rooms, *tatami*, and regular seating.

Kurosawa

Ⓥ   ⓎⓎ

2-7-9 Nagata-cho, Chiyoda-ku **Tel** *(03) 3580-9638*   **Map** *2 F3*

The great Japanese film director Akira Kurosawa loved *soba* noodles, hence the inspiration for this restaurant whichreplicates a house in his movie, *Yojimbo*. A casual dining room on the ground floor serves fresh, hand-cut noodles. Private rooms upstairs serve full meals, focusing on *shabu-shabu* and *nabe* hotpots.

Kuu

🔁 Ⓥ   ⓎⓎ

50F Shinjuku Sumitomo Bldg, 2-6-1 Nishi-Shinjuku, Shinjuku-ku **Tel** *(03) 3344-6457*   **Map** *1 A1*

A high-rise dining spot, Kuu offers a brilliant view of the city of Tokyo while serving reasonably priced grilled seafood, free-range chicken, and seasonal vegetables. It also has a good selection of sake, taking the traditional *izakaya* into the 21st century.

Maisen

🔁 ⧉ ⑪⦿🅘   ⓎⓎ

4-8-5 Jingumae, Shibuya-ku **Tel** *(03) 3470-0071*   **Map** *1 C4*

The attraction here is *tonkatsu* – deep-fried pork cutlets with a crisp, breaded coating and soft, juicy meat inside. This is served with grated cabbage and slathered in Worcestershire sauce. Various grades of pork are used; choose between lean and fatty. The set meals are a popular choice, featuring a range of side dishes.

Ninja

🔲 🔁 Ⓥ ⑪⦿🅘   ⓎⓎ

1F Akasaka Tokyu Plaza, 2-14-3 Nagatacho, Chiyoda-ku **Tel** *(03) 5157-3936*   **Map** *2 F3*

An informal restaurant, Ninja is a fun place to take kids. Located in a basement decked out to evoke an ancient Japanese castle, the waiters dress as ninjas, black-clad spies trained in martial arts. The menu features light *izakaya* dishes, such as sushi rolls.

Pintokona

⑪⦿🅘   ⓎⓎ

B2F Hollywood Plaza, 6-4-1 Roppongi, Minato-ku **Tel** *(03) 5771-1133*   **Map** *2 E5*

A *kaiten* (conveyor-belt) sushi counter with a difference – you do not just wait to see what comes past, but can also order from the menu. A small range of non-sushi items is also on offer. It is classier (and a bit more expensive) than other conveyor-belt sushi joints, as expected in the affluent Roppongi Hills.

Reikyo

🔲   ⓎⓎ

2-25-18 Dogenzaka, Shibuya-ku **Tel** *(03) 3461-4220*   **Map** *1 B5*

Popular as much for its atmosphere as for the quality of its food, this bustling little restaurant has been serving up stir-fries and other Taiwanese dishes for decades. The imported sausages, served steamed and sliced, go perfectly with a glass or two of warmed, sticky rice wine (*shaoxing-jiu*).

Rice Terrace

🅱 🔳 ⑪⦿🅘   ⓎⓎ

2-7-9 Nishi-Azabu, Minato-ku **Tel** *3498-6271*   **Map** *2 D5*

With a look less overtly "ethnic" than other Thai eateries, this bistro-sized place in the back streets of Nishi-Azabu serves up sophisticated and flavorsome Thai cuisine. In hot weather, the two outside tables are popular as the small upstairs dining room can get stuffy. The location is a bit hard to find, but it is worth tracking down.

Roti Brasserie

🆃 🔁 Ⓥ ⑪⦿🅘   ⓎⓎ

1F Tokyo Midtown Garden Terrace, 9-7-4 Akasaka, Minato-ku **Tel** *(03) 5413-3655*   **Map** *2 E5*

Set inside Tokyo Midtown, this elegant, brasserie-style diner serves a varied menu of modern American cooking, including pasta, rotisserie chicken, and burgers (the spicy Cajun catfish burger is a novelty). Roti Brasserie is also a wine bar, with a good cellar of New World wines and a choice of imported ales on tap.

Tsunahachi

⑪⦿🅘   ⓎⓎ

3-31-8 Shinjuku, Shinjuku-ku **Tel** *(03) 3352-1012*   **Map** *1 B1*

Tempura was originally street food, and Tsunahachi keeps it much simpler than at other gourmet tempura restaurants. It is housed in a rambling, wooden building that has somehow survived in the Shinjuku back streets. A bit dingy, the meals, however, are delicious and very reasonably priced.

Vietnam Alice

🔁 Ⓥ ⑪⦿🅘   ⓎⓎ

2F Belle Vie Akasaka, 3-1-6 Akasaka, Minato-ku **Tel** *(03) 3588-5020*   **Map** *2 F3*

Waitresses dressed in *aozai* (Vietnamese national dress) flit through the Neo-Colonial interior of this restaurant, serving noodles and delicate dim sum-like snacks (ask for the Spring Roll Basket), authentically seasoned with fish sauce and coriander. This is an ideal place for a light meal in the sweltering summer heat in Tokyo.

Beacon
1-2-5 Shibuya, Shibuya-ku **Tel** *(03) 6418-0077*

Map *1 B5*

The plush but understated decor and attention to detail make this a good place for entertaining clients or just unwinding at the end of the day. Deviating from the highly popular Japanese fare, Beacon is the place to go for charcoal-grilled, prime, grain-fed beef, free-range chicken, or wild Scottish salmon.

Bincho
2F Marina Bldg, 3-10-5 Roppongi, Minato-ku **Tel** *(03) 5474-0755*

Map *2 E5*

A rare oasis of calm so close to the Roppongi Crossing, the focal point of this genteel *yakitori* house is the charcoal grill in the center of the room, where top-quality chicken is cooked to perfection over premium Bincho charcoal. The traditional sake and an appetizing range of side dishes are also on offer.

Brasserie Paul Bocuse Le Musée
3F National Arts Center, 7-22-2 Roppongi, Minato-ku **Tel** *(03) 5770-8161*

Map *2 D5*

The French master chef's first overseas restaurant is worth a visit, if only for its remarkable setting in the dazzling concrete and glass building of the National Arts Center. The cuisine is simple and light. The fixed price lunches are hugely popular, so it is best to go for a late lunch after the crowds subside.

Fonda de la Madrugada
Villa Bianca B1, 2-33-12 Jingumae, Shibuya-ku **Tel** *(03) 5410-6288*

Map *1 C4*

Bordering on kitsch but promising great fun, this restaurant is located three flights below street level in the central courtyard of a transplanted hacienda. Mariachi singers serenade guests as they sip margaritas or Dos Equis lager, and dine on sophisticated Mexican food.

Fukuzushi
5-7-8 Roppongi, Minato-ku **Tel** *(03) 3402-4116*

Map *2 E5*

This elegant sushi restaurant feels worlds away from the high-decibel clamor of the neon Roppongi night. Fukuzushi is stylish but casual, with none of the snobbery found at many traditional Tokyo sushi counters. This is a good place for visitors not fluent in the argot of the sushi shop.

Hassan
6-1-20 Roppongi, Minato-ku **Tel** *(03) 3403-8333*

Map *2 E5*

Hassan's satisfying all-you-can-eat meals shatter the myth that *sukiyaki* and *shabu-shabu* can only be procured at exorbitant Ginza prices. Wafer-thin slices of marbled beef are served in quantities to challenge the heartiest of appetites. The decor is classic Japanese – all wooden beams and paper *shoji* screens.

Inakaya
4-10-11 Roppongi, Minato-ku **Tel** *(03) 5775-1012*

Map *2 E5*

Diners sit around a market array of produce and seafood, watching as chefs in *happi* (traditional coats) grill food and hand it over on long paddles. Just point to whatever you want to eat. This is a place for snacking with sake or beer, rather than filling the stomach, and it is boisterous, theatrical, and fun.

Mikawa
Roppongi Hills Residence B, 6-12-2 Roppongi, Minato-ku **Tel** *(03) 3423-8100*

Map *2 E5*

The gilt façade of this tempura house looks gaudy, but inside it is serene and traditional. Mikawa prepares "Edomae" tempura with utter precision, using seafood that used to be netted in Tokyo Bay, but which now comes from farther afield. The lunch menu is particularly good value.

Nodaiwa
1-5-4 Higashi-Azabu, Minato-ku **Tel** *(03) 3583-7852*

Map *2 F5*

Housed in a beautifully converted ancient storehouse, Nodaiwa is Tokyo's finest *unagi* (eel) restaurant, elevating this humble fish to gourmet status. Broiled over charcoal, daubed with a sweet-savory sauce, and served over rice, the *unagi* is delicious. Light meals are served on the ground floor; full-course meals upstairs.

Sushi Ouchi
2-8-4 Shibuya, Shibuya-ku **Tel** *(03) 3407-3543*

Map *1 C5*

The chef at this restaurant, Hisashi Ouchi, does not use commercial seasonings and cultivated fish; he uses free-range eggs and organic soy sauce for his preparations. The dining room is as relaxed as a coffee shop and the sushi is excellent. Highly recommended.

Union Square Café
B1F Tokyo Midtown Garden Terrace, 9-7-4 Akasaka, Minato-ku **Tel** *(03) 5413-7780*

Map *2 E4*

The Union Square Café's ethos of premium burgers and quality Italianesque cuisine translates perfectly from New York to Tokyo Midtown. The waiters are informal but helpful, and the outdoors tables are always in great demand. There is a small bar area for those dining solo or in a hurry.

Yuuan
B1F Shinjuku Park Tower, 3-7-1 Nishi-Shinjuku, Shinjuku-ku **Tel** *(03) 5322-6427*

Map *1 A2*

The decor at Yuuan blends *kaiseki*, farmhouse, and urban sensibilities. You can sit at the massive wood counter, sip sake, and nibble on seasonal delicacies or take a low table in the main restaurant for inventive multi-course meals of fish, wild herbs, mushrooms, and premium Kobe beef *shabu-shabu*.

Zakuro
V ⫴●⫴ ¥¥¥

B1F Nihon Jitensha Kaikan, 1-9-15 Akasaka, Minato-ku **Tel** *(03) 3582-2661*
Map *2 F4*

This long-established restaurant in front of the US embassy serves traditional Japanese cuisine with refinement and decorum. Full-course evening meals feature *shabu-shabu*, sukiyaki, teppanyaki, and other seasonal specialties. The lunchtime menu is especially good value.

Gesshinkyo
⩩ V ¥¥¥¥

4-24-12 Jingumae, Shibuya-ku **Tel** *(03) 3796-6575*
Map *1 C4*

The interior of Gesshinkyo looks as traditional as a tea ceremony hut, but chef Tanahashi's unorthodox Buddhist cuisine is quite unlike anything you would find in a temple. His handmade *goma-dofu* (savory sesame mousse) is delicious. He serves just one set hearty meal each day. Reservations are essential.

Heichinrou
⛪ Y ⩩ ⫴●⫴ ¥¥¥¥

27F Sanno Park Tower, 2-11-1 Nagatacho, Chiyoda-ku **Tel** *(03) 3593-7322*
Map *2 F4*

Superlative nouvelle Hong Kong cuisine prepared by chefs from the former crown colony and matched by the bold, contemporary decor and dramatic cityscape from the 27th-floor picture windows. Start and finish the evening with drinks in the suave "hidden" cocktail bar.

Kozue
⛪ Y ⩩ ⫴●⫴ ¥¥¥¥

40F Park Hyatt Hotel, 3-7-1 Nishi-Shinjuku, Shinjuku-ku **Tel** *(03) 5323-3460*
Map *1 A2*

Traditional *kaiseki* meets the 21st century at Kozue, high up in the Park Hyatt Hotel *(see p116)*. Inventive, multi-course meals feature seasonal seafood and premium Wagyu beef. From this ultra-modern, high-ceiling restaurant, you can catch glimpses of Mount Fuji *(see pp96-7)* in the distance on clear days.

New York Grill
⛪ Y ⩩ ⫴●⫴ ¥¥¥¥

52F Park Hyatt Hotel, 3-7-1-2 Nishi-Shinjuku, Shinjuku-ku **Tel** *(03) 5323-3458*
Map *1 A2*

In the soaring, glass-fronted apex of the Park Hyatt Hotel, splurge on modern American food at its finest – superb seafood, juicy steaks, and robust rotisserie fare. The lavish Sunday brunches are terrific value and hugely popular with Tokyo's expat population. It is worth getting dressed up for dinner here.

Oak Door
⛪ Y ⩩ ⫴●⫴ ¥¥¥¥

6F Grand Hyatt Hotel, 6-10-3 Roppongi, Minato-ku **Tel** *(03) 4333-8784*
Map *2 E5*

This is the place to relish the best steaks in town, prepared and cooked to juicy perfection. There is a lovely terrace in summer and an extensive range of international wines. A romantic spot, as nighttime sees well-heeled couples gazing at each other over candlelit tables.

Roku Roku
⛪ Y ⩩ ⫴●⫴ ¥¥¥¥

6F Grand Hyatt Hotel, 6-10-3 Roppongi, Minato-ku **Tel** *(03) 4333-8788*
Map *2 E5*

Seafood is the core of the menu at this sleek, modern restaurant inside the Grand Hyatt Tokyo *(see p115)*. A range of fish dishes, both cooked and raw, are on offer here. The sushi is superb. Whether seated at the counter or in the main dining room, you can choose from the *à la carte* menu or impressive set meals.

Tofuya Ukai
⩩ ⫴●⫴ ¥¥¥¥

4-4-13 Shiba Koen, Minato-ku **Tel** *(03) 3436-1028*
Map *2 F5*

With its rambling garden, carp ponds, and traditional architecture, Tofuya Ukai resembles a feudal mansion. One of the city's must-visit dining destinations, even though it opened only a year ago, this restaurant serves traditional Japanese cuisine. As the name suggests, tofu plays a central role in the complex *kaiseki* meals.

Yama-no-ue
⩩ V ¥¥¥¥

3F Tokyo Midtown Garden Terrace, 9-7-4 Akasaka, Minato-ku **Tel** *(03) 5413-3577*
Map *2 E4*

After half a century at the Hillside Hotel in Kanda, the owners of this prestigious tempura house were coaxed into setting up a branch in the far more glamorous setting of Tokyo Midtown. The attention to service and quality have not changed, but the view is certainly better here. Reservations recommended.

FARTHER AFIELD

AZABU-JUBAN Banreki-ryukodo
⫴●⫴ ¥¥¥

2-33-5 Higashi-Azabu, Minato-ku **Tel** *(03) 3505-5686*

Rustic sophistication meets contemporary *kaiseki* at this designer dining bar. Many seasonal delicacies from sea and mountain are served on dishes of hand-crafted lacquer and ceramic. The main dining area is a single massive wooden counter; the downstairs seating is more discreet. A lighter menu is served after 10pm. Reservations required.

Cicada
⦿ Y ⩩ V ⫴●⫴ ¥¥¥

5-2-40 Minami-Azabu, Minato-ku **Tel** *(03) 5447-5522*

Cicada's Spanish-accented pan-Mediterranean tapas cuisine is the best of its kind in Tokyo. The excellent modern cooking of American chef David Chiddo, great ambience, well-stocked bar, and no-smoking dining room explain this restaurant's popularity with locals and expats alike.

EBISU Afuri

1-1-7 Ebisu, Shibuya-ku **Tel** *(03) 5795-0750*

The Ebisu district has numerous *ramen* shops. This one stands out from the pack, both in its appearance – concrete minimalist – and its subtle flavors, especially its *yuzu* (citrus) flavored soup. Buy a ticket from the machine by the entrance (there are pictures to guide you) and then wait till a seat is free at the long counter.

EBISU Ebisu 18-ban

2-3-13 Ebisu-Minami, Shibuya-ku **Tel** *(03) 3794-1894*

A combination of Japanese *izakaya* food and Spanish tapas is served at this convivial late night bar in Ebisu. If you cannot get a seat at the counter that runs around the central kitchen area, then prop yourself up at one of the large barrels by the door. Shochu and wine are the drinks of choice, depending on which genre of food is ordered.

EBISU Delizioso Italia

4-27-17 Ebisu, Shibuya-ku **Tel** *(03) 3440-5510*

An intimate trattoria with a casual, rustic look and doors that open onto a quiet side street. Parma hams hang over the counter; a wood-fired pizza oven glows in the kitchen. The pasta is good and so are the grill platters. There is a fine selection of grappa to close the meal.

EBISU Ebisu Imaiya Sohonten

1-7-11 Ebisu-Nishi, Shibuya-ku **Tel** *(03) 5456-0255*

Akita Prefecture, on the northern Japan Sea coast, is famous for its local Hinai chicken. Here, the chicken is grilled as *yakitori* or served in delectable *nabe* hotpots featuring a good mix of vegetables and rice dumplings. There is a fine selection of sake too.

EBISU Cardenas Charcoal Grill

1-12-14 Ebisu-Nishi, Shibuya-ku **Tel** *(03) 5428-0779*

Sleek, spacious, and stylish, CCG is a big favorite with the expat population, thanks to its modern cuisine – plentiful fresh produce, seafood, and steaks prepared on the eponymous grill, and a good cellar of Californian wines. With its high ceiling and mezzanine bar, it is easy to forget that it is two floors below street level.

IKEBUKURO Chion Shokudo

1-24-1 Ikebukuro, Toshima-ku **Tel** *(03) 5951-8288*

Mandarin, not Japanese, is the *lingua franca* at this no-frills basement eatery run by and for the mainland Chinese community. With a menu including chili-laden hotpots, fiery stir-fries, and spicy stews, this is the best Sichuan street food in the city, and the prices are unbeatable too.

IKEBUKURO Chugoku Chakan

1-22-8 Nishi-Ikebukuro, Toshima-ku **Tel** *(03) 3985-5183*

Ikebukuro has more authentic Chinese food than Yokohama's Chinatown, thanks to its sizeable population of visiting Chinese students and businessmen. Chugoku Chakan serves Taiwan-style dim sum, prepared in-house and served to order (not from a trolley). Their all-you-can-eat specials are great value.

IKEBUKURO Sasashu

2-2-2 Ikebukuro, Toshima-ku **Tel** *(03) 3971-9363*

With its fine range of lesser-known regional brews and a strong food menu, this is one of the best sake pubs in the area. The specials of the day vary according to the season, but the duck dishes are always worth ordering. Even though this area is well off the beaten tourist track, locals are quite used to foreigners dropping in.

KAGURAZAKA Stefano

6-47 Kagurazaka, Shinjuku-ku **Tel** *(03) 5228-7515*

Chef Stefano Fastro presents the flavors of his native Veneto region here. He is especially strong on meat dishes and his *gnocchi* (dumplings made of starched potato, semolina, or flour) are among the best in town. It is a small restaurant with Chef Fastro and one sous-chef which means the service is excellent.

NAKA-MEGURO Kuro-Hitsuji

1-11-6 Kami-Meguro, Meguro-ku **Tel** *(03) 5457-2255*

Kuro-Hitsuji specializes in the Japanese version of Mongolian barbecue known as "Genghis Khan" – slices of lamb and vegetables cooked over a dome-shaped cast-iron pan. It is smoky but fun, and priced to please the students and young families who come here. Do not wear your best clothes.

NAKA-MEGURO Higashiyama

1-21-25 Higashiyama, Meguro-ku **Tel** *(03) 5720-1300*

Designer-casual, modern Japanese food in a setting to match on the fringes of the hip enclave of Naka-Meguro. Sit at the counter and watch the chefs in the open kitchen or settle down at tables in the spacious dining room. The easiest approach is to order one of the set meals, which change with the seasons.

ODAIBA Icho

Hotel Nikko Tokyo 3F, 1-9-1 Daiba, Minato-ku **Tel** *(03) 5500-5500*

Ensconced in JAL's flagship hotel, Icho specializes in teppanyaki. Light morsels of seafood, vegetable, and meat are cooked to perfection on a heated metal plate right in front of diners. If visitors get bored with watching the chef work, they can gaze out over the Odaiba waterfront and the Rainbow Bridge *(see p83)*.

Key to Price Guide *see p132* **Key to Symbols** *see back cover flap*

SHIBUYA Sorano-niwa

4-17 Sakuragaoka-cho, Shibuya-ku **Tel** *(03) 5728-5191*

This youthful dining bar serves tofu, *yuba* (the protein-rich skin that forms on hot soy milk), and other traditional soy-based foods in a hip, modern context. Several dishes are vegetarian. Do not miss the *hiki-age yuba*, cooked right by your table. The food is light on the stomach and the wallet.

SHIMO-KITAZAWA Champuru

5-32-7 Daizawa, Setagaya-ku **Tel** *(03) 3413-6489*

Okinawa, Japan's southernmost prefecture, lies halfway between Japan and China, and its food reflects this mixture of tastes and cultures. Champuru offers three floors of dining options, from simple Okinawa *soba* noodles to substantial dishes of fish, pork, and goat (often raw). The drink of choice is *awamori* (fire water).

SHIROKANEDAI Luxor

Barbizon 25 2F, 5-4-7 Shirokanedai, Minato-ku **Tel** *(03) 3446-6900*

Nothing to do with Egypt, this restaurant's name has lots to do with the luxury standards of this affluent neighborhood. Chef Mario Fritolli prepares sumptuous cuisine blending Tokyo refinement with the earthy, herb-infused traditions of his native Tuscany. The dining room is a bit cramped but the terrace is perfect for early summer brunch.

TENNOZU T.Y. Harbor Brewery

2-1-3 Higashi-Shinagawa, Shinagawa-ku **Tel** *(03) 5479-4555*

This converted dockland warehouse is home to Tokyo's first and best brew-pub. Sip ale in the hi-tech bar, or adjourn to the spacious restaurant next door for creative modern pub food. The canalside tables are always in hot demand on summer nights. More exclusive still is Waterline, the floating bar moored close by.

BEYOND TOKYO

FUJI FIVE LAKES Mama-no-mori

N side of Yamanaka, Lake Yamanaka, 401-0305 **Tel** *(0555) 620-346*

This is a classic, old thatched-roof restaurant, sitting on the north side of Yamanka Lake, offering good food (*kaiseki ryori*) and gorgeous views of picturesque Mount Fuji on a clear day. The restaurant is named after the popular area mother who started this restaurant.

HAKONE Fujiya Hotel

359 Miyanoshita, 250-0404 **Tel** *(0460) 82-2211*

Good Western food is served in Hakone's oldest and grandest hotel. The bright dining room is from "an age gone by," complete with crisp, white tablecloths and attentive, bow-tied staff. There are good views and great food – everything from spaghetti to rainbow trout to sirloin steak. Reservations are required for dinner.

IZU PENINSULA Fujiichi

Ito 7-6 Shizumi-cho Shizuoka, 414-0002 **Tel** *(0557) 37-4705*

Fujiichi is located right on the waterfront, next to the fish market. Well-loved by locals, this simple, second-story restaurant serves great fresh food at very reasonable prices. There are fantastic views of the harbor. Diners can choose either the excellent *teishoku* or a more expansive (and expensive) set.

KAMAKURA Nakamura-an

1-7-6 Komachi, Kamakura-shi, Kanagawa-ken **Tel** *(0467) 25-3500*

Hearty, honest, hand-made *soba* noodles, rolled and chopped as guests watch. There is always a line outside at lunchtime, since it is just as popular with the locals as the visitors. The specialty is chilled *soba* with shrimp tempura; ask for *ten-seiro* or just point to the plastic models in the window.

NIKKO Kanaya Hotel

1300 Kami-Hatsuishi-machi, Nikko-shi, Tochigi-ken **Tel** *(0288) 54-0001*

The historic Kanaya, one of the oldest Western-style hotels in Japan, is one of the main sights of Nikko – especially its beautiful wood-clad dining room. The Continental cuisine is not outstanding, but they make the best breakfast in town. Failing that, stop by for coffee in the adjoining lounge.

YOKOHAMA Shin-Yokohama Ramen Museum

2-14-21 Shin-Yokohama, Kohoku-ku, Yokohama-shi, Kanagawa-ken **Tel** *(045) 471-0503*

The ground floor has displays on the history and Chinese origins of Japan's favorite home-grown fast food – *ramen* noodles. But the fun part is in the cavernous basement, where half a dozen stalls offer *ramen* styles from all over Japan in a movie-set re-creation of Tokyo *circa* 1960.

YOKOHAMA Tung Fat (Dohatsu Honkan)

148 Yamashita-cho, Naka-ku, Yokohama-shi, Kanagawa-ken **Tel** *(045) 681-7273*

One of the longest-serving Chinese restaurants in Yokohama, Tung Fat is still one of the most popular restaurants. Plenty of Cantonese specials, including good wind-dried duck, home-made sausages, and noodles, are available. It is easy to find as it stands on the central street of Chinatown.

SHOPPING IN TOKYO

Often described as the "warehouse of the world," it is possible to procure anything under the sun in Tokyo, from handcrafted boxwood combs to robot pets. The constant innovation and commercial ingenuity that characterizes the city has resulted in a new rash of mini shopping cities such as Tokyo Midtown and

Decorative cat, a goodwill charm

Omotesando Hills; hi-tech convenience stores and high-end fashion towns such as Harajuku and Ginza; and Akihabara, an almost exotic electronic market. The world's highest concentration of vending machines is also visible at every turn. And, compared with other global cities, the prices are no longer as outrageous as presumed.

PRICES AND SALES TAX

The Japanese yen continues to be regarded as a stable currency. Cash is by far the easiest method to pay for most goods. International credit cards are still unpopular in smaller shops. VISA, American Express, Diners Club, and MasterCard are the most widely accepted.

In department stores and boutiques, and in inner-city areas, prices are nearly always marked in Arabic numerals. In local shops and supermarkets, and in areas where non-Japanese are few and far between, prices may be written only in kanji characters. All purchasable items and services are subject to a consumption tax of five percent. The price displayed should by law include the tax, although in practice this may not be the case.

TAX-FREE SHOPPING

Tokyo's tax-free shops offer a good range of domestic and imported brand items without the five percent sales tax added elsewhere. The best authorized outlets are the **Tokyo International Arcade**, near the Imperial Hotel *(see p112)* and **Laox** *(see p45)* for electronic goods.

In some shops, particularly department stores *(depatos)*, you may have to pay the full price for an item, then obtain a refund and customs document from a tax-exemption counter. This document is retained by customs when you leave Tokyo. Most major department stores offer tax exemption, but usually on

Youth entertainment area in Shibuya

goods over the value of ¥10,000. One advantage of shopping at *depatos* is that they usually have tax-exemption counters with English-speaking staff. The counters will issue a customs document, which they will attach to your passport for presentation when you depart. Large electronic stores in Akihabara *(see p45)*, such as **Yodobashi Camera** and Laox provide this service.

SHOPPING ZONES

Tokyo has many shopping zones identified by the popular goods they display. **Akihabara** *(see p45)* is the world's largest and most up-to-date electronic and camera center. **Aoyama/Omotesando** *(see p68 & p65)* is known for its high fashion in the city. Visit **Asakusa** for traditional Japanese souvenirs, foods, toys, and pop culture trinkets. **Daikanyama Address 17dixsept** *(see pp146–7)* has several reputed boutiques, catering to the young and trend conscious. High-end department stores and art galleries make their home in **Ginza** *(see pp38–9).*

Harajuku *(see p65)*, a fun street-oriented clothing, accessories, and cuddly toy district, caters to high-teens shoppers on small budgets. **Jimbocho** *(see p44)* is Tokyo's oldest book center. **Shibuya** *(see pp66–7)* with its department stores and fashion buildings, is one of the city's most diverse shopping zones. **Shinjuku**, to the west side of the station, is all electronics and software; the east side has department stores and multipurpose shopping complexes.

DEPARTMENT STORES

Many stores are owned by railroad companies, so that passengers coming off from their platforms are fed through passages bulging with advertising and display goods. Apart from selling a vast variety of top-range items, *depatos*, like convenience stores, also sell tickets for concerts and exhibitions. Roofs are often set aside as children's attraction parks, mini-golf ranges, and beer gardens. One early innovator was **Mitsukoshi**, perhaps Tokyo's most famous store. The great flagship stores such as **Takashimaya** and **Isetan** follow a similar layout, with delectable foods in the basement, a wide range of Western and Japanese restaurants on the top floor, and every conceivable type of goods between. Some stores are known for certain commodities – **Matsuya** for top fashion brands and for Japanese crafts, quality souvenirs, and furnishings; **Matsuzakaya** for its textiles, kimonos, and food basement; **Tokyu Hands** for household goods, and **Wako** for watches and jewelry.

MULTI-PURPOSE COMPLEXES

Roppongi Hills *(see p69)*, with its high-end shopping options, a prestigious art gallery, observation lounge, cinemas, and live events, led the trend a few years ago. The **Marunouchi Building** in the Tokyo Station area has turned into a skyscraper shopping, restaurant, and office space. **Shiodome**, another shopping, office, and residential nexus seems to grow exponentially with each visit. The shopping centerpiece of this millennium complex, **Caretta Shiodome**, attracts a young office crowd intent on keeping up with the latest in clothing. **Omotesando Hills** *(see p65)* features many Japanese and overseas designer stores. **Tokyo Midtown** houses several fashion and lifestyle outlets.

MARKETS

Food markets provide an insight into the Japanese enthusiasm for food and cooking. The basement food floor of a major department store is a good place to start. A whole street of highly visible plastic food and kitchenware suppliers along **Kappabashi-dori** *(see p54)* creates the mood of a lively market place along this well patronized street. The ultimate market experience is **Tsukiji Fish Market** *(see p40);* the area to the east is full of small restaurants and shops with pungent crates of *wasabi* (horseradish) and dried fish hanging from storefronts.

CONVENIENCE STORES AND VENDING MACHINES

Convenience stores (*konbini*) are easy to spot. They have catchy names such as 7-Eleven and AM-PM. Many people depend on these stores for more than just foods, toiletries, and magazines: they also book concert tickets and use ATMs and photocopiers. The quality of *konbini* food is surprisingly high and fresh. Among the popular take-out food items are boxed lunches, steamed

Automatic vending machine

buns, and cup noodles. Beverages include soft drinks, hot coffee, beer, and sake. Stores open 24/7. A Tokyo fixture since 1926, besides drinks and snacks, vending machines dispense batteries, flowers, eggs, underwear, disposable cameras, and even oxygen.

ARCADES AND MALLS

Many arcades and malls date from the postwar period and, being generally located in downtown areas, are old-fashioned in style and appearance. Adjoining Senso-ji Temple *(see pp56–7)* is an arcade of shops selling a mixture of tourist souvenirs, traditional crafts, snacks, and kitsch pop culture items.

Fuji Torii antique shop displaying Japanese pottery, Omotesando-dori

ANTIQUE STORES AND FLEA MARKETS

Flea markets, a Sunday only institution, are often held in the grounds of old shrines, adding extra interest. These are attractive to professionals and to those just looking to pick up a bargain. The antique market in the basement of the **International Antique House** along Ometsando-dori may be a little gloomy, but the glassware, swords, and antique jewelry brighten up the setting. Five minutes walk on the same side of the road in the direction of Harajuku, the **Oriental Bazaar** has genuine and replica antique furniture, pottery, and a good deal more. Nearby **Fuji-Torii** is known for the quality of its antiques, woodblock prints, *tansu* chests, scrolls, and lacquerware craft.

The market at the **Tomioka-Hachimangu Shrine**, held on the first two Sundays of the month, is a lively event. **Togo Shrine** holds a similar, though smaller, event in the heart of Harajuku every first and fourth Sunday. Closer to the center, the market at **Hanazono Shrine**, near Shinjuku's legendary watering hole Golden Gai *(see p61)*, is open every Sunday.

Beautiful glass building of Prada store, Aoyama

An elegant display of jewelry in Omotesando

COSMETICS, JEWELRY, AND ACCESSORIES

Mikimoto sells its pearls and jewelry in opulent surroundings. For a selection of silver and jewelry, visit **Mori Silver** in the Oriental Bazaar and **Takane Jewelry**. Nakamise-dori at Senso-ji Temple *(see pp56–7)* is the place to find Japan's traditional jewelry. **Matsuzakaya** sells *kanzashi*, (hairpins) plus other jewelry, and nearby **Ginkado** sells *kanzashi*, costume swords, and fans. Next door is **Bunsendo**, also selling fans. The last maker of handmade wooden combs is **Jusanya** in Ueno. The red, stucco façade of the **Shiseido Building** in Ginza is complemented by the Shiseido Cosmetics Garden in Omotesando. For "cute" culture accessories, **Takeshita-dori** is hard to beat.

TRADITONAL ARTS AND CRAFTS

Maruzen in Nihonbashi is an excellent source of traditional arts and crafts including ceramics, woodcraft, and lacquerware, as is **Takumi** in Ginza. **Itoya**, also in Ginza, is packed with crafts, especially fine *washi* (Japanese paper). **Kuroeya**, at Senso-ji Temple, has been selling *washi* for over 140 years and stocks everything from modern stationery to traditional kites. The **Japan Folk Craft Museum** *(see p77)* has a small, high-quality selection.

The **Japan Traditional Craft Center** in Ikebukuro is an excellent place for purchasing affordable traditional crafts.

CONTEMPORARY ART AND DESIGN

The Spiral Garden in Minami-Aoyama's Spiral Building *(see p68)* usually has something interesting by Japanese artists. In Ginza, you can find works by Japanese artists at **Galleria Grafica**, **Plus Minus Gallery**, and **Yoseido Gallery**. **Ginza Graphic Gallery** exhibits both Japanese and foreign works. The **Karakuri Museum** in Shibuya displays and sells artworks based on optical illusions. In Shinjuku the **NTT Intercommunication Center** in Tokyo Opera City *(see p183)* features exhibits and installations using the latest technology. In the same building is the **Shinjuku Opera City Gallery** which displays Japanese painting, and graphic art. Contemporary prints can be found at the **Tolman Collection** near Tokyo Tower. For ceramics, try **Koransha** in Ginza. Good sources of modern houseware are the department stores **Tokyu Hands** and **Matsuya**. For cutting edge interior design head to **Axis** in Roppongi, a complex of galleries selling kitchenware, ceramics, furniture, and more. Shibuya's **Loft** has several floors of contemporary novelty housewares, jewelry, accessories, and toys.

Ironware kettle, Japan Traditional Crafts Center

BOOKS, MUSIC, AND MANGA

Isseido, an Art Deco Jimbocho institution, keeps used and rare books. The biggest stock of secondhand English titles though, can be found at the friendly **Good Day Books** in Ebisu. Another specialty store, **Crayon House** in Omotesando, caters exclusively to children. The younger of the two Shinjuku **Kinokuniya** stores has the best selections of titles in Tokyo. **Maruzen** has a good choice of titles in its Marunouchi shop. **Tower Records** boasts an up-to-date collection of books. **Cisco**, also in Shibuya, rates high among Tokyo's young and savvy. For used CDs and vinyl, the Shinjuku branch of the **Disk Union** chain has the best stock. Manga fans will love **Mandarake** in the Shibuya Beam building for its secondhand magazines and related products. **Sekaido** in Shinjuku has a good range of manga.

Boxed sweets decorated with characters in a Kabuki play

SPECIALTY SHOPS

Tokyo has many niche shops. **Sanbido** sells religious statues and beautiful dolls; **Nishijima Umbrellas** has traditional umbrellas; **Tokiwado** has been selling *kaminari okoshi* crackers for 200 years; **Nakatsuka** sells candies and sweet crackers. **Kappabashi-dori** *(see p54)* is Tokyo's center for kitchenware and plastic food. **Isetatsu** specializes in *chiyogami* designs taken from textiles worn by samurai. A few minutes walk from Iidabashi station, **Puppet House** is shop, gallery, and workshop.

DIRECTORY

DEPARTMENT STORES

Isetan
3-14-1 Shinjuku.
Map 1 R1
Tel (03) 3352-1111.
www.isetan.co.jp

Matsuya
3-6-1 Ginza. **Map** 5 C2.
Tel (03) 3567-1211.
www.matsuya.com/ginza

Matsuzakaya
6-10-1 Ginza. **Map** 5 B2.
Tel (03) 3572-1111.

Mitsukoshi
1-4-1 Nihonbashi.
Map 5 C1.
Tel (03) 3241-3311.
www.mitsukoshi.co.jp

Takashimaya
5-24-2 Sendagaya. **Map** 1
B2. *Tel (03) 5361-1122.*

Tokyu Hands
12-18 Udagawacho,
Shibuya. **Map** 1 B5.
Tel (03) 5489-5111.

Wako
4-5-11 Ginza.
Tel (03) 3562-2111.

MULTI-PURPOSE COMPLEXES

Marunouchi Building
2-4-1 Marunouchi.
Map 5 B1.
Tel (03) 5218-5100.

Omotesando Hills
Omotesando-dori,
Omotesando. **Map** 1 C4.
Tel (03) 3497-0310.

Caretta Shiodome
1-8-2 Higashi-Shimbashi.
Map 5 B3.
Tel (03) 6218-2100.

Tokyo Midtown
9-7-1 Akasaka.
Map 2 E3.
Tel (03) 3475-3100.

ANTIQUE STORES AND FLEA MARKETS

Fuji-Torii
6-1-10 Jingumae.
Map 1 C4. **Tel** (03) 3400-
2777. www.fuji-torii.com

International Antique House
B/F Hanae Mri Bldg, 3-6-1
Kita Aoyama. **Map** 1 C4.
Tel (03) 3407-2675.

Oriental Bazaar
5-9-13 Jingumae.
Map 5 C1.
Tel (03) 3400-3933.

Togo Shrine Market
1-5-3 Jingumae.
Map 1 B4.
Tel (03) 3425-7965.

Tomioka-Hachimangu Shrine Market
1-20-3 Tomioka. **Map** 6
E2. *Tel (0276) 383-417.*

COSMETICS, JEWELRY, AND ACCESSORIES

Bunsendo
1-20-2 Asakusa.
Map 4 F3.
Tel (03) 3841-0088.

Ginkado
1-30-1 Asakusa.
Map 4 F3.
Tel (03) 3841-8540.

Jusanya
2-12-21 Ueno.
Tel (03) 3831-3238.

Mikimoto
4-5-5 Ginza. **Map** 5 B3.
Tel (03) 3535-4611.

Shiseido Building
7-8-10 Ginza. **Map** 5 B3.
Tel (03) 3571-7731.

Takane Jewelry
1-7-23 Uchisawaicho.
Map 5 A3.
Tel (03) 3591-2764.

TRADITIONAL ARTS AND CRAFTS

Itoya
2-7-15 Ginza. **Map** 5 C2.
Tel (03) 3561-8311.

Japan Folk Craft Museum
4-3-33 Komaba.
Tel (03) 3467-4527.

Japan Traditional Craft Center
1st/2nd F, Metropolitan
Plaza Bldg, 1-11-1 Nishi-Ikebukuro.

Kuroeya
2F, 1-2-6 Nihonbashi.
Tel (03) 3272-0948.

Maruzen
Oazo Bldg, 1-6-4
Marunouchi. **Map** 5 C1.
Tel (03) 5288-8881.

Takumi
8-4-2 Ginza. **Map** 5 B3.
Tel (03) 3571-2017.

CONTEMPORARY ART AND DESIGN

Axis
5-17-1 Roppongi.
Map 2 E5.
Tel (03) 3587-2781.

Galleria Grafica
Ginza S2 Bldg, 6-13-4
Ginza. **Map** 5 B3.
Tel (03) 5550-1335.

Ginza Graphic Gallery
DNP Ginza Bldg, 7-7-2
Ginza. **Map** 5 B3.
Tel (03) 3571-5206.

Koransha
6-12-12 Ginza. **Map** 5 B3.
Tel (03) 3543-0951.

Loft
21-1 Udagawacho,
Shibuya. **Map** 1 B5.
Tel (03) 3462-3807.

Plus Minus Gallery
2F, TEPCO Ginza-kan,
6-11-1 Ginza.
Tel (03) 3575-0456.

Tolman Collection
2-2-18 Shiba Daimon.
Map 5 A4.
Tel (03) 3434-1300.

Tokyu Hands
12-18 Udagawacho.
Map 1 B5.
Tel (03) 5489-5111.

Tsutsumo Factory
37-15 Udagawacho,
Shibuya. **Map** 5 A4.
Tel (03) 5478-1330.

Yoseido Gallery
5-5-15 Ginza. **Map** 5 B2.
Tel (03) 3571-1312.

BOOKS, MUSIC, AND MANGA

Cisco
11-1 Udagawacho,
Shibuya. **Map** 1 A5.
Tel (03) 3462-0366.

Crayon House
3-8-15 Kita-Aoyama.
Map 1 C5.
Tel (03) 3406-6409.

Isseido
1-1-4 Kanda-Jimbocho.
Map 3 B5. *Tel (03) 3292-0071.*

Disk Union
3-31-4 Shinjuku. **Map** 1
B5. *Tel (03) 3352-2691.*

Good Day Books
3F, 1-11-2 Ebisu.
Map 4 F3.
Tel (03) 5421-0957.
www.gooddaybooks.com

Kinokuniya
5-24-2 Sendagaya. **Map** 1
B1. *Tel (03) 5361-3301.*

Mandarake
B2 fl, Shibuya Beam Bldg,
31-2 Udagawacho,
Shibuya. **Map** 1 A5.
Tel (03) 3477-0777.

Maruzen
Oazu Bldg, 1-6-4
Marunouchi. **Map** 5 C1.
Tel (03) 5288-8881.

Sekaido
3-1-1 Shinjuku. **Map** 1 B1.
Tel (03) 5379-1111.

Tower Records
1-22-14 Jinnan, Shibuya.
Map 1 B5.
Tel (03) 3496-3661.

SPECIALTY SHOPS

Isetatsu
2-18-9 Yanaka. **Map** 3 B1.
Tel (03) 3823-1453.

Nakatsuka
1-37-1 Asakusa. **Map** 4
F3. *Tel (03) 3843-4455.*

Nishijima Umbrellas
1-30-1 Asakusa.
Map 4 F3.
Tel (03) 3841-8560.

Puppet House
1-8 Shimomiyabi-cho,
Shinjuku.
Tel (03) 5229-6477.

Sanbido
1-33-3 Asakusa. **Map** 4
F3. *Tel (03) 5827-0070.*

Tokiwado
1-3-2 Asakusa. **Map** 4 E3.
Tel (03) 3841-5656.

Clothing

The pace of change in a city where everything seems temporary, is perfectly suited to Tokyo's fast-moving fashion world. Extensive media coverage of the fashion industry, relatively high disposable incomes among the young, and an active nightlife have made Tokyo one of the trendiest, most visible fashion centers on the globe. Snapping at the heels of the fashion establishment with their Paris and New York outlets, are brat packs of new, young Japanese designers creating a host of new trendy labels. Some of the leading fashion houses in the world now call Tokyo their home.

![Young shoppers browsing through readymade Western wear, Shibuya 109]

Young shoppers browsing through readymade Western wear, Shibuya 109

FASHION BUILDINGS

Fashion buildings house exclusive boutiques, often with a collective theme, target age group, or approach to design. The modern, innovative architecture of the buildings themselves adds much interest to the entire shopping experience. **Shibuya 109** is a silver, circular tower housing several boutiques known for radical designs. It also stages fashion promotion events in front of the building. **Mark City**, a towering modern building connected by passageways to Shibuya station, is a more ambitious project. Labyrinthine floors of boutiques and accessory stores aimed at the 20s and 30s age group, provide a social setting with restaurants, bakeries, and trendy cafés. The **LaForet Building**, a Harajuku landmark, is strictly for teen shoppers. **Venus Fort**, *(see p82)* a retail outlet for young women in Odaiba, looks more like an Italian film set than a fashion store. Restaurants, cafés, and trinket stalls create a faux Italian street scene. Unless voices are raised to halt the plan, the whole building is due to be dismantled at the end of 2008.

WOMEN'S FASHIONS

Ginza has always been synonymous with high-chic and prices to match. Large department stores such as **Mitsukoshi** *(see p142)* and **Matsuzakaya** *(see p143)* have always been the arbiters of taste here, offering classic design cuts, which appeal to women in their 30s upwards.

Trendy women's wear, Dolce and Gabbana showroom, Omotesando

Luxury foreign brands such as Gucci and Chanel have opened super-modern outlets, providing designer shoes, handbags, cosmetics, and other chic accessories. Aoyama's **Comme Des Garcons** store, the brainchild of radical designer Kawakubo Rei, is well worth a look for the building alone. Also in the contiguous Aoyama/Omotesando/Jingumae districts, **Prada Aoyama**, the latest addition to Minami-Aoyama's high-end fashion scene, is another shopping-plus-architecture experience. The flowing fabrics and colorful embroidery that characterize **Tsumori Chisato** designs, on show in her Shibuya store, enjoy an almost cult following among women. The more radical but fun **Hysteric Glamour** has had a similar effect on the tastes of punk-inclined customers not afraid to wear T-shirts with provocative messages. For a good mix of women's fashions, accessories, and cosmetics, **Daikanyama Address 17dixsept**, a retail complex with an open-air plaza and interesting interior consisting of suspension bridges, makes for an interesting half-day fashion shopping trip. The complex is a little northwest of Daikanyama station.

MENSWEAR

Young males are almost as fashion conscious as women, though there are few exclusive menswear shops in Tokyo. The following recommendations also feature women's fashions. **Muji** design aesthetics – cool, simple, understated – are well known the world over. Besides clothes and accessories, their Roppongi store has an interesting line in simple homeware designs. The singular and arresting designs of **Yohji Yamamoto**, another household name in the Japanese fashion cosmos, seem to go from strength to strength. The interior of the bronze-faced store in Omotesando is well worth a look. The name **Issey Miyake** needs no introduction. The

Western wear for men, Uniqlo store, Aoyama

anarchist designer burst onto the scene in the 1980s with his innovative use of fabrics, design forms, and shapes to create expensive but highly regarded work. The window displays are a joy. Nearby **Undercover** is the brainchild of Jun Takahashi, a punk musician whose designs are inspired by the music his band plays.

The menswear at **Uniqlo**, a popular clothing chain with branches overseas, is simple, contemporary, and bottom-line for many shoppers at this store along Jingumae's Meiji-dori. The fashions here target all age groups.

TEXTILES AND KIMONOS

Silk, cotton, linen, hemp, and wool all feature in Japan's long and rich textile history. While some traditional techniques are fading, most are alive and well. Department stores are often the best places to find a range of textiles. **Matsuzakaya** (in Ginza) grew from a Nagoya kimono merchant and stocks bolts of kimono cloth made in Kyoto and textured *furoshiki* (square wrapping cloths). The **Tokyo National Museum shop** *(see pp50–53)* has a good selection of *furoshiki* and scarves made using traditional techniques. Also good is **Bengara**. **Miyashita Obi** on Nakamise-dori at Senso-ji

Kimono with an *obi* sash

Temple *(see pp56–7)* has wonderful *obi* sashes, used to wrap the waist of a kimono. **Hayashi Kimono** in Yurakucho, sells classic outfits but also a light cotton summer version called *yukata*, which can be comfortable house wear. The **Oriental Bazaar** *(see p143)* and **Uniqlo** also offer a good range of *yukata*. Asakusa's **Nakamise-dori** *(see p56)* has a lot of less expensive fabric kimono in bright colors, the assumption being that foreigners like brilliant, gaudy designs. And do not forget that there are some terrific kimonos and textile bargains to be found at the eclectic Sunday flea markets *(see p143)*.

A colorful *yukata* with traditional floral motifs

Gifts, Gizmos, and Toys

Handmade combs

In the first months after the Second World War, de-mobbed men and displaced persons would spread a towel or newspaper on the incinerated wasteland around main stations, and display a saucepan or worn kimono in the hope of finding a customer. These were the tentative beginnings of the black markets. Since then consumers have long moved from desiring just basic necessities to acquiring gifts, gizmos, and the novelties that flood Tokyo's markets.

GIFT SHOPS

The Japanese are not only avid buyers of souvenirs when they venture overseas, but excellent customers for the interesting products of their own country. The result is countless gift shops.

The traditional and modern stationery, origami paper, and calligraphy tools sold at **Itoya** (*see p145*) in Ginza, make light, affordable, and portable gifts. The articles at **Japan Sword**, the oldest dealer in authentic Japanese blades, are a little heavier and more expensive. Replicas of the swords are also sold. The shop and exhibition space are located in the business district of Toranomon.

Sagemonoya in Yotsuya, where the staff is multi-lingual, specializes in *netsuke* (miniature sculpture) and *sagemono,* small, ornate objects designed as accessories to hang from kimono belts, medicine flasks and, more likely these days, desk lamps, ceiling fixtures, and cell phones. Craft and gift sections of reputed

An eye-catching chopsticks box, a traditional souvenir

department stores (*see p142*) are logical places to do one-stop shopping. Large railroad terminuses, especially Tokyo Station, are crammed with souvenir and gift shops.

FOOD AND DRINK

Department store basements have the largest and most interesting single selections of ready-to-go Japanese foods of the kind that make interesting gifts. Markets (*see p143*) and

even supermarkets will have interesting and unfamiliar food items as well, from rice crackers to traditional Japanese confections. The main ingredient of Japanese sweets is *anko*, red bean paste, which may be an acquired taste for some Westerners. These beautifully made confections are called *wagashi* in Japanese, and are often taken with green tea. **Toraya** is famous – they supply to the imperial family. This Akasaka institution changes its sweet motifs to reflect the seasons. Branches of **Akebono** selling exquisite sweets can be found in the food basements of some of the best Tokyo department stores. The origins of **Iidabashi Mannendou** in Iidabashi, date back to the 17th century, when it began making sweets based on recipes from the old imperial city of Kyoto.

Alcohol is freely available in Tokyo. Individual sake shops and, once again, department store basements, have shelves full of *Nihonshu*, the generic name for all indigenous Japanese drinks. The choice, though, can be quite bewildering, involving some knowledge of grades and provenance. For an initiation into the mysteries of the drink, the **Sake Plaza** in Shimbashi has excellent displays. Entrance to the plaza is free, and for a small fee visitors can enjoy a five-cup sampling.

GADGETS AND GIZMOS

The novelty goods found in the basement of **Tokyu Hands**, a treasure trove of inventive and original household goods, is a good place to start for general items from fancy dress costumes to trick store treats evoking a sense of fun. The **Don Quixote** stores, such as the popular one in Shinjuku, are stuffed to the ceilings with novelty, "character" goods, costume wear, mixed in with snacks, camping gear, and ironing boards. For a combination of electronics and eccentricities, **Akihabara** (*see p45*) is hard to

Bewildering variety of sweets in a store on Nakamise-dori, Akihabara

Electronics store stacked with low-priced gadgets, Akihabara

beat. **Ishimaru** and **Yamagiwa** are two huge electronic department stores here. **Akky** and **Takarada Musen** are also duty free stores. **Sato Musen** and **Onoden** are also names to look out for in this "Electronic Town." Young women dressed as anime characters from classic series such as Sailor Moon and Neon Genesis Evangelion greet customers outside **AsoBitCity**, where, beside the software games and peripherals, are "character" goods and large model train sets. More Akihabara wonders await at **Tsukumo Robocon Magazine Kan**, where the specialty are cute, owner-friendly robots – mechanized turtles, cats, dogs, insects, and fictitious creatures.

TOYS

One of the nice things about Tokyo toy stores is that nobody seems to mind if you pick things up and play with them, even if you are a lone adult. Customers are treated with a measure of

tolerance and indulgence in Tokyo. And there are a surprising number of adults shopping for themselves in the toy stores, a reminder that a sense of playfulness is alive and well among the hard-working Tokyoites. These places are among the best in the world to pick up souvenirs and the latest craze among children before it hits the international market. The **Hakuhinkan** in Ginza has always been a Mecca for toys and still is, with several crowded floors to prove it. Try not to go on a weekend. The six floors of toys, games, and novelties at **Kiddyland** in Jingumae are a wonder to behold. Besides conventional toys, kits, and games, all the popular anime characters are here too, from Pokemon to Hello Kitty. For a slightly more personal experience, **Astro Mike** in Harajuku has many loyal followers. The store traces the history of toy making, both Japanese and Western, from the action figures and models of the 1960s, up to the present day.

DIRECTORY

GIFT SHOPS

Itoya
2-7-15 Ginza. **Map** 5 C2.
Tel (03) 3561-8311.

Japan Sword
3-8-1 Toranomon.
Tel (03) 3434-4321.
www.japansword.co.jp

Sagemonoya
Yabane KK, 4-28-20-703 Yotsuya.
Tel (03) 3352-6286.

FOOD AND DRINK

Akebono
5-7-19 Ginza.
Tel (03) 3571-0483. **www**.ginza-akebono.co.jp/top.html

Iidabashi Mannendou
1F Toku Bldg, 2-19 Ageba-cho.
Tel (03) 3266-0544.

Sake Plaza
1F, 4F Nihon Syuzo Centre Bldg, 1-1-21 Nishi-Shimbashi.
Map 5 B3 & 5 C2. **Tel** (03) 3519-2091. **www**.japansake.or.jp/sake/english/index

Toraya
4-9-22 Akasaka.
Tel (03) 3408-4121.
www.toraya-group.co.jp

GADGETS AND GIZMOS

AsoBitCity
1-13-2 Soto-Kanda.
Tel (03) 3251-3100.

Don Quixote
1-16-5 Kabuki-cho. **Map**1 B1.
Tel (03) 5291-9211.

Tokyu Hands
12-18 Udagawacho, Shibuya.
Map 1 B5. **Tel** (03) 5489-5111.

Tsukumo Robocon Magazine Kan
1F Yamaguchi Bldg, 3-2-13 Soto-Kanda. **Tel** (03) 3251-0987.

TOYS

Astro Mike
5-25-2 Jingumae.
Tel (03) 3499-2588.

Hakuhinkan
8-8-11 Ginza. **Map** 5 B3.
Tel (03) 3571-8008.

Kiddyland
6-1-9 Jingumae. **Map** 1 B4.
Tel (03) 3409-3431.

Stuffed toys in all sizes at Kiddyland, a major kids' toy store in Jingumae

ENTERTAINMENT IN TOKYO

Entertainment in Tokyo is a wonderful mix of the old world and the cutting-edge modern. Traditional performing arts span the vibrancy of Kabuki theater to the haunting tones of a *shakuhachi* recital. Tokyo is the best place to catch the latest in movies and music from around the world. The abundance of live music on offer ranges from jazz and blues to pop

Man playing a traditional *shakuhachi* instrument

and techno, and even western classical music. Tokyo enjoys a pulsating and truly international club culture; at most places you can dance till dawn. Sports fans have a choice between baseball and soccer, or the more traditional forms of martial arts, especially sumo. At night the city puts on a new face, the brightly lit leisure districts show how serious Tokyo is about fun.

Kabuki performance in Kabuki-za Theater

INFORMATION SOURCES

Metropolis, a free weekly magazine and website is a good source of information on leisure activities in the city. **Japanzine**, another free magazine, also covers other cities in Japan if you plan to travel out of the city. The *Japan Times, Asahi Shimbun, Daily Yomiuri,* and *Tokyo Journal* also have comprehensive listings. All of these publications are available at station kiosks and major stores including **Kinokuniya** (see p60), **Tower Records** (see p67), and **Maruzen** (see p145). Information on current events in and around Tokyo is also given on the **JNTO** (see p163) website. Other useful online resources include **Japan Visitor**, **RealTokyo**, and **Tokyo Food Page**.

BOOKING TICKETS

Popular traditional Japanese entertainment, such as Kabuki or sumo, are best reserved ahead of time through a travel

agent or hotel travel desk. For concerts and sporting events, the two major ticket agencies are **Ticket PIA** and **CN Playguide**. They can be hard to reach by phone. It is easier to book in person; a convenient office is Ticket PIA at Ginza's Sony Building (see p38). Department stores also have ticket desks, sometimes with English-speaking assistants. Alternatively, book directly by phoning the venue; payment is made when the tickets are picked up. Most agencies speak only Japanese, so having a

Japanese-speaker at hand will help. Reservations can also be made online, at convenience stores such as **Lawson**, or through **Metropolis**.

CINEMA

There are several specialist cinemas that screen movies from Asia, as well as Europe and the US. However, most non-Japanese films are shown in the original language with Japanese subtitles. The **Tokyo International Film Festival** (see p30) is becoming increasingly high profile. Several other interesting film festivals, showcasing both domestic and international movies, have also sprung up in the recent years.

Cinema prices are not cheap, averaging around ¥1,800. On Cinema Day, usually the first of each month, tickets are reduced. In Shibuya, **Bunkamura** (see p66) sometimes shows Japanese films with English subtitles and is known for screening independent and European films. Also in Shibuya, **Theater Image Forum** uses the most advanced digital technology. The more

Movie poster in Shinjuku, one of Tokyo's centers for cinema

Ebisu Garden Cinema, a popular cinema hall for foreign films

centrally located **Hibiya Chanter** shows art-house and independent films. For mainstream cinema, **Koma** is just one of the six cinemas around the main square in Kabukicho *(see p60)*. **Marunouchi Piccadilly** in the Mullion Building in Yurakucho *(see p38)* has five screens, while **Ebisu Garden Cinema** *(see p76)* has two. Currently, the most comfortable cinema in the city is at the nine-screen complex in Roppongi Hills *(see p69)*, part of the **Toho Cinema** group, with an in-house bar and late-night screenings.

Anyone with an interest in classic Japanese cinema should visit the superb **National Film Center** *(see p42)*. Fans of animation should visit **Ghibli Museum**; it displays the work of pioneering anime director Hayao Miyazaki, whose films include *Spirited Away* and *Howl's Moving Castle*.

INTERNATIONAL THEATER

The international theater scene in Tokyo encompasses everything from Shakespeare and Broadway musicals to comedy, classical ballet, and modern dance. The main venues are in Shinjuku, Shibuya, and Marunouchi. Although some foreign touring companies come through Tokyo, most shows are in Japanese, with local actors of a consistently high standard. The **Tokyo Comedy Store** offers non-Japanese and Japanese the chance to exhibit their comedy skills in English on the fourth Friday of the month at the Crocodile club in Harajuku.

LIVE MUSIC

The finest venues for orchestral concerts are the **New National Theater, Suntory Hall, NHK Hall, Orchard Hall** in Bunkamura *(see p66)*, **Sumida Triphony Hall**, and the two halls of the **Tokyo International Forum** *(see p43)*. The New National Theater and Orchard Hall also stage opera and ballet performances.

Tokyo has a vibrant jazz scene too, reflected in the large number of clubs and the quality of the visiting artists. **Blue Note Tokyo** is the best-known club (although prices are high and sets are short). Other places that attract world class performers include **B Flat, Shinjuku Pit Inn**, and the **Cotton Club. STB139 Sweet Basil** offers an eclectic mix of music, with mostly Japanese artists. **Blues Alley Japan** is a small club featuring blues and jazz artists.

Ever since the Beatles played at **Nippon Budokan** in 1966, Tokyo has been an essential stop on the world itinerary of pop and rock bands. Both the aging Budokan and the cavernous Tokyo Dome stadium have poor acoustics. Smaller and far better venues include **Koseinenkin Kaikan, Shibuya AX**, the inconveniently located **Zepp Tokyo, Nakano Sun Plaza**, and **Liquid Room**. As with jazz, though, it is the more intimate venues where

gigs come alive. **Club Quattro** can be claustrophobic but gets top international acts; **Duo Music Exchange** and **O-West** often specialize in techno and J-pop. **Eggman** and the ever-eclectic **SuperDeluxe** showcase experimental, fringe, and upcoming talent. Live bands also play at many of the Irish pubs as well as the **Pink Cow**, a casual, artsy hangout, popular with expats.

KARAOKE

The boom for belting out popular hits to backing music tracks dates from the 1960s but remains as popular as ever today in Japan, the birthplace of karaoke. Translated as "empty orchestra," karaoke is enjoyed in traditional bars, lively pubs, at home, and in major entertainment districts, at karaoke "boxes." These complexes range from small, cozy rooms for couples to much larger spaces for groups of friends or office parties. Food and drinks can be ordered. The most performed numbers are local pop songs, current and classic; *enka*, the Japanese equivalent of French chanson; and some western pop hits. **Karaoke-kan** in Shibuya *(see pp66–7)* is the famed location used in the movie *Lost in Translation*. For the best selection of songs in English follow the expats to **Smash Hits**.

Street musician giving a live performance

An extravagant opera performance in New National Theater

Sumo wrestlers compete at Tokyo's National Sumo Stadium

SUMO

Three sumo tournaments (*basho*) are held in Tokyo each year, in January, May, and September, all at the impressive 10,000-seat **National Sumo Stadium** in Ryogoku (*see p74*). The 15-day tournaments begin on a Sunday, with each wrestler fighting one bout a day. The action starts at 2:30pm with the lowest-ranking wrestlers; the top ranked appear from 5–6pm. The highest-ranking wrestler, usually a *yokozuna* (grand champion) will compete in the last bout.

The best views are on the north side of the stadium. Seating in the main auditorium is Japanese-style, in individual boxes. These are cramped and more expensive than the seats upstairs, but much closer to the action. Tickets should be booked in advance. Easiest to get are midweek tickets in the first week of a tournament. If you cannot buy tickets via an agency, try asking your hotel to check for returns, or just line up at the stadium itself.

It is possible to watch practice sessions at sumo stables, or *beya*. They are open to anyone who wants to watch, with a few basic rules – do not eat or use a camera flash, and be silent. Most of the *beya* are situated near Ryogoku station. Visitors can make a trip to the **Kasugano Beya**, a tall new building with a green copper gable over the entrance, the **Izutsu Beya**, or the **Dewanoumi Beya**.

OTHER MARTIAL ARTS

The center for martial arts in Japan is the **Nippon Budokan**, and this is where the top tournaments in judo, karate, and *kendo* (wooden sword fighting) are held. There are *dojo* (practice halls) for the various martial arts throughout Tokyo. Not all are open to non-Japanese as observers or participants. Contact **Tokyo TIC** (*see p173*) for a list of *dojos* that allow spectators. To participate in martial arts training, contact one of the national regulatory bodies.

Nippon Budokan, an important center for all martial arts

BASEBALL AND SOCCER

Baseball is Japan's de facto national sport. Professional baseball teams are split between the Central League and the Pacific League. The Tokyo-based Yomiuri Giants (Central League) are Japan's most popular team. Their engaging games in the soaring **Tokyo Dome** are always sold out. The Yakult Swallows (also Central

League) play at the beautiful **Jingu Stadium**. Book tickets ahead of time.

The **National Stadium** is used for occasional professional soccer (J-League) matches, and the final of the Emperor's Cup on January 1 each year. The **Ajinomoto Stadium** is home to FC Tokyo and Tokyo Verdy 1969, both J-League teams. Tickets are available at the stadium on the day of the match.

OTHER SPECTATOR SPORTS

Other sports with a significant presence include rugby, tennis, volleyball, swimming, athletics, basketball, cycling, and motor sports. Racing (horses, speedboats, or cycling) generates fervent interest, especially since gambling is allowed through official channels. Details of competitions are given in the sports pages of **Metropolis**.

PACHINKO

Pachinko (*see p67*) is like an electronic vertical pinball and its practitioners appear hypnotized by the blinding-bright lights and trance-inducing electronic music. Not just a pastime, it is a form of gambling. Winnings are exchanged for goods, which are then bought back (off the premises, to remain within the law). To experience pachinko firsthand, try the **Maruhan Pachinko Tower** in Shibuya. Here, each floor has a different theme and there are love seats for couples.

Sportsgear on display at the Baseball Hall of Fame, Tokyo Dome

DIRECTORY

INFORMATION SOURCES

Japanzine
www.japanzine.com

Japan Times
www.japantimes.co.jp/
entertainment.html

Japan Visitor
www.japanvisitor.com

Metropolis
www.jnto.go.jp

RealTokyo
www.realtokyo.co.jp/
english

Tokyo Food Page
www.bento.com/
tokyofood.html

Tokyo Journal
www.tokyo.to

BOOKING TICKETS

CN Playguide
Tel (0570) 08-9999.

Lawson
www.lawsonticket-ir.com

Ticket PIA
Tel (0570) 02-9999.

CINEMA

Bunkamura
2-24-1 Dogenzaka,
Shibuya-ku. **Map** 1 A5.
Tel (03) 3477-9111.

Ghibli Museum,
1-1-83 Shimorenjaku,
Mitaka-shi.
Tel (0570) 055777.

Hibiya Chanter
1-2-2 Yurakucho,
Chiyoda-ku.
Tel (03) 3591-1511.

Koma Theater
1-19-1 Kabukicho,
Shinjuku-ku. **Map** 1 B1.

Theater Image Forum
2-10-2 Shibuya,
Shibuya-ku. **Map** 1 C5.
Tel (03) 5766-0114.

Toho Cinema
Keyakizaka Complex,
6-10-2 Roppongi,
Minato-ku.
*Tel (03) 5775-6090 (press
9 for English).*

INTERNATIONAL THEATER

Tokyo Comedy Store
4-1-1 Taishido, Setagaya-
ku. **Map** 1 B5.
Tel (03) 5351-3011.
www.tokyocomedy.com

LIVE MUSIC

B Flat
B1, 6-6-4, Akasaka,
Minato-ku. **Map** 2 F4.
Tel (03) 5563-2563.

Blue Note Tokyo
Raika Building, 6-3-16
Minami-Aoyama,
Minato-ku. **Map** 2 D5.
Tel (03) 5485-0088.

Blues Alley Japan
Hotel Wing International
Meguro, 1-3-14 Meguro,
Meguro-ku. **Map** 1 B1.
Tel (03) 5496-4381.

Club Quattro
4F Parco Quattro,
32-13 Udagawa-cho,
Shibuya-ku. **Map** 1 A5.
Tel (03) 3477-8750.

Cotton Club
2 F Tokia Tokyo Building,
2-7-3 Marunouchi,
Chiyoda-ku. **Map** 5 B2.
Tel (03) 3215-1555.

Duo Music Exchange
2-14-8 Dogenzaka,
Shibuya-ku. **Map** 1 A5.
Tel (03) 5459-8716.

Eggman
1-6-8 Jinnan, Shibuya-ku.
Map 1 B5.
Tel (03) 5738-1151.

Koseinenkin Kaikan
5-3-1 Shinjuku,
Shinjuku-ku. **Map** 1 C1.
Tel (03) 3356-1114.

Liquid Room
3-16-6 Higashi,
Shibuya-ku.
Tel (03) 5464-0800.

Nakano Sun Plaza
4-1-1 Nakano,
Nakano-ku.
Tel (03) 3388-1151.

New National Theater
1-1-1 Honmachi, Shibuya-
ku. **Map** 1 A2.
Tel (03) 5351-3011.

NHK Hall
2-2-1 Jinnan, Shibuya-ku,
391B Orchard Road.
Map 1 B4. *Tel (03) 3465-
1751.*

Nippon Budokan
2-3 Kitanomaru-Koen,
Chiyoda-ku. **Map** 3 A5.
Tel (03) 3216-5100.

Orchard Hall
Bunkamura, 2-24-1
Dogenzaka, Shibuya-ku.
Map 1 A6.
Tel (03) 3477- 9111.

O-West
2-3 Maruyama-cho,
Shibuya-ku. **Map** 1 A5.
Tel (03) 5458-4646.

Pink Cow
Villa Moderuna B1, 1-3-18
Shibuya, Shibuya-ku.
Map 1 B5.
Tel (03) 5412-0515.

Shibuya AX
2-2-1 Jinnan,
Shibuya-ku. **Map** 1 B4.
Tel (03) 5738-1151.

Shinjuku Pit Inn
B1 Accord Building, 2-12-
4 Shinjuku, Shinjuku-ku.
Map 1 B1.
Tel (03) 3354-2024.

STB139 Sweet Basil
6-7-11 Roppongi,
Minato-ku. **Map** 2 E5.
Tel (03) 5474-0139.

Sumida Triphony Hall
1-2-3 Kinshi, Sumida-ku.
Tel (03) 5608-1212.

Suntory Hall
1-13-1 Akasaka,
Minato-ku. **Map** 2 F4.
Tel (03) 3584-9999.

SuperDeluxe
B1F 3-1-25 Nishi-Azabu,
Minato-ku. **Map** 2 E5.
Tel (03) 5412-0515.

Zepp Tokyo
Palette Town, 1 Aomi,
Koto-ku. **Map** 2 E5.
Tel (03) 3599-0710.

KARAOKE

Karaoke-kan
K&F Building, 30-8
Udagawa-cho, Shibuya-ku.
Map 1 B5.
Tel (03) 3462-0785.

Smash Hits
M2 Building B1F,
5-2-26 Hiroo,
Shibuya-ku.
Tel (03) 3444-0432.

SUMO

Dewanoumi Beya
2-3-15 Ryogoku,
Shibuya-ku.
Map 4 E5.
Tel (03) 5458-4646.

Izutsu Beya
2-2-7 Ryogoku,
Sumida-ku.
Map 4 E5.
Tel (03) 6733-1111.

Kasugano Beya
1-7-11 Ryogoku,
Sumida-ku.
Map 4 E5.

National Sumo Stadium
1-3-28 Yokoami,
Sumida-ku.
Map 4 E4.
Tel (03) 3623-5111.

BASEBALL AND SOCCER

Ajinomoto Stadium
376-3 Nishimachi,
Chofu City.
*Tel (0424) 40-0555;
(03) 3465-1751.*

Jingu Stadium
13 Kasumigaoka,
Shinjuku-ku.
Map 2 D4.
Tel (03) 3404-8999.

National Stadium
15 Kasumigaoka,
Shinjuku-ku.
Map 1 C3.
Tel (03) 3404-8999.

Tokyo Dome
1-3-61 Koraku,
Bunkyo-ku.
Map 3 A3.
Tel (03) 5800-9999.

PACHINKO

Maruhan Pachinko Tower
28-6 Udagawa-cho,
Shibuya.
Tel (03) 5458-3905.

Traditional Performing Arts

Despite Tokyo's ultra-modern exterior, its heart still moves to a traditional beat. The rarified, otherworldly court music known as *gagaku* dates back much further than the city itself, as does the Noh Theater *(see p16)*. It is however, the performing arts of the Edo Period *(see p25)*, especially Kabuki and the Bunraku puppet theater *(see p17)*, that capture the rich, vibrant cultural life of premodern Japan. As at the Kabuki-za theater, it is not so hard to find – just walk in off the busy street, buy a one-act ticket, and travel back in time.

An elegant cypress performance stage, Noh National Theater

TRADITIONAL THEATER

Kabuki and Noh, the two main forms of traditional theater *(see pp16–17)*, are well represented in Tokyo. Of the two traditions, Kabuki provides a much more flamboyant spectacle, with rousing stories, elaborate sets, and amazing costumes. However, dramatic action sequences can often be interspersed with extended soliloquies. The **Kabuki-za Theater** is the main

The grand façade of Kabuki-za Theater, Ginza

venue for Kabuki, with almost daily performances starting mid-morning and lasting three or more hours. It is also possible to buy a ticket to see just one act if you are short of time. Prices range from around ¥2,500 to as much as ¥16,000; one-act tickets are around ¥700. Earphone guides giving explanations and commentary in English are available to hire. The **National Theater** also stages Kabuki performances in January, March, October, November, and December. A number of unorthodox versions of Kabuki have been developed to make it more contemporary. Super Kabuki, introduced in 1985 and staged at the **Shinbashi Enbujo**, adds high-tech special effects (such as actors flying through the air) to the traditional plots. Cocoon Kabuki, a project launched in 1994, brings the traditional plays and costumes each summer to an uncustomary setting, the **Theater**

A giant Bunraku puppet

Cocoon in Shibuya, best known for visiting foreign theatrical productions.

In contrast, a Noh performance can be heavy going for those unprepared for its slow pace. As a theatrical experience, however, it can be exceptionally powerful. The **Noh National Theater** near Sendagaya JR station usually has weekend performances. Tickets vary from ¥2,300 to ¥4,300. It is also possible to see plays at a Noh school, for instance **Kanze Nohgakudo**. Outdoor Noh performed by torchlight (*"Takigi Noh"*) can be wonderfully atmospheric, especially when staged in front of an ancient shrine or temple, such as the annual fall performances at the Kamakura-gu shrine, in the hills of Kamakura. More information is readily available from **JNTO** *(see p163)* or the **Kamakura Tourist Association**.

The puppet theater, Bunraku, predates Kabuki, and many of its plays were later adapted to the stage. The black-robed puppeteers are so skillful, you soon ignore their presence and just watch the lifelike movements of the puppets themselves. Performances can be seen at the National Theater's Small Hall.

Kyogen (short comic farces) is Japan's oldest form of drama, and includes acrobatics and juggling. Now played to comic effect, Kyogen is performed as part of Noh, or as individual plays between Noh plays. Another lighthearted theatrical tradition is Rakugo. Dressed in a kimono and sitting on a *zabuton* (cushion), the storytellers act out comic situations, often retelling old and well-loved stories. Held at intimate theaters such as **Suzumoto** in Ueno or **Suehirotei** in bustling Shinjuku, they give great insight into characteristic Japanese traditional humor, even without understanding the language. A few Rakugo artists have also started doing occasional shows in English.

Takarazuka Theater, a venue for dance and theater performances

TRADITIONAL AND CONTEMPORARY DANCE

Performances of traditional dance are staged regularly by the **Nihon Buyo Kyokai**. The Azuma Odori, an annual production of dance and drama usually held at the end of May, brings Tokyo's geisha community on stage at the **Shinbashi Enbujo**.

A unique theater experience is Takarazuka, a company divided into five troupes and composed entirely of women. With their own state-of-the-art **Takarazuka Theater** in Yurakucho, they perform traditional adaptations in Japanese of Western musicals and historic love stories, and are famed for their extravagant productions.

Butoh is a distinct and compelling form of contemporary dance developed in the 1960s that draws on elements of mime and traditional ascetic practice. Often shaven-headed and almost naked with body makeup, the dancers follow a slow choreography that seeks to create beauty out of self-imposed grotesqueness. Look out for performances by established troupes such as Dairakudakan or Buto-sha Tenkei, staged at **Setagaya Public Theater** but more often at small fringe theaters in outlying areas.

TRADITIONAL MUSIC

The oldest Japanese musical traditions are those of the *matsuri* or festivals *(see pp28–31)*, featuring instruments such as drum and flute. Performances of captivating ancient court music, known as *gagaku*, are given occasionally at the **National Theater** or at major temples in the city. The **Ono Gagaku-kai Society** holds major concerts featuring other regional instruments such as the stringed *koto* and *shamisen*, and the *sakuhachi* (flute). Do not miss a chance to catch a concert by one of the troupes of Japanese drummers, performing on *taiko* drums ranging from the size of small snares to huge barrels two meters or more in diameter. The most dynamic of the performing groups is Kodo, who play an annual series of concerts at venues such as the popular Bunkamura *(see p66)* in Shibuya each December.

A woman playing a shamisen instrument

DIRECTORY

TRADITIONAL THEATER

Kabuki-za Theater
4-12-5 Ginza, Chuo-ku.
Map 5 C3.
Tel (03) 3541- 3131.

Kanze Nohgakudo
1-16-4 Shoto, Shibuya-ku.
Map 1 A5.
Tel (03) 3469-5241.

National Theater
4-1 Hayabusa-cho, Chiyoda-ku.
Map 2 F3.
Tel (03) 3265-7411.

Noh National Theater
4-18-1 Sendagaya, Shibuya-ku.
Map 1 C3.
Tel (03) 3423-1331.

Kamakura Tourist Association
Tel (0467) 23-3050.

Shinbashi Enbujo
6-18-2 Ginza, Chuo-ku.
Map 5 C3.
Tel (03) 3541-2600.

Suehirotei
3-6-12 Shinjuku, Shinjuku-ku.
Map 1 B1.
Tel (03) 3351-2974.

Suzumoto
2-7-12 Ueno, Taito-ku.
Map 3 C3.
Tel (03) 3834-5906.

Theater Cocoon
Bunkamura, 2-24-1 Dogenzaka, Shibuya-ku. **Map** 1 A5.
Tel (03) 3477-9999.

TRADITIONAL AND CONTEMPORARY DANCE

Nihon Buyo Kyokai
2-18-1 Kachidoki, Chuo-ku.
Map 5 D4.
Tel (03) 3533-6455.

Setagaya Public Theater
4-1-1 Taishido, Setagaya-ku.
Tel (03) 5432-1526.
www.onoteru.com

Takarazuka Theater
1-1-3 Yurakucho, Chiyoda-ku.
Map 5 B2.
Tel (03) 5251-2001.

TRADITIONAL MUSIC

Ono Gagaku-kai Society
www.onoteru.com

Japanese women performing traditional opera dance

Nightlife

Evening does not signal any let-up in the pace of life in Tokyo. If anything, it seems to intensify, especially in areas where the neon burns brightest. Fashionable Ginza, the cosmopolitan party district of Roppongi, sophisticated Nishi-Azabu, youthful Shibuya or vibrant Shinjuku – there are plenty of choices. Tokyo is rapidly becoming an all-night city, and it is one of the most exciting places in the world to party. It is not just the clubs and cabarets, many restaurants, bars, and traditional *izakayas (see p120)* now stay open until 2am or later.

A DJ performing at La Fabrique, Shibuya

HIGH-RISE BARS

The best place to get into the mood for an evening out is at one of the city's high-rise hotel bars. The Conrad's **Twenty Eight Bar** has a brilliant view over the Rainbow Bridge and the Odaiba waterfront. In Shibuya, there is the Cerulean Tower Hotel, with its 40th-floor **Bello Visto Bar**. Best of all is the Park Hyatt Hotel's *(see p116)* luxurious 52nd-floor **New York Bar**, as seen in the film *Lost in Translation*. Cradle a cocktail,

New York Bar offers superb views of the city below

watch the dusk fall and the lights come on, then descend to street level and plunge into the neon night.

CLUBS AND BARS

Ginza remains one of Tokyo's most exclusive and priciest nightlife districts. But alongside the costly hostess bars, there are also more affordable spots, such as the standing-only **300 Bar** where the food or drink all cost around ¥300. The Ginza Corridor, a row of bars and restaurants built right under the expressway between Ginza and Shinbashi, also offers good options.

Central to the city's nightlife since postwar occupation, Roppongi stays lively through the night. Popular places to start the evening include **Hobgoblin**, Tokyo's largest British pub, and longtime Irish pub **Paddy Foley's**. For more recreation, catch one of the retro-themed shows at **Kaguwa** *(see p181)*, a unique dinner theater (entrance

Logo of British pub, Hobgoblin

¥3,500). Dance the night away at **Salsa Sudade** or **El Café Latino**. Smoke a Havana cigar and sip premium aged tequila at **Agave** or rub shoulders with celebrities at **NewLex Edo**.

The scene is more relaxed in nearby Nishi-Azabu. **The Baron** offers tapas and weekend DJ events. **SuperDeluxe** is an eclectic bar-cum-event space with performance art and live music. The enduringly lively bar **Acaraje Tropicana** swings to a Brazilian rhythm.

Shibuya is the center of Tokyo youth culture and the Center-Gai pedestrian alley is its promenade and fast-food kitchen. Good watering holes in the area include **Tasu-Ichi**, a standing bar with very reasonable prices; and **The Aldgate**, an Anglophile pub with an extensive selection of ales on draught.

Chic, upscale Akasaka also has a good range of clubs and bars. Shinjuku's Kabuki-cho, with its maze of streets and future-world feel, boasts numerous restaurants and clubs. It is also the city's most notorious red-light district. It is safe to explore, but beware of pickpockets and venues that do not post their prices. A more restful neighborhood is Shinjuku Sanchome, close to Isetan Department Store. Recommended watering holes include the **Marugo** wine bar.

If sightseeing in Asakusa leaves you thirsty, cross the Sumida river to the **Flamme D'Or** bar in the premises of the Asahi Breweries headquarters. Close to Kaminarimon Gate is the **Kamiya Bar**, the oldest bar in Tokyo. Near the sumo stadium, look for **Beer Station Ryogoku**, a German-style bierkeller.

DJ AND DANCE CLUBS

Tokyo's clubbing scene has exploded in the last decade, attracting top DJs from around the world. Roppongi, Shinjuku, and Shibuya offer a wealth of options. In terms of scale, the topspot is **ageHa**, in Shin-Kiba, on the other side of Odaiba. Other substantial

A row of clubs and bars, Shinjuku Sanchome

The leading online magazine **Cyberjapan** carries up-to-date listings. Dance clubs warm up around 11pm and keep going all night. Expect a cover charge of between ¥2,000 and ¥4,000.

GAY AND LESBIAN

The undisputed center of Tokyo's gay world is the concentration of bars, clubs, and saunas in the small area of Shinjuku called "Ni-Chome" ("2nd Block"). Many of the venues here cater exclusively to the local gay community, but there are still a good

number of bars that are open to non-Japanese speakers. The most popular places to meet are **GB** and **Advocates Café**, a tiny, lively venue where the action spills out onto the street. The second-floor **Kinsmen** bar is more sedate, attracting a mix of all persuasions. Its lesbian counterpart, the women-only **Kinswomyn**, is equally relaxed and welcoming. Ni-Chome is also the location for the mega-scale **24 Kaikan** bath-house complex which also has branches in Asakusa, Ueno, and Shinjuku. Two good sources of online information are the **Utopa-Asia** and **Out Japan** websites.

venues include longtime favorite **Space Lab Yellow**; hip **Air**; cavernous **Womb**; the upmarket **The Orbient**; and the impersonal **Club Complex Code**. On a more manageable scale, **La Fabrique** and **Loop** are also worth checking out.

DIRECTORY

HIGH-RISE BARS

Bello Visto Bar
26-1, Sakuragaoka-cho,
Shibuya-ku.
Tel (03) 3476-3000.

Twenty Eight Bar
1-9-1 Higashi-Shinbashi,
Minato-ku. **Map 5** B4.
Tel (03) 6388-8000.

CLUBS AND BARS

Acaraje Tropicana
B2, 1-1-25 Nishi-Azabu,
Minato-ku. **Map 2** E5.
Tel (03) 3479-4690.

Agave
B1, 7-15-10 Roppongi,
Minato-ku. **Map 2** E5.
Tel (03) 3497-0229.

Beer Station Ryogoku
1-3-20 Yokoami,
Sumida-ku. **Map 4** E5.
Tel (03) 3623-5252.

300 Bar
B1, 5-9-11 Ginza, Chuo-ku. **Map 5** B3.
Tel (03) 3572-6300.

El Café Latino
3-15-24 Roppongi,
Minato-ku. **Map 2** E5.
Tel (03) 3402-8989.

Flamme D'or
1-23-36 Azumabashi,
Sumida-ku. **Map 4** F3.
Tel (03) 5608-5381.

Hobgoblin
3-16-33 Roppongi,
Minato-ku. **Map 2** E5.
Tel (03) 3568-1280.

Kamiya Bar
1-1-1 Asakusa, Taito-ku.
Map 4 F3.
Tel (03) 3841-5400.

Marugo
3-7-5, Shinjuku,
Shinjuku-ku. **Map 1** B1.
Tel (03) 3350-4605.

NewLex Edo
B1, 3-13-14 Roppongi,
Minato-ku. **Map 2** E5.
Tel (03) 5575-6600.

Paddy Foley's
B1, 5-5-1 Roppongi,
Minato-ku. **Map 2** E5.
Tel (03) 3423-2250.
www.paddyfolleystokyo.
com

Salsa Sudade
3F, Rue Palette, 7-13-8
Roppongi, Minato-ku.
Map 2 E5.
Tel (03) 5474-8806.

SuperDeluxe
B1, 3-1-25 Nishi-Azabu,
Minato-ku. **Map 2** E5.
Tel (03) 5412-0515.

Tasu-Ichi
1F, 33-14 Utagawa-cho,
Shibuya-ku. **Map 1** B5.
Tel (03) 3463-0077.

The Aldgate
3F, 30-4 Udagawa-cho,
Shibuya-ku. **Map 1** B5.
Tel (03) 3462-2983.

The Baron
1-8-21 Nishi-Azabu,
Minato-ku. **Map 2** D5.
Tel (03) 6406-4551.

DJ AND DANCE CLUBS

Ageha
2-2-10 Shin-Kiba,
Koto ku.
Tel (03) 5534-2525.

Air
Hikawa Bldg, B1, 2-11
Sarugaku-cho, Shibuya-ku.
Tel (03) 5784-3386.

Club Complex Code
4F, 1-19-2 Kabuki-cho,
Shinjuku-ku. **Map 1** B1.
Tel (03) 3209-0702.

Cyberjapan
www.cyberjapan.tv

La Fabrique
Zero Gate B1F, 16-9
Udagawa-cho, Shibuya-ku.
Map 1 A5.
Tel (03) 5428-5100.

Loop
2-1-13 Shibuya,
Shibuya-ku. **Map 1** B5.
Tel (03) 3797-9933.

Space Lab Yellow
B1, 1-10-11 Nishi-Azabu,
Minato-ku. **Map 2** D5.
Tel (03) 3479-0690.

The Orbient
Crystal Bldg B1, 3-5-12
Kita-Aoyama, Minato-ku.
Map 1 C4.
Tel (03) 5775-2555.

Womb
2-16 Maruyama-cho,
Shibuya-ku.
Map 1 A5.
Tel (03) 5459-0039.

GAY AND LESBIAN

Advocates Café
2-18-1 Shinjuku,
Shinjuku-ku.
Map 1 C1.
Tel (03) 3358-8638.

GB
2-12-16 Shinjuku,
Shinjuku-ku.
Map 1 C2.
Tel (03) 3352-8972.

Kinsmen
2F, 2-18-5 Shinjuku,
Shinjuku-ku.
Map 1 C1.
Tel (03) 3354-4949.

Kinswomyn
3F, Dai-ichi Tenka Bldg,
2-15-10 Shinjuku,
Shinjuku-ku. **Map 1** B1.
Tel (03) 3354-8720.

24 Kaikan
2-13-1 Shinjuku,
Shinjuku-ku.
Map 1 C1.
Tel (03) 3354-2424.

Out Japan
www.outjapan.com

Utopia-Asia
www.utopia-asia.com

SURVIVAL GUIDE

PRACTICAL INFORMATION

From a practical point of view, Tokyo is much easier for foreign visitors to negotiate than is generally believed. Being unable to speak or read Japanese is rarely a serious problem in the city. Many everyday signs in major suburbs and at tourist attractions are displayed in Roman script along with Japanese characters. English-speaking locals are generally quick to offer their assistance. The infrastructure for tourism (public transportation, accommodations,

Street sign in Japanese and Roman script

sight-seeing) is highly developed, because the Japanese are well used to traveling extensively around their own country. Where problems can arise for visitors, however, is in the surprising contrasts in Tokyo's unique East-West culture – for instance, the contrast between the ease with which even visitors can get around on the efficient rail network compared with the difficulty everyone, including the Japanese, have with locating an address in the city (*see p171*).

Picnics in Tokyo's Ueno Park at cherry-blossom time

WHEN TO VISIT

The best times to visit Tokyo are spring (April and May) with crisp, clear skies, and fall (October and November). July and August are mostly very humid and better avoided.

Tokyo has numerous festivals throughout the year (*see pp28–31*). Cherry blossom time brings out large blossom-viewing groups who fill the parks day and night, while late summer is a time when city dwellers return home to celebrate the O-Bon festival. Peak vacation periods for the Japanese are New Year (December 29 to January 4), "Golden Week" (April 29 to May 5), and the period around O-Bon, the Buddhist Festival of the Dead (in mid-August). At these times flights and some accommodations are sold out, and some hotels, offices, and tourist attractions may close for up to a week.

WHAT TO BRING

It is a good idea to take a variety of clothing, as modern buildings tend to be overheated in winter and overcooled in summer, while traditional buildings are relatively vulnerable to the elements. The weather can be changeable – an umbrella is more useful than a raincoat,

A colorful display of practical and souvenir fans for sale

especially in midsummer heat. Clothes, even if casual, should be neat, clean, and not too revealing; a short, tight skirt makes it awkward to sit on the floor. Comfortable footwear is a good idea; shoes will be removed frequently, so wear some that are easily slipped on and off, and make sure there are no holes in your socks or tights. Keep luggage to a minimum, and choose items that are easy to carry. Stations have many steps and few porters.

Almost anything you need can be bought in Tokyo, although it may be expensive, and clothes or shoes may be available only in small sizes. Film can be pricey but is reasonable in general discount stores or electrical shops (note that slide film is not usually process-paid); developing is quite cheap, and of good quality, although standard print size is small.

As with any destination, good travel insurance is advisable. If you plan to travel around within Japan, consider obtaining a Japan Rail Pass before you go (*see pp174-5*).

VISAS AND PASSPORTS

Citizens of most Western countries may enter Tokyo for short visits as a Temporary Visitor simply with a valid passport. There is no need to obtain a visa. The usual period of stay for a Temporary Visitor is 90 days. Visitors are allowed to enter for tourism, sports, visiting friends or

Film and cameras in a discount camera shop

relatives, study, or business, but may not undertake paid employment in Tokyo or stay longer than the specified period. (Journalists with US passports are an exception and must obtain a visa before traveling to Tokyo on business, even for a short stay.)

Citizens of some countries, including the UK and Germany, may extend this 90-day stay by up to another 90 days at immigration offices in Tokyo (at least 10 days before the original expiration date), but the length of extension is at the discretion of immigration officers.

On the plane you will be given a landing card – you need fill in only the first part, relating to arrival – the second part will be attached to your passport to be completed when you depart. There are no immunization requirements for entering Tokyo.

Any visitor planning on undertaking paid work, long-term study, or voluntary work in Tokyo should obtain a visa from a Japanese embassy before going to Tokyo. It is generally not possible to obtain a visa, or change status, once in the city. Foreigners who stay in Tokyo for more than 90 days must also apply for a Certificate of Alien Registration from the Ward Office of the area in which they are living, within 90 days of arrival in the city.

This certificate, or your passport, must be carried at all times – not doing so can occasionally lead to arrest. Visa-holders who want to leave the country and return within the duration of their visa need to obtain a re-entry permit from an immigration office. In Tokyo, contact the **Tokyo Regional Immigration Bureau** for more information.

CUSTOMS

There is no need to fill in a written declaration of your belongings unless you are arriving in Tokyo by ship, have unaccompanied baggage, or if you are exceeding the duty-free allowances.

Duty-free allowances on entering the country are 400 cigarettes or 500 grams of tobacco or 100 cigars; three 0.76 liter (27 oz) bottles of alcohol; 57 g (2 oz) of perfume; and gifts and souvenirs

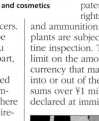

Shop selling perfume and cosmetics

of a total value up to ¥200,000 (not counting items less than ¥10,000). Certain articles are prohibited – narcotic drugs or stimulants; counterfeit money; pornography; articles that infringe on patents or copyrights; and firearms and ammunition. Animals and plants are subject to quarantine inspection. There is no limit on the amount of currency that may be taken into or out of the country, but sums over ¥1 million must be declared at immigration.

For guidelines on tax-free shopping in Tokyo, see page 142. Guns, swords, and some high-quality personal computers require an export license, obtained from the Ministry of International Trade and Industry. Art objects may be subject to restrictions.

FACILITIES FOR DISABLED VISITORS

Facilities for the disabled are of mixed quality. Blind people are well provided for, but the elderly and those in wheelchairs may face problems with stations and pedestrian overpasses, as there are endless steps and sometimes no escalator or elevator; the situation is improving, but slowly. Most modern offices and hotels have excellent toilet facilities.

FACILITIES FOR CHILDREN

Children are welcomed, and parents can forget their usual worries about safety. Taking children to a restaurant poses no problems, discreet breast-feeding in public is accepted, and baby food, milk, disposable diapers, and boiled water are easily obtainable. Hotels tend to be geared toward adults, but top ones usually offer baby-sitting and nurseries, while at traditional inns a maid may be willing to baby-sit. Many theme parks and museums are great fun for kids, but some very cultured temples and galleries do not allow children. Rush hour travel and very hot *onsen* pools should also be avoided.

Children playing on the sidewalk

Logo of the Japan National Tourist Organization (JNTO)

INFORMATION CENTERS

Outside Japan, it is possible to obtain tourist information from branches of the **Japan National Tourist Organization (JNTO)**. The JNTO has a range of useful material – background information, practical leaflets, and brochures on particular locations and specialist interests. The JNTO does not, however, make recommendations or reservations or sell Rail Pass vouchers, but can provide a list of travel agents that do.

In Tokyo, the **Tourist Information Center** or TIC has knowledgeable staff, and offers information, travel literature, and suggestions on tour itineraries in and outside the city, though they cannot make transport bookings. The TIC also has a counter for the **Welcome Inn Reservation Center** *(see pp106-7)*, where staff will arrange hotel reservations at locations beyond Tokyo. This service is free of charge. For areas beyond Tokyo and farther afield, information on a local level can be obtained from the Tourist Information Offices found in almost every town, usually in or near the station. Nearly 100 of these offices are designated **"i"** Tourist Information Offices, meaning they have multilingual staff and carry pamphlets in English.

EVENTS INFORMATION AND TICKETS

Details of attractions and events in Tokyo can be gleaned from local publications such as *Tokyo Journal* and *Metropolis*, as well as their online editions. Free listings brochures are available at hotels, bookstores, and the TIC.

Hotels will usually help reserve tickets for entertainment venues. Ticket-agency booths located inside department stores, convenience stores, and near train stations also book seats in advance and sell tickets up to the last minute. **Ticket PIA**, **CN Playguide** *(see p153)*, and **Ticket Saison** are the main agencies.

WELCOME CARDS

Several cities have begun to issue a Welcome Card to foreign visitors, and there are now a number of different ones available. Intended to reduce the cost of a visit, the card can be used to obtain discounts on accommodations, shopping, food and drink, and various other tourist facilities and services. For example, the Tokyo Museum Guide Welcome Card can be used to obtain a discount on the admission price at more than 40 galleries and museums in Tokyo, and the Mount Fuji Welcome Card allows discounts or special services at more than 200 hotels, restaurants, and sights in the Fuji, Hakone, and Izu regions. Obtain these or other cards with a booklet of participating services from a TIC or an "i" information center.

OPENING HOURS AND ADMISSION FEES

Most temple buildings are typically open from 8 or 9am to 4pm in winter, and until 5pm in summer, though exact times and the number of buildings closed vary widely. Shrines are often open 24 hours. Admission to many temples and shrines is free; others charge a small admission fee, usually between ¥200 and ¥500.

Museums, art galleries, and many other tourist attractions such as technology centers and aquariums are usually open from 10am until 4 or

Roppongi's National Art Center has extended opening hours on Fridays

Tokyo Midtown, a busy commercial center, home to over 40 embassies

to the reigning Japanese emperor. The present era, Heisei (meaning "achieving peace"), began when Emperor Akihito came to the throne in 1989, so that year was known as "Heisei 1"; Akihito's father's era was called "Showa." The Japanese system is generally used within the country, especially on official documents, while Western years are often used in international contexts.

Misunderstandings about timings and dates are common, and it is advisable to confirm arrangements when booking accommodations, to state the number of nights as well as the dates of your stay.

5pm. Many of these sights are open every day except Monday; when Monday is a public holiday, they often close on Tuesday instead. Most of these attractions may close for a week or more over the New Year period. Entrance fees to tourist attractions are occasionally under ¥1,000, but are usually more.

Shopping hours are mostly from 10am–8pm; for banking hours see page 168; and for post offices see page 171.

TIME AND THE CALENDAR

Tokyo is 9 hours ahead of Greenwich Mean Time and 14 hours ahead of US Eastern Standard Time. There is no daylight-saving time; when countries that use daylight-saving time switch to summer time, the time difference is one hour less.

The Japanese calendar combines the Western system with the Chinese system – years are designated Year of the Tiger, Rabbit, and so on, but they begin on January 1 and not, as in China, in mid-February. Years are numbered both by the Western system and according

Stamps to mark the 10th year of the Heisei era

ELECTRICITY

The electric current in Tokyo is 100 volts, AC, 50 cycles – a system similar to that of the US. The country, however, has two different cycles – 50 cycles in eastern Japan (including Tokyo) and 60 cycles in western Japan. Plugs with two flat pins are standard; this means that appliances that can be used in America can also be used in Tokyo, but sometimes at a reduced efficiency.

Most British and other European appliances can be used only with transformers suitable for US voltage (which are large and expensive). If in doubt, consult the appliance's instructions. Some international hotels have two outlets, of 110 and 220 volts, although these accept only two-pin plugs – adapters are available from electrical stores. In older buildings, ceiling lights are often operated by both a switch on the wall and a pull cord on the light itself; each pull of the cord gives a different degree of brightness.

Attitudes and Etiquette

Etiquette is important in Tokyo – the social lubricant for a crowded community. In recent decades attitudes have relaxed, yet even the most apparently rebellious Tokyoite will not break certain rules. What constitutes correct behavior often varies according to the situation and status of individuals. Foreigners will be forgiven most gaffes, but good manners will earn you respect. The best approach is to be as sensitive as possible to situations, avoid loud or dogmatic behavior, and follow the lead of those around you.

Gauze mask, worn to prevent the spread of colds

TABOOS

Few allowances are made even for foreigners on certain points, mainly relating to Japanese standards of hygiene. It is considered unforgivable to get soap or shampoo in a bathtub; washing belongs to the shower area *(see p109)*. It is also a serious mistake to wear shoes indoors or to wear the wrong slippers into or out of a toilet area.

Eating while walking is frowned upon, though eating on longer train trips is fine. Emissions from the body are considered very rude, while anything drawn inward is acceptable. Thus, sniffing is fine, but blowing your nose in public is reviled. Gauze face masks are worn in public to prevent the spread of colds.

THE HIERARCHY

Respect for seniors is fundamental to Japanese society; not only parents, grandparents, company bosses, and teachers but even those a year or two senior in school or employment. The term *sensei* (teacher) is used for all elders and experts.

In the Japanese language, different vocabulary is used to speak to those above and those below, so it is vital for a Japanese to know the relative status of other people – one reason why business cards *(meishi)* are so widely used.

The ultimate parent in such a social system is the imperial family, worshiped as the ancestors of the nation. Even today, most people show great respect for the emperor, but stop short of veneration.

BOWING

The traditional greeting in Tokyo is a bow, its depth reflecting the relative status of participants. Visitors, however, rarely need to bow – a handshake is fine. In many situations, bows are part of the service, for instance, in department stores, restaurants, and hotels. They can be ignored or met with a brief smile. If you wish to bow, hold your arms and back straight, and bend from the waist, and pause for a moment at the low point.

ATTITUDES TO PHYSICAL CONTACT AND SEX

Members of the same sex are physically at ease with each other. The atmosphere in single-sex public baths is relaxed. Between the sexes, however, public display of contact is very limited. Although more couples hold hands in public these days, kissing is rarely seen. A "hello" kiss on the cheek would cause embarrassment. In general, sex is seen as free from shame, but something to be indulged in discreetly. Homosexual activity is less openly accepted than in many Western nations. Sadly, the sleazier side of the sex trade includes schoolgirl prostitution, and cartoon pornography is widely sold in convenience stores. Nonetheless, everyday life is relatively sanitized, and it is important to remember that geisha and most bar hostesses are not prostitutes.

Embracing in public; a rarity, even in Tokyo

Bow between business colleagues close in status to each other

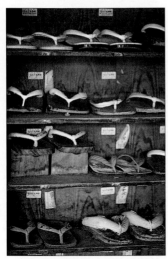

Traditional footwear neatly lined up on racks outside a temple

ETIQUETTE AT TEMPLES AND SHRINES

The atmosphere in temples and shrines is casual. Visitors should show respect, and not be noisy, but there are few of the taboos found in some other Buddhist nations.

If you enter buildings in a shrine or temple, except those with stone floors, leave your shoes at the entrance or carry them with you. Plastic bags are often provided for this, especially if you can use a different exit. Some temples allow photography, some only without flash, others not at all.

TIPPING

Tipping is not necessary unless stated, and may even cause offense. If a receipt or change is placed on a tray, this is through a sense of decorum when handling money, not in expectation of a tip for services.

SHOES

Shoes are an important element of social etiquette. When you enter a Japanese house or restaurant, take off your outdoor shoes and put on slippers, if provided, before you step on to the raised floor. If there are no slippers, go in socks or stockings. The principle is not to contaminate clean interiors with dirt from the outside, so be careful not to rest a shoe on the indoor floor or put a stockinged foot on the dirty part.

In a Western-style hotel, however, "indoors" starts when you enter your own room. If you are unsure where "indoors" begins or, for instance, whether to take your shoes off to enter a restaurant, take your cue from other shoes or slippers at the entrance. To walk on *tatami* matting, remove slippers and go in stockinged feet. Most restrooms, public and private, have special toilet slippers waiting outside.

LANGUAGE DIFFICULTIES

Tokyo is well signposted in English and not hard for visitors to find their way around. While there are many Japanese who do not speak English and few are comfortable with everyday spoken English, this is less of a problem in Tokyo. However, do not expect English to be understood by all taxi drivers, policemen, or station clerks.

JAPANESE NAMES

The order of Japanese names is traditionally family name followed by given name. However, many Japanese automatically reverse this order when giving names to Westerners, so you may need to check which is the "first" name and "surname." Japanese generally call each other by the family name, even if they are close friends, but will happily call you by your first name if you prefer.

When speaking to or about an adult other than yourself, add "-san" to their name, which stands for Mr., Mrs., Ms., – for instance, Smith-san or John-san. For babies and young girls add "-chan," for young boys "-kun."

GIFT-GIVING

Gift-giving is an important aspect of social etiquette in Japan. Any trip means bringing home souvenirs for colleagues and friends, usually something edible. Small gifts may be exchanged at a first business meeting, and if you visit someone's home, never go empty-handed – buy a luxury food item or take a small gift from your home country, such as a local specialty or fine tea.

Keep gifts small, to avoid placing obligation on the recipient. Do not expect them to be opened in front of you. Likewise, if someone offers you a gift, it may be best not to open it in front of the giver.

Appearance matters – a gift is expected to be beautifully wrapped. A shop will usually do the wrapping for you. Wine, chocolates, or flowers are acceptable as gifts, but avoid chrysanthemums, which are used at funerals; do not give four of anything, because in Japanese the words for "four" and "death" sound similar; nor knives, lest they cut the friendship.

Box of cookies gift-wrapped first in paper, then cloth

LINING UP AND JAYWALKING

When waiting, such as for a train, people line up neatly. To get off a crowded train, gently push your way through. If you are completely stuck and cannot reach the door in time, call out *"orimass"* ("I'm getting off").

Jaywalking is heavily discouraged. Pedestrians in Tokyo invariably wait for the crossing lights, even when there is no traffic coming.

Personal Security and Health

Hygiene standards in Tokyo are as high as in Western countries, and crime rates are low. Pickpockets occasionally operate in crowds, but bags can generally be put down freely in a store or at a station, and there is little risk in carrying large amounts of cash. *Koban* (manned police boxes) are found in every neighborhood; their presence helps to keep crime down.

A uniformed Tokyo policeman

IN AN EMERGENCY

Emergency calls are free. Your hotel, embassy, or consulate may also be able to help, while Tokyo Police have an assistance phone line for foreign visitors. The **Tokyo Metropolitan Health and Medical Information Center** provides health information; their operators speak English, Chinese, Korean, Thai, and Spanish. In case of translation difficulties during treatment, contact the **Emergency**

Translation Services. Lost possessions are very likely to be returned to you; contact the appropriate local police or transport authorities.

EARTHQUAKES, TYPHOONS, AND VOLCANOES

Each year, Japan experiences more than 1,000 earthquakes large enough to be felt by humans, although most are no more disruptive than the vibrations of a passing truck and are nothing to worry about. Earthquakes are more noticeable in tall buildings, which sway markedly but usually have mechanisms to absorb the motion. In a larger earthquake, especially in an old building, open doors (to prevent them from buckling and jamming) and turn off any gas. Do not rush outside, where debris may fall on you, but shelter under something protective such as a reinforced doorway or sturdy table. Don't sleep close to a TV or computer shelf, or next to heavy furniture, such as a wardrobe, not securely fixed to the wall.

Typhoons may cause flooding or landslides, and the worst bring winds so strong

that it is wise to stay indoors. The main typhoon season is in September. Active volcanoes usually have fences around them to ensure that no one goes dangerously close. Poisonous fumes occasionally seep from the ground nearby; look out for warning notices.

THINGS TO AVOID

Paddy fields are areas under cultivation and are private property so you should not walk in them. There are few "off-limits" areas in Tokyo, but it is advisable to avoid the *yakuza* (mafia), extremist political groups, and some religious sects.

WOMEN TRAVELERS

Official statistics for sexual assault in Tokyo are very low, and any unwanted propositions from men can usually be shaken off with a simple "no." However, groping hands on crowded trains are acknowledged to be a problem, and increasing evidence suggests that sex crimes tend to go unreported or unprosecuted in Tokyo. Thus, women are best advised to take due care everywhere they go and with whom they associate. Avoid mountain paths after dark and be wary of men outside train stations who try to initiate a conversation – it may be a prelude to an unwanted advance. On a practical level, tampons are widely available, but the Pill is hard to obtain.

FOOD SAFETY

Food poisoning is rare thanks to good hygiene standards, and an upset stomach is likely to be simply due to a change in diet. The problem, if anything, is over-reliance on science – organic foods are uncommon. Tap water is drinkable throughout Tokyo, although it may taste chlorinated. Avoid drinking from mountain streams.

Raw fish in sushi and sashimi is not a risk, nor are oysters. *Fugu* (blowfish) is safe provided it is correctly prepared. Only eat raw meat in a good restaurant, and

Schoolchildren practicing earthquake drill

Well-stocked Mitsukoshi food supermarket at a basement floor, Ginza

DIRECTORY

EMERGENCY NUMBERS

Fire/Ambulance
Tel 119.

Police
Tel 110 (emergencies only) Tokyo.
Tel (03) 3503-8484 (assistance service for foreigners).

Emergency Translation Services
Tel (03) 5285-8185.
☐ 5–8pm Mon–Fri, 9am–8pm Sat, Sun, public hols.

Tokyo Metropolitan Health and Medical Information Center
Tel (03) 5285-8181.
☐ 9am–8pm daily.

MEDICAL FACILITIES AND HOSPITALS

AMDA International Medical Information Center
Tel (03) 5285-8088.

American Pharmacy
B1 Marunouchi Bldg,
2-4-1 Chiyoda-ku, Tokyo.
Tel (03) 5220-7716.

International Catholic Hospital
2-5-1 Naka-Ochiai,
Shinjuku-ku, Tokyo.
Tel (03) 3951-1111.

Japanese Red Cross Medical Center
4-1-22 Hiroo, Shibuya-ku, Tokyo.
Tel (03) 3400-1311.

National Medical Clinic
2nd floor, 5-16-11,
Minami-Azabu,
Minato-ku, Tokyo.
Tel (03) 3473-2057.

St. Luke's International Hospital
9-1 Akashicho, Chuo-ku, Tokyo.
Tel (03) 3541-5151.

Tokyo Medical and Surgical Clinic
3-4-30, 32 Mori Bldg,
Shiba-koen, Minato-ku, Tokyo.
Tel (03) 3436-3028.

avoid raw bear (*kuma*) and raw wild boar (*inoshishi*) because of risk of trichinosis, borne by parasites. Fruit and vegetables are clean, although insecticides and chemicals are widely applied so it is wise to peel the fruit before eating.

MEDICAL FACILITES

Facilities are generally as good as in the US or Europe but can be expensive. If you are sick, go to a hospital; for minor problems, consulting a pharmacist is another option.

To find a hospital, doctor, or dentist, contact the International Affairs Division of the prefectural office, the **AMDA (Asian Medical Doctors Association) International Medical Information Center**, or a TIC. The hospitals listed in the directory have some English-speaking doctors. Look, too, for advertisements in foreign-language magazines; international hotels have doctors on call.

Dental care varies in quality and may not meet Western aesthetic standards. Medicines are dispensed at hospitals and pharmacies; a prescription from abroad is more likely to be understood at a hospital. Western brands are available, if expensive, at international pharmacies such as Tokyo's **American Pharmacy**. Contact lenses can be obtained with relative ease, and

Western-brand lens solutions are very reasonably priced. Tokyo is big on pick-me-ups containing ginseng, caffeine, and the like, which can work wonders with a hangover. Local mosquito repellents and bite medicines are also good, as are pocket handwarmers (*kairo*), sold in pharmacies and convenience stores. Chinese herbal medicine is widely available.

PUBLIC CONVENIENCES

Japanese toilets range from highly sophisticated to very basic. The latter are simple troughs to squat over, facing the end with the hood, making sure nothing falls out of trouser pockets. If squatting is difficult, seek out Western-style toilets; many public facilities, including trains, have both. The usual way of finding out if a cubicle is occupied is to knock on the door and see if anyone knocks back. Toilet paper and hand towels are often not provided, so carry tissues with you.

Sign for a men's public bath

Sign for a women's public bath

Older Western-style toilets often have the option of small or large flush. They may also have a panel that, if pressed, plays a tune or makes a flushing sound to discreetly mask natural noises. Newer hi-tech toilets may have heated seats, automatic seat covers, and hot-air-drying facilities. For protocol on toilet slippers, see page 165.

Banking and Local Currency

For visitors used to easy and instant access to cash 24 hours a day in their home country, Japan's banking system can prove frustrating. Japan is largely a cash economy – personal checks are unknown – and cash is still the most popular way to pay for almost everything. After the economic "bubble" burst in late 1989, various scandals resulted in the closure of several banks and financial institutions. A comprehensive restructuring was undertaken and the economy is now recovering.

ATM with signs indicating that it accepts some foreign cards

BANKS AND BANKING HOURS

The nation's central bank, the Bank of Japan (Nippon Ginko), issues newly minted yen currency; it is also the banks of banks and the government bank. However, this and the local city banks are not geared to visitors. Buying yen, exchanging travelers' checks, and any other regular banking transactions may be more easily conducted via major Japanese banks that are authorized money exchangers, such as **Tokyo-Mitsubishi UFJ**, **Sumitomo Mitsui**, **Mizuho Bank**, and **Citibank**. Some foreign banks also offer useful services.

Most banks open 9am to 3pm on weekdays, and are closed on weekends and national holidays. The exchange rate is posted at about 10am for US dollars, and after that for other currencies. Banks usually exchange currency between 10am and 3pm; some city banks offer exchange facilities from 9am.

Logo of Mizuho Bank

TRAVELERS' CHECKS

Although travelers' checks provide a convenient way to carry money around Japan, they are usually accepted only in major city banks and large hotels. Travelex, American Express, and VISA checks are the most widely recognized. It is advisable to bring cash as well as checks, especially if you are traveling away from main tourist centers.

CREDIT AND DEBIT CARDS

International credit cards such as American Express, MasterCard, VISA, and Diners Club are generally accepted by leading banks, hotels, and stores in major cities. There may be a charge to use a credit card. Obtaining cash with credit cards is rarely possible. Even if a machine displays the sticker for your card (e.g. at gas stations and ATMs), there may be a problem reading it. Some places only accept Japanese-issued cards such as JCB.

CHANGING MONEY

It is possible to change cash and travelers' checks at banks, major hotels (which offer the same exchange rates as banks), *ryokan*, main post offices, and some department stores in cities. Banks and post offices may also offer money transfer facilities. Even leading city banks may be unfamiliar with foreign currency apart from dollars, so be prepared for bank tellers to check with their superiors if they have not experienced such notes before. In city centers, staff may speak English, and forms are often supplied in English – if not, staff will indicate to a customer where to write. Transactions are relatively simple, but usually time-consuming. Always carry your passport as your identity will be checked.

At major airports handling international flights, currency exchange counters may be

DIRECTORY

open for longer than regular banking hours; at Tokyo International Airport at Narita, for example, the counter is open from 6:30am to 11pm. It is illegal for public transportation, stores, and restaurants to accept payment in foreign currencies, so a small amount of Japanese yen will be required on arrival to cover immediate needs. It is always wise to obtain cash before traveling in the countryside.

ATM SERVICES

Automatic Teller Machines are commonly available in large urban areas throughout Japan, although many do not accept foreign credit cards or cash cards. Post office ATMs are more likely to accept foreign cards; stickers on display inside indicate which cards are accepted. Many convenience stores and supermarkets now have ATMs that stay open all night. Contact your bank or credit card company beforehand for locations of suitable ATMs.

CURRENCY

The Japanese currency is the yen, indicated by the symbol ¥. Coins are minted in denominations of ¥1, ¥5, ¥10, ¥50, ¥100, and ¥500. Bank notes are printed in denominations of ¥1,000, ¥2,000 (introduced in mid-2000), ¥5,000, and ¥10,000. Unused Japanese bank notes (but not coins) can be reconverted to foreign currency at the point of departure; the amount is limited only by the funds carried by the airport exchange center.

JTB COUPONS

Japan Travel Bureau, a travel agency with branches in North America, Europe, Asia, and Australia, sells hundreds of different kinds of coupons that can be exchanged by visitors for services (such as travel, car rental, and accommodations) inside Japan. These can be a convenient means of paying, but work best when combined with a JTB-planned itinerary. Contact a nearby JTB office for further details.

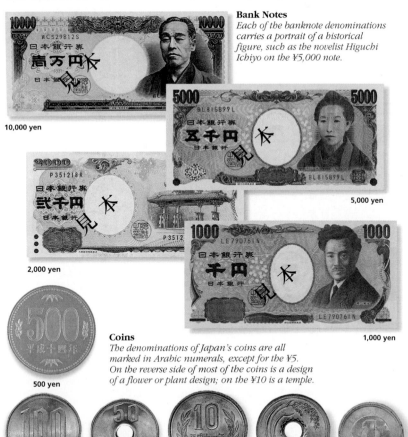

Bank Notes
Each of the banknote denominations carries a portrait of a historical figure, such as the novelist Higuchi Ichiyo on the ¥5,000 note.

10,000 yen

5,000 yen

2,000 yen

1,000 yen

Coins
The denominations of Japan's coins are all marked in Arabic numerals, except for the ¥5. On the reverse side of most of the coins is a design of a flower or plant design; on the ¥10 is a temple.

500 yen

100 yen

50 yen

10 yen

5 yen

1 yen

Communications

Phonecard dispenser

Tokyo has embraced the digital age with enthusiasm, and the range of communication tools available is extensive and state-of-the-art. It is, however, far from being the wired, computer-geek capital it is sometimes portrayed as. Just about everyone has mobile phones, but Internet cafés and wifi hotspots are still surprisingly rare. English-language newspapers and magazines are readily available, the postal system is fast and efficient, and public phones are easy to find, though not all suitable for making international calls.

Three of the popular English-language dailies

NEWSPAPERS AND MAGAZINES

Three English-language newspapers are printed in Tokyo – *The Japan Times, The Daily Yomiuri,* and the *International Herald Tribune-Asahi Shimbun.* All are sold at kiosks in train stations, major hotels, and foreign-language bookstores.

There are several English-language magazines easily available, many of them free, with extensive listings and classified advertisements. These include *Metropolis* and *Tokyo Journal.* Imported magazines can be found at foreign-language bookstores.

English, *Japanzine* magazines

TELEVISION AND RADIO

The state public broadcaster, NHK, has two terrestrial and three satellite TV channels. Its 7pm and 9pm news bulletins (7pm on weekends) can be heard in English on bilingual TVs, which are often found in

hotels. Other nationwide networks include Nihon TV, TBS, Fuji TV, and TV Asahi. Overseas networks are also widely available via cable or satellite. NHK Radio airs news and classical music, on both AM and FM. There are several commercial radio stations in Tokyo; J-WAVE and Inter FM offer some programs in English. Check up-to-date listings pages for frequencies and for times of programs.

TYPES OF TELEPHONES

The almost total saturation of mobile phones in Tokyo has led to fewer public phones, but they are readily found in train stations (and even inside trains), outside convenience stores, and on street corners. Green-colored public phones accept ¥10, ¥50, ¥100, and ¥500 coins, plus telephone cards. These phones are for domestic calls only. Gray public phones have an LCD display, a button for converting information into English, volume control (handy in noisy places), and an emergency button for dialing police, fire, and ambulance *(see pp166–7)*. These phones are the most likely to offer international direct-dialing. They also have digital jacks for data transmission. The old-styled pink phones, sometimes found in restaurants, are for local calls and accept ¥10 coins only.

TELECOM COMPANIES AND PHONE CARDS

Calls from public phones are automatically connected via **NTT Communications** unless you use readily available phone cards issued by other operators such as **Softbank Telecom** or **KDDI**.

A red call box with a gray phone, suitable for international calls

MAKING INTERNATIONAL CALLS

Some public phones accept international credit cards as well as phone cards. As with domestic calls, the call will be routed via **NTT** unless you purchase a phone card issued by one of the other major telecom companies offering international calls. Dial the appropriate company's access code *(see directory)*, then the country code, area code (minus any initial zero), then the number. The major telecom companies are in competition, so charges and services are constantly changing; each has a toll-free number for information.

All major hotels in Tokyo offer international direct-dialing. But remember, you may be surcharged for calls from your room. **KDDI** and **NTT** offer international collect calls; dial the appropriate access code and then ask the operator to place a collect call. The cheapest times for making international calls are from 11pm to 8am daily; the next-cheapest are between 7pm and 11pm.

Gray public phone, the most widespread type

LOCAL CALLS

The charge for a local call is ¥10 per minute. Use small coins or phone cards in a public phone; unused coins will be returned to you. In this guide area codes are given in brackets; omit the code if calling from inside the area.

MOBILE PHONES

Some foreign mobile phones may be used in Japan via Japanese operators such as **Softbank Telecom** and **DoCoMo**. Check with your mobile operator before traveling. If you are staying for a while, mobiles are cheap to buy and there is a huge choice. For shorter stays, it is possible to rent mobiles from all the big providers through their service desks at Narita and Haneda airports.

FAX, E-MAIL, AND INTERNET FACILITIES

Fax machines for public use are located at a number of convenience stores and at most of the main post offices, as well as in hotels and stores such as Kinko's.

Internet cafés are not as plentiful as might be expected but access to the Internet is slowly on the rise. Kinko's provides Internet access at its branches throughout the city. Some computer stores, including Apple, provide free Internet access. For a list of hotspots, check *www.hotspot-locations.com.*

MAIL

Post offices (*yubin-kyoku*) and mailboxes in Tokyo can easily be identified by the character looking like the letter "T" with an extra horizontal bar across the top. Main post offices are usually open 9am–5pm on weekdays and (9am–12:30pm on Saturdays). Smaller post offices may open 9am–5pm on weekdays but are often closed on weekends. Stamps are also sold at some convenience stores and larger hotels.

International mail is best sent from a main post office. Express mail service is a speedy way to send top priority mail. For urgent mail, **Tokyo Central Post** and **Tokyo International Post Office** both have all-night counters.

Some mailboxes have two slots; the one on the left is for domestic letters, and the one on the right is for other mail, including international express mail.

COURIERS AND OTHER MAIL SERVICES

Several door-to-door delivery services (*takkyubin*) offer prompt and efficient services throughout Japan, including **Yamato** and **Sagawa-Kyubin**. Small packages can be sent via these courier services from convenience stores. International courier services include FedEx, DHL, and Nippon Courier Services.

Japanese mailbox

FINDING AN ADDRESS

Only the main thoroughfares in Tokyo have street names, and there is no consistent numbering system in place for buildings. In an address, the first number of, for example, 2-3-4 Otemachi refers to the *chome*, or main block. The second number points to a smaller block of buildings within the original *chome*. The last is the number of the building itself. Local police boxes are used in large part to help people reach their destinations.

DIRECTORY

TELECOM COMPANIES, PHONE CARDS, AND ACCESS CODES

KDDI
Tel 001 (access code).
Tel 0057 (toll-free information).
KDDI Super World Card.

NTT Communications
Tel 0033 (access code).
Tel 0120 54-0033 then dial 8 # (toll-free information).
World Prepaid Card.

Softbank Telecom
Tel 0061 (access code).
Tel 0066-11 (toll-free information).
Love Love Homecard.

Softbank Telecom
Tel 0041 (access code).
Tel 0088-41 (toll-free information).
Super Moshi Moshi Card.

OTHER USEFUL NUMBERS

Domestic Directory Enquiries
Tel 104.

Domestic Operator
Tel 100.

International Directory Enquiries
Tel 0051.

INTERNATIONAL DIALING CODES

Use these codes after the international access codes to dial the following countries:
Australia **61**, Brazil **55**, Canada **1**, China **86**, France **33**, Germany **49**, Hong Kong **852**, India **91**, Indonesia **62**, Ireland **353**, Israel **972**, Republic of Korea **82**, Malaysia **60**, Netherlands **31**, New Zealand **64**, Peru **51**, Philippines **63**, Russia **7**, Singapore **65**, Spain **34**, Sweden **46**, Switzerland **41**, Taiwan **886**, Thailand **66**, United Kingdom **44**, and US **1**.

TRAVEL INFORMATION

Tokyo is served by flights from across the world, virtually all of them arriving at Narita Airport. Although Narita is a long way from the city center, this gives visitors their first introduction to the prompt and highly efficient public transportation system that makes traveling so easy in Tokyo and the rest of the country. Tokyo can be used as the hub for travel to other parts of the country, either by air from Haneda

Logo of Japan Airlines

Airport or by *shinkansen* bullet train *(see p178)*. There are direct bus and train connections from Narita to Haneda. The Japan National Tourist Organization (JNTO) website *(see p163)* provides useful travel information for visitors, including lists of travel agents that can make reservations and sell travel tickets and Rail Pass vouchers *(p174–5)*. In Tokyo, the JNTO has a Tourist Information Center, which provides travel information in English.

Japan Airlines (JAL) airplane

ARRIVING BY AIR

All major international airlines fly to Tokyo. Virtually all flights land at Narita Airport, formally known as Tokyo New International Airport. Tokyo's other airport, Haneda (also referred to confusingly as Tokyo International Airport) is served by a few flights from Taiwan, as well as being the major hub for domestic flights. The two airports are linked together by an efficient network of train, bus, and helicopter services. **Japan Airlines (JAL)** and **All Nippon Airways (ANA)** are the main airlines of Japan. JAL is particularly popular with foreign travelers.

GETTING TO AND FROM NARITA AIRPORT

Tokyo's Narita Airport has two terminals connected by a free shuttle bus, which takes about 10 minutes. Narita Tourist Information Offices are located in the arrival lobby of each terminal, and have a multi-lingual staff.

Visitors who have bought a Japan Rail Pass Exchange Order *(see p179)* before arriving in Tokyo should visit the Japan Railways (JR) ticket counter. If validated from the day of arrival in Tokyo, the pass can be used to make the trip from the airport into central Tokyo by JR train. Narita Airport is located 35 miles (60 km) northeast of the center of Tokyo, thus the journey by taxi will cost at least ¥22,000. Airport Limousine Buses cover an extensive network of destinations with frequent non-stop services to Tokyo, Yokohama, and other nearby cities, with drop-offs at most major hotels.

The **Narita Express (N'EX)** train, located beneath the terminal buildings, travels non-stop and in some luxury to Tokyo station in less than one hour, and then on to Shinjuku and Ikebukuro in the capital,

or to Yokohama and Ofuna, near Kamakura. The Japan Rail Pass can be used on this train, but you will need to reserve a seat (free of charge) at the ticket booth. All signs and announcements for the N'EX are in Japanese and English, and English-language information is available via an onboard telephone service. Remember to reserve a seat when returning to the airport on the N'EX.

Travelers without a JR Pass will find Keisei trains cheaper than the N'EX and almost as fast. The Keisei line connnects with JR at Nippori, with an easy transfer. Board the Keisei Skyliner at Keisei Narita airport station (also below the terminal buildings); it terminates at Keisei Ueno station, within walking distance of JR Ueno train station and Ueno subway station.

Local Keisei trains are the cheapest but slowest form of transportation to the city from the airport.

Terminal 2 of Tokyo New International Airport, at Narita

Entrance to Terminal 2, Haneda Airport

GETTING TO AND FROM HANEDA AIRPORT

Operational since 1931, Haneda Airport lies just to the south of central Tokyo. Serving more than 60 million passengers every year, it is amongst the world's five busiest airports. It has three terminals – two for domestic flights, and one for a limited number of international flights. These are connected by a free shuttle bus service.

Taxis can be picked up outside the terminals – fares into the city will be at least ¥5,000. Limousine Buses run to destinations in central Tokyo (including major hotels), for about ¥1,000. By train, the Keikyu private line connects with the JR network at Shinagawa (in as little as 11 minutes; ¥400) from a station underneath the airport. The Tokyo Monorail, built in time for the 1964 Tokyo Olympics, links the airport with Hamamatsucho station, also on the JR Yamanote line (20 minutes; ¥470). It is cramped and crowded in rush hour, but it gives a fascinating view over the Tokyo dockland.

LUGGAGE DELIVERY

Luggage can be delivered from airports to either a hotel or a private address the following day, and it can be picked up for the return trip. A number of companies offering this service operate counters at Narita and Haneda airports. It costs about ¥2000 for one bag weighing no more than 70 lb (32 kg).

DOMESTIC FLIGHTS

The airlines JAL and ANA maintain an extensive network of flights covering the four main islands and many of the smaller ones, too. For trips up to 350 miles (600 km), bullet trains *(see p178)* are often faster and more convenient than planes. On domestic flights JAL and ANA offer economy seats and, at an extra cost, a "Super Seat" service, which is a combination of first and business class. The domestic "no-frills," low-cost airline **Skymark** operates flights between Haneda Airport (Tokyo), Fukuoka, Tokushima, and Kagoshima.

Luxurious red and silver Narita Express, connecting several stations

DEPARTURE

Since it takes 60–90 minutes to reach Narita Airport from central Tokyo, it is best to set out approximately 4 hours before the departure time of your flight. If traveling by the Narita Express, seats should be reserved well ahead of time. However, standing is allowed, if you hold a valid ticket. All trains stop at Terminal 2 and then terminate at Terminal 1. The departure lobbies of both terminals are on the 4th floor. If arriving by train with luggage, it is easier to take the elevator rather than trying to negotiate the many escalators. Many flights from Terminal 2 are boarded at the satellite terminal, reached via a driverless shuttle train. Other flights require shuttle bus connections.

Narita Airport is exceptionally busy during the New Year holiday travel rush. Around this time, buses and trains are booked well in advance, and the crowds ensure that there are long waits at security checks and passport control.

DIRECTORY

TOURIST INFORMATION

Tokyo office (TIC)
10F Tokyo Kotsu Kaikan Bldg,
Yurakucho, Chiyoda-ku
Tel (03) 3201-3331.

Narita Airport offices
Arrivals floor, Terminal 1.
Tel (0476) 30-3383.
Terminal 2. *Tel (0476) 34-6251.*

Kansai Airport office
Arrivals floor. *Tel (072) 455-2500.*

AIRPORT INFORMATION

Narita Airport
www.narita-airport.jp

Kansai Airport
www.kansai-airport.or.jp

AIRLINES

Japan Airlines (JAL)

In Japan:
Tel 0120-25-5931 (toll-free) for international reservations.
Tel 0120-25-5971 (toll-free) for domestic reservations.
www.jal.co.jp

In USA and Canada:
Tel 1-800 525 3663.
www.ar.jal.com/en/

In UK:
Tel (0845) 7-747-700.
www.uk.jal.com

All Nippon Airways (ANA)
Tel 0120-029-222 (toll-free).
www.ana.co.jp

Skymark
Tel (03) 3433-7670 (Tokyo).

Using the Subway

Given the traffic that invariably clogs the streets of central Tokyo, there is only one practical way to get around the city – by the subway. For the most part, this is a pleasure not a penance, since the entire system is clean, efficient, and punctual. The Tokyo Metro line and the Toei subway line are both safe and surprisingly easy to negotiate, with color-coded train lines and maps, directional arrows, and bilingual sign posts. Trains run daily from around the early hours of the morning to just after midnight, every five minutes during peak daytime hours. There is only one cardinal rule to remember – avoid the rush hour if at all possible.

Swanky and comfortable interior of a metro car

Uniformed subway staff assisting train commuters

ROUTES, FARES, AND TICKETS

Besides being color-coded, each subway line has been designated a letter (G for the Ginza Line), and each station assigned a number. Hence, Shibuya, the western terminal of the Ginza Line is G-01 (on the Hanzomon Line it is Z-01) (see Back Endpaper). Metro maps in English are available at all major train and metro stations, tourist hotels, and the TIC (see p173). An online route planner is also available on the **Jorudan** website.

Directions to various platforms are indicated with appropriate color codes and sometimes the distance given in meters. All platforms have prominent signboards in both Japanese and English giving the name of the station, as well as those on either side. These help a commuter to confirm which direction they should follow. Inside many trains, there are bilingual indicators above the doors indicating the name of the next station. Some important

announcements are also made in English to assist foreign travelers in orientation.

Tickets are dispensed from automatic vending machines, usually located next to the entrance gates at each station. Most accept banknotes, although some accept coins only. Change will be dispensed with the ticket. Newer subway ticket vending machines (with electronic touch screens) also have instructions in English.

To reach the platforms, feed the ticket into the slot in the automatic ticket gate. Retrieve your ticket and keep it with you until you reach your final destination, as you will need it to get out.

Fares are charged according to distance, starting at ¥160 (¥170 on **Toei** lines), with children between 6–11 years charged half-fares. At some

Metro ticket machine

stations, route maps are provided in English translation, showing in which fare zone your destination lies (the current station is indicated with a red dot). If you are unsure or cannot work out the exact fare to your destination, just purchase the cheapest ticket available, and then pay any excess when you arrive at your station. There are "Fare Adjustment" machines by the exit gates that dispense and adjust tickets and provide you with change.

Unlimited-use one-day tickets can be bought from some ticket machines. There are two types – ¥710 for Tokyo Metro lines; or ¥1,000 for all lines, including the Toei subway line. However, these will only be economical if you intend to make five or more separate journeys in a day. There is also a **Tokyo**

Metro platform with prominent signs displaying station names

Free Pass (¥1,580) that allows
use of Japan Railways (JR)
trains and city buses (*see
p176*), as well as all metro
lines throughout the wards of
central Tokyo. Tourist discount one-day (¥600) and
two-day (¥980) Tokyo Metro
tickets can be bought at the
Narita Airport terminals and
the railroad ticket counters.

Strips of yellow tiles on the floor marking the routes to the ticket barriers

PASSNET AND PASMO CARDS

Prepaid cards can be bought
from ticket machines in most
stations in the city of Tokyo.
Known as **Passnet** cards, they
are issued in denominations
of ¥1,000, ¥3,000, and ¥5,000.
Designs range from utilitarian
to gorgeous enough to keep
as a souvenir. The most
colorful cards, often
commemorative or advertising
art exhibitions,
have to be bought
from ticket offices.
Similar in size to a
credit card, they
must be fed into
the ticket slots in
the automatic gates
as you enter and
exit. These cards can be used
on any metro line, and also
on all private railroads in the
Tokyo region. A new smart
card system known as **Pasmo**
has been introduced, similar

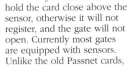

JR East train card,
usable on the subway

to the Suica smart cards
currently used on the JR East
network (*see p179*). Once you
have bought these smart
cards (¥500, refundable), you
can charge them in denominations of ¥1,000, ¥3,000,
¥5,000, and
¥10,000. As you
enter a station, sen-
sors in the gates
deduct the mini-
mum fare (¥160);
the balance (if any)
is deducted on exit.
Just remember to
hold the card close above the
sensor, otherwise it will not
register, and the gate will not
open. Currently most gates
are equipped with sensors.
Unlike the old Passnet cards,

the Pasmo smart cards are
interoperable with the JR
Suica system. This allows you
to use the same card for all
subway, private railroad, and
JR lines, as well as some bus
networks. The demand for
Pasmo cards has grown so
rapidly that some of its utilities
have had to be restricted.

Subway turnstile at entry and exit
points at the train stations

COMMUTER CULTURE

Commuters packed into trains are a common sight morning
and evening at Tokyo's major train stations. High urban
land prices force families to look farther out of the city for
affordable housing. A commute of at least an hour each way
is practically the standard. By far the majority of commuters
are men, as they are still the prime earners in most families.
The commute effectively removes them from family life –
they leave before children get up, come back after they are
in bed, and collapse on weekends with fatigue. The other
major group on the trains is unmarried young women (after
marriage women are generally expected to stay home and
raise the children).
An industry has
grown up around
these commuters:
dozens of maga-
zines are produced
for killing time,
and stand-up
restaurants offer
cheap meals to
those with a long
ride ahead.

Crowding onto a commuter train

DIRECTORY

ROUTES, FARES, AND TICKETS

Jorudan
www.jorudan.co.jp/english/

Toei
www.kotsu.metro.tokyo.jp/
english/

Tokyo Metro
www.tokyometro.jp/e/

PASSNET AND PASMO CARDS

Pasmo Cards
www.pasmo.co.jp/en/

Passnet Cards
www.tokyometro.jp/e/card/

Using Public Transport

Equipped to handle a daytime population swelling to well over 10 million every weekday, Tokyo's public transport system has evolved a remarkable diversity. Besides using the efficient subway, visitors can explore the city by bus, "overground" train (notably the Japan Railways Yamanote loop line), tram, monorail, boat, taxi or even rickshaw. Lack of signs in English can make commuting by bus a bit challenging. However, for areas not connected by the subway or train line, buses are a good option. Taxis can be easily hired for short trips within the city. Maps and other details are available at the Tourist Information Center (*see p173*).

Visitors on a city tour of Tokyo in an open-topped sightseeing bus

RAILROAD NETWORK

The **Japan Railways' (JR) Yamanote Line** (*see p178*) forms a loop encircling and defining most of central Tokyo. Many of its stations act as hubs, connecting with long-distance JR lines, suburban private railroads, and the city's subway stations.

Three other JR lines run through the city. The Sobu Line (yellow) cuts east-west across the center of the loop, from Shinjuku to Akihabara and then farther eastward. Running next to it is the express Chuo Line (orange), linking Tokyo JR station with Shinjuku and the western suburbs. The Keihin Tohoku line (turquoise) runs north-south along the eastern side of the Yamanote loop.

A convenient alternative to the subway system, these JR lines offer fascinating above-ground glimpses of the metropolis and its suburbs. The Chuo Line between Ochanomizu and Shinjuku is particularly scenic, as it runs along the old city moat.

For more on JR trains beyond Tokyo read the "Traveling by Train" section on page 178. The **East Japan Railway Company** is also an option.

BUSES

Several local bus companies, including **Keio**, **Toei**, and **Tokyu**, operate in Tokyo connecting just about every corner of the city. However they can get quite crowded during city rush hour and, unlike the subway, there are fewer signs or maps in English.

Buses in central Tokyo are all driver-operated and have a flat-fare system. You pay as you enter by the door, placing your fare into a collecting box by the driver. Prepaid bus cards can also be bought, which are valid for all operators in the Tokyo region. These are available from the bus driver as well as from offices around Tokyo.

MONORAIL

The **Tokyo Monorail** opened in 1964, to carry visitors to the Olympics into the city from Haneda Airport.

In Tokyo, the monorail skims above a post-industrial dockland landscape, terminating at Hamamatsucho Station (on the JR Yamanote Line). The journey takes 20 minutes and costs ¥470.

Much of the fun of visiting the Odaiba waterfront development area is getting there on the **Yurikamome Line**, which gives spectacular views. A one-day Open Pass allowing unlimited travel on the line costs ¥800. A combined ticket with the Water Bus costs ¥900.

WATER BUS

Ferry trips make an interesting alternative for getting around Tokyo. The most popular route is the Sumida River water bus (in Japanese, *suijo* bus) between Asakusa and the Hama Detached Palace Garden, operated by the **Tokyo Cruise Ship Company**. Others ply to various points along the waterfront, including Odaiba.

"Himiko" water bus speeding across Sumida River alongside skyscrapers

All services depart from the Hinode Pier, close to Hinode station on the Yurikamome monorail line, and a 10-minute walk from Hamamatsucho JR Station (Yamanote Line). The Asakusa ferry can also be picked up at the Hama Palace Garden (only during the garden's opening hours). Boats run approximately every half hour and the fare is ¥620.

A ride on the old-fashioned rikshaw service

TRAMS

Tokyo's last remaining tramline or Toden, the **Arakawa Line** (*see p73*), serves few neighborhoods on the tourist trail. It trundles at a relaxing pace along a circuitous route through the backstreets of the less-visited parts of Tokyo. The stations at either end have subway connections. It can also be boarded at Otsuka, where it crosses the JR Yamanote loop. You pay a ¥160 flat-fare.

The still operational Toden Arakawa line

CAR RENTAL

Tokyo's roads are narrow and crowded, with few signs in English, so renting a car in Tokyo is not recommended for short-term visitors. Those wishing to explore the Japanese hinterland are advised to head out of town by train, and then rent cars in provincial cities. The **Japan Automobile Federation** (JAF) provides useful details about authorized car rental companies such as **Nippon Rent-a-Car**, **Toyota Rent-a-Car**, or **Nissan Rent-a-Car**.

RICKSHAWS

The rickshaw (*jin-riki-sha*) has made a remarkable comeback to the streets of Tokyo – but only as a convenient vehicle for sightseeing. In Asakusa, look for the rickshaw men in their *happi* coats and shorts in front of the Kaminarimon gate. Although they will pull two slender Japanese people at a time, bigger-built foreigners may be asked to ride solo. This can be expensive and costs up to ¥10,000 per hour per person.

TAXIS

Taxis are numerous and convenient for shorter journeys. Most fares start at ¥660, and the meter rises fast. A trip across town can run to ¥2-5,000, especially if you get stuck in traffic. Tipping is required or expected.

Taxis can be hailed on almost every street corner, and are easily found at major hotels and railroad stations. A red light is visible in the front window if it is available. Few taxi drivers speak English, so it helps to have your destination written in Japanese. Large luggage is usually carried on the front seat.

One of Tokyo's taxis; the door is remote-controlled by the driver

DIRECTORY

JAPAN RAILWAYS

East Japan Railway Company (JR East)
www.jreast.co.jp/e/

Japan Railways
www.japanrail.com

BUSES

Keio Bus
www.keio–bus.com

Limousine Buses
www.limousinebus.co.jp/e/

Toei Bus
www.kotsu.metro.tokyo.jp/
english/bus_op.html

Tokyu Bus
www.tokyubus.co.jp

WATER BUS

Tokyo Cruise Ship Company
www.suijobus.co.jp/english

MONORAIL

Tokyo Monorail
www.tokyo-monorail.co.jp/
english

Yurikamome Line
www.yurikamome.co.jp/english/
index.php

TRAMS

Arakawa Line
www.kotsu.metro.tokyo.jp/
english/toden_op.html

CAR RENTAL

Japan Automobile Federation
www.jaf.or.jp/e/index.htm

Nippon Rent-a-Car
Tel 0800-500-0919 (Toll Free).
(03) 3485-7196.
www.japaren.co.jp/

Nissan Rent-a-Car
Tel Freedial: 0120-00-4123.
http://nissan-rentacar.com

Toyota Rent-a-Car
Tel 0070-8000-10000 (Toll Free),
(03) 5954-8008.
http://rent.toyota.co.jp

Traveling by Train

With roads often clogged with traffic, trains are the best way of exploring Tokyo and the surrounding area. Japan's rail system leads the world in terms of safety, efficiency, and comfort. The city and surrounding area are served by numerous lines. Besides the Japan Railways (JR) trains, there are also many private railroads serving suburban areas. For many destinations, such as Nikko, travelers have a choice of lines. Generally, fares on private lines are cheaper than on JR trains. In rural areas, the names of stations may not be in English, but railroad staff and co-passengers are helpful.

Ticket office and advance reservation center at a JR train station

THE RAILROAD NETWORK

The Japan Railways Group, known as **JR**, is the main operator. It includes all the *shinkansen* super expresses (bullet trains) and a nationwide network of over 13,000 miles (21,000 km) of tracks. There are also many private railroads linking smaller communities in more remote regions. Often travelers have a choice of lines to the same destination.

THE SHINKANSEN: BULLET TRAIN

The first "bullet train," as it was quickly nicknamed by a marveling media worldwide, drew out of Tokyo Station in 1964, the year of the Tokyo Olympics. Symbolic of Japan's economic recovery and future drive, it became, and remains, a source of national pride.

They are no longer the world's fastest trains, and there are still only a few *shinkansen* lines linking the major cities, but their efficiency, as proved by the long-distance journeys timed

to the minute, is legendary. There are five *shinkansen* lines serving Tokyo. The **Tokaido** Line runs south to Nagoya, Kyoto, and Osaka (continuing as the Sanyo Line to Hiroshima and Fukuoka). The **Joetsu** Line serves Niigata and there are also lines to Nagano and Yamagata. All *shinkansen* services start from Tokyo Station. Many Tokaido line trains can be boarded at Shinagawa. Trains on the Tohoku, Joetsu, Nagano, and Yamagata *shinkansen* lines

Aerodynamic nose of the fabled *shinkansen*, or "bullet train"

also stop briefly at Ueno. Announcements in English and clear signs make the *shinkansen* super express an appealing form of transportation, more convenient than flying, though there is little space for large suitcases.

It is advisable to reserve a seat, especially during a holiday period, as the non-reserved carriages can get very crowded.

OTHER TRAINS AND LINES

Many of the sites around Tokyo are also served by private train lines, which tend to be cheaper than JR. These lines also operate express trains, some of which try to rival the *shinkansen* for luxury.

The Odakyu line (from Shinjuku) runs its Romance Car trains to the Hakone hills; it also has services to Enoshima, on the Shonan coast close to Kamakura. Tobu operates the fastest and most economical route to Nikko (from Asakusa). Tokyu trains (from Shibuya) are a good alternative if you are going to Yokohama's port area or Chinatown. Other lines include Seibu (various destinations, including the Chichibu Hills); Keisei (to Chiba and Narita); and Keikyu (Yokohama and Yokosuka).

STATION SIGNS AND FACILITIES

Tokyo's Shinjuku station (*see p63*) is the world's busiest, and several others – including Tokyo JR station – are vast warrens built on several levels. Finding a particular line or exit during rush hour can be intimidating for newcomers with heavy baggage. It is a good idea to find out which named or numbered exit is best for you before arriving at one of the major stations.

Shinkansen lines are clearly marked, and signs for other lines are color-coded. The yellow bobbles on the floor are intended to help blind people navigate but can be a problem for suitcases with wheels. Escalators are readily available for commuters.

The elegant Romance Car train halting at a station, Odakyu line

Note that trains, especially the *shinkansen*, stop only briefly in order to maintain their timetables. Thus, travelers are encouraged to line up on some platforms. Look out for floor markings relating to each set of doors. There may also be numbers correlating to carriage numbers for trains with reserved seats.

Stations in major tourist areas have baggage lockers and information booths, where staff may speak English.

ON-BOARD FACILITIES

Services on *shinkansen* and other long-distance routes usually include trolleys for snacks and beverages, and the sale of *bento* lunchboxes and edible *omiyage* (souvenirs). There is often a choice of Western- (sit-down) and Japanese-style (squat) toilets. Toilets and washrooms may be electronically operated, requiring a hand to be passed in front of a panel for flushing, or under a tap to start water flowing.

THE JAPAN RAIL PASS

In a country with some of the world's highest train fares, the Japan Rail Pass is a wonderful deal specially devised for people visiting Japan on tourist visas. However, the Pass must be purchased from an agent abroad, before the visit. It is not for sale inside Japan itself.

The Pass gives unlimited travel on all JR lines and affiliated buses and ferries,

The Japan Rail Pass

including the N'EX train *(see p172)* from Narita into Tokyo, city-center JR trains including Tokyo's Yamanote loop line, and *shinkansen*, except Nozomi. (If you board a Nozomi, you will be asked to pay for the entire fare). Subways and private railroads are not included. You may still have to reserve a seat on long-distance trains, but the reservation will be free.

You can choose a 7-day, 14-day, or 21-day Pass, first or standard class. If you intend to travel any greater distance than a return train trip from, say, Tokyo to Kyoto for example, the Pass will save money. Showing it to railroad staff at station ticket barriers also saves the hassle of purchasing tickets and negotiating turnstiles with luggage. If you want to explore Japan by train for more than 21 days, or prefer to break up your travels by staying in one place for more than a few days, then consider buying more than one Pass.

Staffed exit lane for holders of the Japan Rail Pass

JNTO offices *(see p163)* will have a full list of Rail Pass agents in your country. The agent will issue a **Japan Rail Pass Exchange Order**, usually at a price based on the day's rate of exchange with the yen. This voucher must be exchanged for the Japan Rail Pass proper at designated JR Travel Service Centers in Japan, including Narita airport and major train stations. When you get your Pass, you must specify the date which you wish to start using it; the date has to be within three months of the issue of the Exchange Order. After the start date of the Pass, its cost cannot be refunded, neither can the Exchange Order or Pass be replaced if lost or stolen.

OTHER PASSES

There are also other less expensive regional rail passes. The **JR East Rail Pass** covers Honshu northeast of Tokyo. **Tobu Railway** issues 2-day and 4-day passes for Nikko. **Odakyu** offers various passes to Kamakura and the Hakone area. **Seibu** also issues passes for Chichubu and Kawagoe. The **Tokyo Free Kippu** covers most of the subway, bus, and tram lines in central Tokyo.

DIRECTORY

JR Infoline
(English-language service)
Tel (050) 2016-1603, 10am–6pm daily.

JR East: www.jreast.co.jp/e/index.html

JR East Rail Pass: www.jreast.co.jp/e/eastpass/index.html

Tobu Railway
Tel *(03) 3841-2871.*
www.tobuland.com/foreign/english/index.html

Odakyu Railway
Tel *(03) 5321-7887.*

Seibu Railway
www.seibu-group.co.jp/railways/tourist/english/index.html

Keisei Line
www.keisei.co.jp/keisei/tetudou/keisei_us/html/o_express.html

TOKYO STREET FINDER

Tokyo is notoriously hard for visitors to find their way around, due to the scarcity of street names and the complex numbering system for buildings. The Tokyo sights covered in this guide, plus Tokyo hotels (*see pp110–17*), restaurants (*see pp132–41*), and many of the city's key landmarks are plotted on the maps on the following pages. Transportation points are also marked, and indicated by the symbols listed in the key below. When map references are given the first number tells you which Street Finder map to turn to, and the letter and number that follow refer to the grid reference. The map below shows the area of Tokyo covered by the six Street Finder maps. The Street Finder index opposite lists street names, buildings, and stations. For a map of the Tokyo subway system, see the inside back cover.

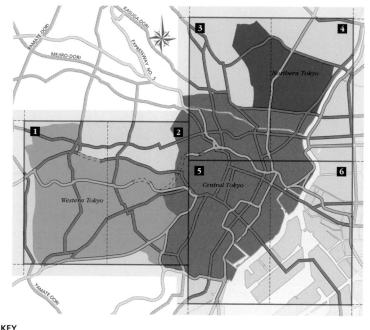

KEY

▪ Major sight	🚓 Police station	0 kilometers 2
▪ Other sight	卍 Temple	0 miles 1
▪ Other building	⛩ Shrine	
S Subway station	✝ Church	
R Train station	✉ Post office	
🚌 Long-distance bus station	JR Rail line	**SCALE OF MAPS 1–6**
🚢 River boat	Other rail line	
i Tourist information	Expressway	0 meters 500
✚ Hospital	Pedestrian street	0 miles 500

Street Finder Index

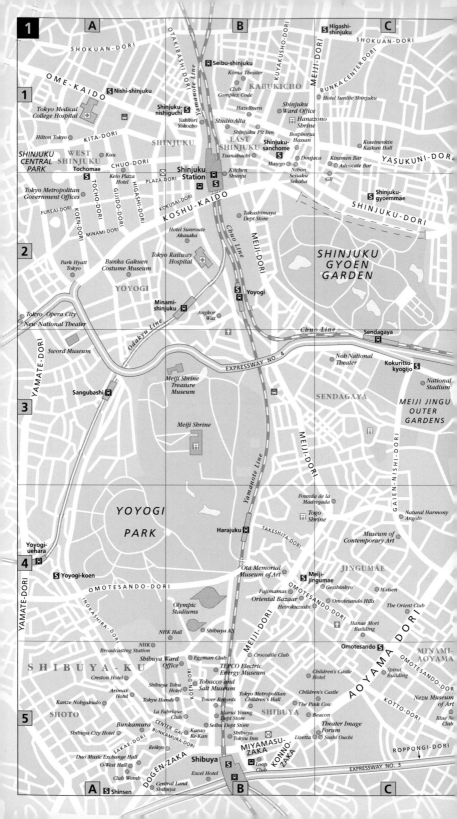

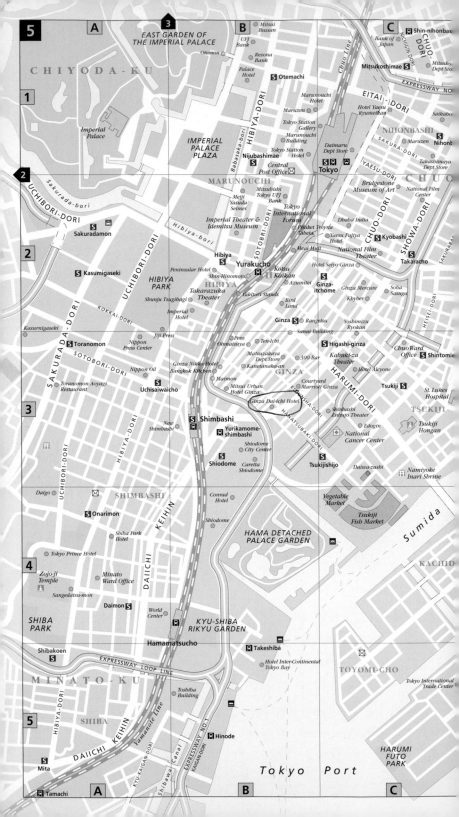

General Index

Acknowledgments

Dorling Kindersley would like to thank the many people whose help and assistance contributed to the preparation of this book.

Main Contributors
Jon Burbank is a travel writer and photographer who lives in Chiba prefecture, to the east of Tokyo, with his family.

Emi Kazuko is a writer and broadcaster who moved to London from Japan in the 1980s. She is the author of several books about the cuisine of her home country.

Stephen Mansfield is a British photojournalist and author based in the Tokyo region. His work has appeared in over 60 magazines, newspapers, and journals worldwide, including *The Geographical*, *South China Morning Post*, *The Traveller*, *Japan Quarterly*, and *Insight Japan*. He is a regular book reviewer for *The Japan Times*. His pieces cover a variety of subjects such as travel, contemporary issues, and cultural and literary themes. His photographs have appeared in several books. He has authored eight books and is currently working on a book on the cultural history of Tokyo. He is also the author of *Japan: Islands of the Floating World*, *Birmanie: Le Temps Suspendu*, and *China: Yunnan Province*.

Robbie Swinnerton moved to Japan in 1980, impelled by his fascination for sake, seaweed, and soba noodles, plus all other aspects of the traditional Japanese diet and culture. For the past 26 years, he has been based in Kamakura, balancing his life by the ocean in the old Japanese capital with writing assignments around Japan and East Asia. While writing extensively on foods of all flavors – his restaurant review column Tokyo Food File has run in the *Japan Times* for over a decade – it is Japanese cuisine in all its intricate simplicity that remains his first and abiding love.

Fact Checker Yumi Shigematsu

Proofreader Gowri Mohanakrishnan

Design and Editorial
Publisher Douglas Amrine
Publishing Manager Jane Ewart
Managing Editor Kathryn Lane
Project Editor Mani Ramaswamy
Project Art Editor Kate Leonard
Senior Cartographic Editor Casper Morris

DTP Designer Natasha Lu
Picture Researcher Ellen Root
Production Controller Shane Higgins

Additional Photography
Stephen Bere, Demetrio Carrasco, Ian O'Leary, Clive Streeter, Linda Whitwam, Peter Wilson.

Additional Illustrations
Gary Cross, John Fox, Nick Gibbard, David Harris, Kevin Jones Associates, Claire Littlejohn, Mel Pickering, John Woodcock.

Special Assistance
Bunka Gakuen Costume Museum; Dolce & Gabbana Showroom, Omotesando; Drum Museum; Goto Art Museum; Isetan Department Store; Isetatsu; Japan Folk Craft Museum; Mikimoto, Ginza; Mitsukoshi, Mitsukoshimae; National Museum of Western Art; National Science Museum, Ueno; Noh National Theater; Shibuya 109; Sony Showroom, Ginza; Tosho-gu Museum of Art

Picture Credits
t=top; tl=top left; tc=top centre; tr=top right; cla=centre left above; ca=centre above; cra=centre right above; cl=centre left; c=centre; cr=centre right; clb=centre left below; cb=centre below; crb=centre right below; bl=bottom left; bc=bottom centre; br=bottom right.

Every effort has been made to trace the copyright holders, and we apologize in advance for any unintentional omissions. We would be pleased to insert the appropriate acknowledgments in any subsequent edition of this publication.

The Publishers are grateful to the following individuals, companies and picture libraries for permission to reproduce their photographs:

ALAMY: Ablestock 148c; allOver photography 95tl; AM Corporation 29cl; Jonah Calinawan 147bc; Chromepix.com 14bc; Corbis Collection 2–3; Alan King Etching 07 9c, 159c; Michele Falzone 46; Frederick Fearn 85b; Jeremy Sutton-Hibbert 125c, 126cl, 168c; Peter Horree 58; Jon Arnold Images 15bl, 28c, 30ca, 41b, 148bl; Look Die Bildagentur der Fotografen GmbH 143bl; Iain Masterton 87tr, 151c; Megapress 19bc; Pacific Press Service 125tl, 130tr; Peter Arnold, Inc. 16c; Photo Japan 16clb, 27crb, 36, 126br; Rollie Rodriguez 4br,

10bc; Eitan Simanor 160cl; Jochen Tack 1c; Tribaleye Images/J Marshall 105c; Chris Willson 127br; Eve Astrid Andersson: 102clb; Axiom Photographic Agency: Steve J Berbow 107bl; Mitchell Coster 18–19c, 18br; Jim Holmes 18tl, 165tl; Paul Quayle 19cr, 19bl.

Dave Bartruff. 17bc, 18tl, 19br; Bridgeman Art Library: British Museum, London, Katsu-shika Hokusai (1760–1849) *Fuji in Clear Weather* from the series *36 Views of Mount Fuji* pub by Nishimura Eijudo in 1831, 25br; Fitzwilliam Museum, University of Cambridge, Katsushika Hokusai (1760–1849) *Block Cutting and Printing Surimono*, 1825 5cl, 55bc; Private Collection Ando or Utagawa Hiroshige (1797–1858) *Mountains and Coastline*, two views from the series *36 Views of Mount Fuji* pub by Kosheihei in 1853, 97crb; Victoria & Albert Museum, London, Utagawa Kuniyoshi (1798–1861) *Mitsukini Defying the Skeleton Spectre* c.1845, 55crb; British Library: Maps Collection Maps 63140 (2) *Map of Yedo Japan*, 1707, 25clb.

Christie's Images Ltd: 21c, 23t, 25tc, 55tc, 55clb; Corbis: 27tl; Asian Art & Archaeology, Inc. 16tr, 55cl; B.S.P.I. 28br; Morton Beebe 128tr; Bettmann 26cb; Burstein Collection 22cr; Christie's Images 8–9; Corbis Sygma/ Annebicque Bernard 164c; Dex Image 155c; Bruno Ehrs 177bl; EPA/Andy Rain 28tc,/Frank Robichon 30clb,/Akio Suga 30bc; Ric Ergenbright 96tr; Eye Ubiquitous/Frank Leather 98bl,/Paul Thompson 86cl; Jon Hicks 70; Historical Picture Archive 97br; Image Plan 87br; Robbie Jack 16crb, Richard T. Nowitz 82bc; Philadelphia Museum of Art 26tl; Photo & Co./Stephane Reix 19cb; Jose Fuste Raga 83tr, 104–5; Ken Straiton 142cr; Liba Taylor 164cla; TWPhoto 152tl; Werner Forman 16bc, 16br, 17tr; Michael S. Yamashita 3c, 17c, 17clb, 17crb, 18cl, 19tc, 96bc, 109cb, 150cl.

Aron Danburg: 93cr. Fast Retailing Co. Ltd 2007: 147tl. Getty Images: AFP/Stringer 27c; Stone/Thierry Cazabon 18clb,/Paul Chesley 166bl,/Chad Ehlers 84,/Charles Gupton 119br, 124cl, 164br.

Martin Hladik: 15tl; Hobgoblin Japan Ltd: 156cb. Ikjeld.com: Kjeld Duits 150tc.

Japan Airlines: 172tc, 172cla; Japan National Tourist Organisation: 162tl; Japanzine: 170cb.

Masterfile: Allen Birnbach 69tl; R. Ian Lloyd 32–3; Jeremy Woodhouse 158–9; Keiko Morita: 171tl.

National Aeronautics and Space Administration: 12tr; New National Theatre, Tokyo: Chikashi Saegusa 151br.

Park Hyatt Tokyo: 156bl; Photographersdirect. com: Mantis Metalworks/Jonathan Christopher Roberts 11tr; Photolibrary: Jtb Photo Communications Inc. 155bl; Private Collection: 33c.

Robert Harding Picture Library: Charles Bowman 172br; Reuters: Toshiyuki Aizawa 31bl; Issei Kato 29br, 176br; Yuriko Nakao 31c; Susumu Toshiyuki 149tl.

Hotel Seiyo Ginza, a Rosewood Hotel: 106cr.

Treasures from the Tokugawa Art Museum: 24tl; Tokyo National Museum Collection: 10tc, 20, 22tl, 22cb, 23c, 35cr, 50bl, 51tl, 51ca, 51cra, 50cl, 50bc, 51cb, 52tr, 52cl, 52cr, 52clb, 52crb, 53tr; 53cla, 53crb, 53bc.

Werner Forman Archive: Victoria & Albert Museum, London. 55cr; Wikipedia, the free encyclopedia: 27br.

Front Endpaper: Alamy Images: Michele Falzone tr, Peter Horree bl, Photo Japan br; Corbis: Jon Hicks tl; Getty Images: Stone/Chad Ehlers tc.

Jacket: Front – Alamy Images: Chad Ehlers main image; Trip clb. Back – Corbis: Jai/Michele Falzone cla; DK Images: Martin Hladik bl, tl; Peter Wilson clb. Spine – Alamy Images: Chad Ehlers t; DK Images: Martin Hladik b. Back Endpapers: Metro Ad Agency Co. Ltd: Tokyo Metro Co, Ltd. © 2006.3

SPECIAL EDITIONS OF DK TRAVEL GUIDES

Phrase Book

The Japanese language is related to Okinawan and is similar to Altaic languages such as Mongolian and Turkish. Written Japanese uses a combination of three scripts – Chinese ideograms, known as *kanji*, and two syllable-based alphabet systems known as *hiragana* and *katakana*. These two latter are similar, *katakana* functioning as italics are used in English. Traditionally, Japanese is written in vertical columns from top right to bottom left, though the Western system is increasingly used. There are several romanization systems; the Hepburn system is used in this guide. To simplify romanization, macrons (long marks over vowels to indicate longer pronunciation) have not been used. Japanese pronunciation is fairly straightforward, and many words are "Japanized" versions of Western words. This Phrase Book gives the English word or phrase, followed by the Japanese script, then the romanization, adapted to aid pronunciation.

Guidelines For Pronunciation

When reading the romanization, give the same emphasis to all syllables. The practice in English of giving one syllable greater stress may render a Japanese word incomprehensible.

Pronounce vowels as in these English words:

a	as the "a" in "cat "
e	as in "red"
i	as in "chief"
o	as in "solid"
u	as the "oo" in "cuckoo"

When two vowels are used together, give each letter an individual sound:

ai	as in "pine"
ae	as if written "ah-eh"
ei	as in "pay"

Consonants are pronounced as in English. The letter *g* is always hard as in "gate," and *j* is always soft as in "joke." *R* is pronounced something between *r* and *l*. *F* is sometimes pronounced as *h*. "*Si*" always becomes "*shi*," but some people pronounce "*shi*" as "*hi*." *V* in Western words (e.g., "video") becomes *b*. If followed by a consonant, *n* may be pronounced as either *n* or *m*.

All consonants except *n* are always either followed by a vowel or doubled; however, sometimes an *i* or *u* is barely pronounced. In this Phrase Book, to aid pronunciation, apostrophes are used where an *i* or *u* is barely pronounced within a word, and double consonants where this occurs at the end of a word.

Dialects

Standard Japanese is used and understood throughout Japan by people of all backgrounds. But on a colloquial level, there are significant differences in both pronunciation and vocabulary, even between the Tokyo and Osaka-Kyoto areas, and rural accents are very strong.

Polite Words and Phrases

There are several different levels of politeness in the Japanese language, according to status, age, and situation. In everyday conversation, politeness levels are simply a question of the length of verb endings (longer is more polite), but in formal conversation entirely different words (*keigo*) are used. As a visitor, you may find that people try to speak to you in formal language, but there is no need to use it yourself; the level given in this Phrase Book is neutral yet polite.

In an Emergency

Help!	たすけて！	Tas'kete!
Stop!	とめて！	Tomete!
Call a doctor!	医者をよんで ください！	Isha o yonde kudasai!
Call an ambulance!	救急車を よんでください！	Kyukyusha o yonde kudasai!
Call the police!	警察を よんでください！	Keisatsu o yonde kudasai!
Fire!	火事！	Kaji!
Where is the hospital?	病院はどこに ありますか？	Byoin wa doko ni arimass-ka?
police box	交番	koban

Communication Essentials

Yes/no.	はい／いいえ	Hai/ie.
… not …	・・・ない／ちがい ます。	… nai/ chigaimass.
I don't know.	しりません。	Shirimasen.
Thank you.	ありがとう。	Arigato.
Thank you very much.	ありがとう ございます。	Arigato gozaimass.
Thank you very much indeed.	どうもありがとう ございます。	Domo arigato gozaimass.
Thanks (casual).	どうも。	Domo.
No, thank you.	結構です。 ありがとう。	Kekko dess, arigato.
Please (offering).	どうぞ。	Dozo.
Please (asking).	おねがいします。	Onegai shimass.
Please (give me or do for me).	・・・ください。	… kudasai.
I don't understand.	わかりません。	Wakarimasen.
Do you speak English?	英語を 話せますか？	Eigo o hanasemass-ka?
I can't speak Japanese.	日本語は 話せません。	Nihongo wa hanasemasen.
Please speak more slowly.	もう少し ゆっくり 話して ください。	Mo s'koshi yukkuri hanash'te kudasai.
Sorry/Excuse me!	すみません。	Sumimasen!
Could you help me please? (not emergency)	ちょっと手伝って いただけません か？	Chotto tets'datte itadakemasen-ka?

Useful Phrases

My name is ….	わたしの 名前は・・・ です。	Watashi no namae wa … dess.
How do you do, pleased to meet you.	はじめまして、 どうぞ よろしく。	Hajime-mash'te, dozo yorosh'ku.
How are you?	お元気ですか？	Ogenki dess-ka?
Good morning.	おはよう ございます。	Ohayo gozaimass.
Good afternoon/ good day.	こんにちは。	Konnichiwa.
Good evening.	こんばんは。	Konbanwa.

Good night.	おやすみなさい。	Oyasumi nasai.
Good-bye.	さよなら。	Sayonara.
Take care.	気をつけて。	Ki o ts'kete.
Keep well (casual).	お元気で。	Ogenki de.
The same to you.	そちらも。	Sochira mo.
What is (this)?	(これは) 何ですか?	(Kore wa) nan dess-ka?
How do you use this?	これをどうやって使いますか?	Kore o doyatte ts'kaimass-ka?
Could I possibly have …? (very polite)	・・・をいただけますか?	… o itadake-mass-ka?
Is there … here?	ここに・・・がありますか?	Koko ni … ga arimass-ka?
Where can I get …?	・・・はどこにありますか?	… wa doko ni arimass-ka?
How much is it?	いくらですか?	Ikura dess-ka?
What time is …?	・・・何時ですか?	… nan-ji dess-ka?
Cheers! (toast)	乾杯!	Kampai!
Where is the restroom/toilet?	お手洗い/おトイレはどこですか?	Otearai/otoire wa doko dess-ka?
Here's my business card.	名刺をどうぞ。	Meishi o dozo.

Useful Words

I	わたし	Watashi
woman	女性	josei
man	男性	dansei
wife	奥さん	ok'san
husband	主人	shujin
daughter	むすめ	musume
son	むすこ	mus'ko
child	こども	kodomo
children	こどもたち	kodomo-tachi
businessman/ woman	ビジネスマン/ウーマン	bijinessuman/ wuman
student	学生	gakusei
Mr./Mrs./Ms. …	・・・さん	…-san
big/small	大きい/小さい	okii/chiisai
hot/cold	暑い/寒い	atsui/samui
cold (to touch)	冷たい	tsumetai
warm	温かい	atatakai
good/ not good/bad	いい/よくない/悪い	ii/yokunai/warui
enough	じゅうぶん/結構	jubun/kekko
free (no charge)	ただ/無料	tada/muryo
here	ここ	koko
there	あそこ	asoko
this	これ	kore
that (nearby)	それ	sore
that (far away)	あれ	are
what?	何?	nani?
when?	いつ?	itsu?
why?	なぜ?/どうして?	naze?/dosh'te?
where?	どこ?	doko?
who?	誰?	dare?
which way?	どちら?	dochira?

Signs

Open	営業中	eigyo-chu
closed	休日	kyujitsu
entrance	入口	iriguchi
exit	出口	deguchi
danger	危険	kiken
emergency exit	非常口	hijo-guchi
information	案内	annai
restroom, toilet	お手洗い/手洗い/おトイレ/トイレ	otearai/tearai/ otoire/toire
free (vacant)	空き	aki
men	男	otoko
women	女	onna

Money

Could you change this into yen please.	これを円に替えてください。	Kore o en ni kaete kudasai.
I'd like to cash these travelers' checks.	このトラベラーズチェックを現金にしたいです。	Kono toraberazu chekku o genkin ni shitai dess.
Do you take credit cards/ travelers' checks?	クレジットカード/トラベラーズチェックで払えますか?	Kurejitto kado/ toraberazu chekku de haraemass-ka?
bank	銀行	ginko
cash	現金	genkin
credit card	クレジットカード	kurejitto kado
currency exchange office	両替所	ryogaejo
dollars	ドル	doru
pounds	ポンド	pondo
yen	円	en

Keeping in Touch

Where is a telephone?	電話はどこにありますか?	Denwa wa doko ni arimass-ka?
May I use your phone?	電話を使ってもいいですか?	Denwa o ts'katte mo ii dess-ka?
Hello, this is ….	もしもし、・・・です。	Moshi-moshi, …dess.
I'd like to make an international call.	国際電話、お願いします。	Kokusai denwa, onegai shimass.
airmail	航空便	kokubin
e-mail	イーメール	i-meru
fax	ファクス	fak'su
postcard	ハガキ	hagaki
post office	郵便局	yubin-kyoku
stamp	切手	kitte
telephone booth	公衆電話	koshu denwa
telephone card	テレフォンカード	terefon kado

Shopping

Where can I buy …?	・・・はどこで買えますか?	… wa doko de kaemass-ka?
How much does this cost?	いくらですか?	Ikura dess-ka?
I'm just looking.	見ているだけです。	Mite iru dake dess.
Do you have …?	・・・ありますか?	… arimass-ka?
May I try this on?	着てみてもいいですか?	Kite mite mo ii dess-ka?
Please show me that.	それを見せてください。	Sore o misete kudasai.
Does it come in other colors?	他の色もありますか?	Hoka no iro mo arimass-ka?
black	黒	kuro
blue	青	ao
green	緑	midori
red	赤	aka
white	白	shiro
yellow	黄色	kiiro
cheap/expensive	安い/高い	yasui/takai
audio equipment	オーディオ製品	odio seihin
bookstore	本屋	hon-ya
boutique	ブティック	butik
clothes	洋服	yofuku
department store	デパート	depato
electrical store	電気屋	denki-ya
fish market	魚屋	sakana-ya
folk crafts	民芸品	mingei-hin
ladies' wear	婦人服	fujin fuku
local specialty	名物	meibutsu
market	市場	ichiba
menswear	紳士服	shinshi fuku
newsstand	新聞屋	shimbun-ya

pharmacist	薬屋	kusuri-ya
picture postcard	絵葉書	e-hagaki
sale	セール	seru
souvenir shop	お土産屋	omiyage-ya
supermarket	スーパー	supa
travel agent	旅行会社	ryoko-gaisha

Sightseeing

Where is …?	…はどこですか？	… wa doko dess-ka?
How do I get to …?	…へは、どうやっていったらいいですか？	… e wa doyatte ittara ii dess-ka?
Is it far?	遠いですか？	Toi dess-ka?
art gallery	美術館	bijutsukan
reservations desk	予約窓口	yoyaku madoguchi
bridge	橋	hashi/bashi
castle	城	shiro/jo
city	市	shi
city center	街の中心	machi no chushin
gardens	庭園／庭	tei-en/niwa
hot spring	温泉	onsen
information office	案内所	annaijo
island	島	shima/jima
monastery	修道院	shudo-in
mountain	山	yama/san
museum	博物館	hakubutsukan
palace	宮殿	kyuden
park	公園	koen
port	港	minato/ko
prefecture	県	ken
river	川	kawa/gawa
ruins	遺跡	iseki
shopping area	ショッピング街	shoppingu gai
shrine	神社／神宮／宮	jinja/jingu/gu
street	通り	tori/dori
temple	お寺／寺	otera/tera/dera/ji
tour, travel	旅行	ryoko
town	町	machi/cho
village	村	mura
ward	区	ku
zoo	動物園	dobutsu-en
north	北	kita/hoku
south	南	minami/nan
east	東	higashi/to
west	西	nishi/sei
left/right	左／右	hidari/migi
straight ahead	真っ直ぐ	mass-sugu
between	間に	aida ni
near/far	近い／遠い	chikai/toi
up/down	上／下	ue/sh'ta
new	新しい／新	atarashii/shin
old/former	古い／元	furui/moto
upper/lower	上／下	kami/shimo
middle/inner	中	naka
in	に／中に	ni/naka ni
in front of	前	mae

Getting Around

bicycle	自転車	jitensha
bus	バス	basu
car	車	kuruma
ferry	フェリー	feri
baggage room	手荷物一時預かり所	tenimotsu ichiji azukarijo
motorcycle	オートバイ	otobai
one-way ticket	片道切符	katamichi kippu
return ticket	往復切符	ofuku kippu
taxi	タクシー	takushi
ticket	切符	kippu
ticket office	切符売場	kippu uriba

Trains

What is the fare to …?	…までいくらですか？	… made ikura dess-ka?
When does the train for… leave?	…行きの電車は、何時に出ますか？	… iki no densha wa nan-ji ni demass-ka?
How long does it take to get to …?	…まで時間は、どのぐらいかかりますか？	… made jikan wa dono gurai kakarimass-ka?
A ticket to …, please.	…行きの切符をください。	… yuki no kippu o kudasai.
Do I have to change?	乗り換えが必要ですか？	Norikae ga hitsuyo dess-ka?
I'd like to reserve a seat, please.	席を予約したいです。	Seki o yoyaku shitai dess.
Which platform for the train to …?	…行きの電車は、何番ホームから出ますか？	… yuki no densha wa nanban homu kara demass-ka?
Which station is this?	この駅は、どこですか？	Kono eki wa doko dess-ka?
Is this the right train for …?	…へは、この電車でいいですか？	… e wa kono densha de ii dess-ka?
bullet train	新幹線	shinkansen
express trains:		
"limited express" (fastest)	特急	tokkyu
"express" (second)	急行	kyuko
"rapid" (third)	快速	kaisoku
first-class	一等	itto
line	線	sen
local train	普通／各駅電車	futsu/kaku-eki-densha
platform	ホーム	homu
train station	駅	eki
reserved seat	指定席	shitei-seki
second-class	二等	nito
subway	地下鉄	chikatetsu
train	電車	densha
unreserved seat	自由席	jiyu-seki

Accommodations

Do you have any vacancies?	部屋がありますか？	Heya ga arimass-ka?
I have a reservation.	予約をしてあります。	Yoyaku o sh'te arimass.
I'd like a room with a bathroom.	お風呂つきの部屋、お願いします。	Ofuro-ts'ki no heya, onegai shimass.
What is the charge per night?	一泊いくらですか？	Ippaku ikura dess-ka?
Is tax included in the price?	税込みですか？	Zeikomi dess-ka?
Can I leave my luggage here for a little while?	荷物をちょっとここに預けてもいいですか？	Nimotsu o chotto koko ni azukete mo ii dess-ka?
air-conditioning	冷房／エアコン	reibo/eakon
bath	お風呂	ofuro
check-out	チェックアウト	chekku-auto
hair drier	ドライヤー	doraiya
hot (boiled) water	お湯	oyu
Japanese-style inn	旅館	ryokan
Japanese-style room	和室	wa-shitsu
key	鍵	kagi
front desk	フロント	furonto
single/twin room	シングル／ツイン	shinguru/tsuin

shower	シャワー	shyawa
Western-style hotel	ホテル	hoteru
Western-style room	洋室	yo-shitsu

Eating Out

A table for one/two/three, please.	一人／二人／三人、お願いします。	Hitori/futari/sannin, onegai shimass.
May I see the menu.	メニュー、お願いします。	Menyu, onegai shimass.
Is there a set menu?	定食がありますか？	Teishoku ga arimass-ka?
I'd like ….	私は…がいいです。	Watashi wa … ga ii dess.
May I have one of those?	それをひとつ、お願いします。	Sore o hitotsu, onegai shimass?
I am a vegetarian.	私はベジタリアンです。	Watashi wa bejitarian dess.
Waiter/waitress!	ちょっとすみません。	Chotto sumimasen!
What would you recommend?	おすすめは何ですか？	Osusume wa nan dess-ka?
How do you eat this?	これはどうやって食べますか？	Kore wa doyatte tabemass-ka?
May we have the check please.	お勘定、お願いします。	Okanjo, onegai shimass.
May we have some more …	もっと…、お願いします。	Motto …, onegai shimass.
The meal was very good, thank you.	ごちそうさまでした。おいしかったです。	Gochiso-sama desh'ta. oishikatta dess.
assortment	盛りあわせ	moriawase
boxed meal	弁当	bento
breakfast	朝食	cho-shoku
buffet	バイキング	baikingu
delicious	おいしい	oishii
dinner	夕食	yu-shoku
to drink	飲む	nomu
a drink	飲みもの	nomimono
to eat	食べる	taberu
food	食べもの／ごはん	tabemono/gohan
full (stomach)	おなかがいっぱい	onaka ga ippai
hot/cold	熱い／冷たい	atsui/tsumetai
hungry	おなかがすいた	onaka ga suita
Japanese food	和食	wa-shoku
lunch	昼食	chu-shoku
set menu	セット／定食	setto (snack)/ teishoku (meal)
spicy	辛い	karai
sweet, mild	甘い	amai
Western food	洋食	yo-shoku

Places to Eat

Cafeteria/canteen	食堂	shokudo
Chinese restaurant	中華料理屋	chuka-ryori-ya
coffee shop	喫茶店	kissaten
local bar	飲み屋／居酒屋	nomiya/izakaya
noodle stall	ラーメン屋	ramen-ya
restaurant	レストラン／料理屋	resutoran/ ryori-ya
sushi on a conveyor belt	回転寿司	kaiten-zushi
upscale restaurant	料亭	ryotei
upscale vegetarian restaurant	精進料理屋	shojin-ryori-ya

Foods (see also Reading the Menu pp122–3)

apple	りんご	ringo
bamboo shoots	たけのこ	takenoko
beancurd	とうふ	tofu
bean sprouts	もやし	moyashi
beans	豆	mame
beef	ビーフ／牛肉	bifu/gyuniku
beefburger	ハンバーグ	hanbagu
blowfish	ふぐ	fugu
bonito, tuna	かつお／ツナ	katsuo/tsuna
bread	パン	pan
butter	バター	bata
cake	ケーキ	keki
chicken	とり／鶏肉	tori/toriniku
confectionery	お菓子	okashi
crab	かに	kani
duck	あひる	ahiru
eel	うなぎ	unagi
egg	たまご	tamago
eggplant/ aubergine	なす	nasu
fermented soybean paste	みそ	miso
fermented soybeans	納豆	natto
fish (raw)	さしみ	sashimi
fried tofu	油揚げ	abura-age
fruit	くだもの	kudamono
ginger	しょうが	shoga
hamburger	ハンバーガー	hanbaga
haute cuisine	会席	kaiseki
herring	ニシン	nishin
hors d'oeuvres	オードブル	odoburu
ice cream	アイスクリーム	aisu-kurimu
jam	ジャム	jamu
Japanese mushrooms	まつたけ／しいたけ／しめじ	mats'take/ shiitake/shimeji
Japanese pear	なし	nashi
loach	どじょう	dojo
lobster	伊勢えび	ise-ebi
mackerel	さば	saba
mackerel pike	さんま	sanma
mandarin orange	みかん	mikan
meat	肉	niku
melon	メロン	meron
mountain vegetables	山菜	sansai
noodles:		
buckwheat	そば	soba
Chinese	ラーメン	ramen
wheatflour	うどん／そうめん	udon (fat)/ somen (thin)
octopus	たこ	tako
omelet	オムレツ	omuretsu
oyster	カキ	kaki
peach	もも	momo
pepper	こしょう	kosho
persimmon	柿	kaki
pickles	つけもの	ts'kemono
pork	豚肉	butaniku
potato	いも	imo
rice:		
cooked	ごはん	gohan
uncooked	米	kome
rice crackers	おせんべい	osenbei
roast beef	ローストビーフ	rosutobifu
salad	サラダ	sarada
salmon	鮭	sake
salt	塩	shio
sandwich	サンドイッチ	sandoichi
sausage	ソーセージ	soseji
savory nibbles	おつまみ	otsumami
seaweed:		
dried	のり	nori
chewy	こんぶ	konbu

shrimp	えび	ebi
soup	汁／スープ	shiru/supu
soy sauce	しょうゆ	shoyu
spaghetti	スパゲティ	supageti
spinach	ほうれんそう	horenso
squid	いか	ika
steak	ステーキ	suteki
sugar	砂糖	sato
sushi (mixed)	五目寿司	gomoku-zushi
sweetfish/smelt	あゆ	ayu
taro (potato)	さといも	sato imo
toast	トースト	tosuto
trout	鱒	masu
sea urchin	ウニ	uni
vegetables	野菜	yasai
watermelon	すいか	suika
wild boar	ぼたん／いのしし	botan/inoshishi

Drinks

beer	ビール	biru
coffee (hot)	ホットコーヒー	hotto-kohi
cola	コーラ	kora
green tea	お茶	ocha
iced coffee:		
black	アイスコーヒー	aisu-kohi
with milk	アイスオーレ	kafe-o-re
lemon tea	レモンティー	remon ti
milk	ミルク／牛乳	miruku/gyunyu
mineral water	ミネラルウォーター	mineraru uota
orange juice	オレンジジュース	orenji jusu
rice wine	酒	sake
(non-alcoholic)	（甘酒）	(ama-zake)
tea (Western-	紅茶	kocha
style)		
tea with milk	ミルクティー	miruku ti
water	水	mizu
whiskey	ウイスキー	uis'ki
wine	ワイン／ぶどう酒	wain/budoshu

Health

I don't feel well.	気分が	Kibun ga
	よくないです。	yokunai dess.
I have a pain in ...	・・・が痛いです。	... ga itai dess.
I'm allergic to ...	・・・アレルギーです。	... arerugi dess.
asthma	喘息	zensoku
cough	せき	seki
dentist	歯医者	haisha
diabetes	糖尿病	tonyo-byo
diarrhea	下痢	geri
doctor	医者	isha
fever	熱	netsu
headache	頭痛	zutsuu
hospital	病院	byoin
medicine	薬	kusuri
Oriental	漢方薬	kampo yaku
medicine		
pharmacy	薬局	yakkyoku
prescription	処方箋	shohosen
stomachache	腹痛	fukutsu
toothache	歯が痛い	ha ga itai

Numbers

0	ゼロ	zero
1	一	ichi
2	二	ni
3	三	san
4	四	yon/shi
5	五	go
6	六	roku
7	七	nana/shichi
8	八	hachi
9	九	kyu
10	十	ju
11	十一	ju-ichi
12	十二	ju-ni
20	二十	ni-ju
21	二十一	ni-ju-ichi
22	二十二	ni-ju-ni
30	三十	san-ju
40	四十	yon-ju
100	百	hyaku
101	百一	hyaku-ichi
200	二百	ni-hyaku
300	三百	san-byaku
400	四百	yon-hyaku
500	五百	go-hyaku
600	六百	ro-ppyaku
700	七百	nana-hyaku
800	八百	ha-ppyaku
900	九百	kyu-hyaku
1,000	千	sen
1,001	千一	sen-ichi
2,000	二千	ni-sen
10,000	一万	ichi-man
20,000	二万	ni-man
100,000	十万	ju-man
1,000,000	百万	hyaku-man
123,456	十二万三千	ju-ni-man-san-
	四百五十六	zen-yon-hyaku-
		go-ju-roku

Time

Monday	月曜日	getsu-yobi
Tuesday	火曜日	ka-yobi
Wednesday	水曜日	sui-yobi
Thursday	木曜日	moku-yobi
Friday	金曜日	kin-yobi
Saturday	土曜日	do-yobi
Sunday	日曜日	nichi-yobi
January	一月	ichi-gatsu
February	二月	ni-gatsu
March	三月	san-gatsu
April	四月	shi-gatsu
May	五月	go-gatsu
June	六月	roku-gatsu
July	七月	shichi-gatsu
August	八月	hachi-gatsu
September	九月	ku-gatsu
October	十月	ju-gatsu
November	十一月	ju-ichi-gatsu
December	十二月	ju-ni-gatsu
spring	春	haru
summer	夏	natsu
fall/autumn	秋	aki
winter	冬	fuyu
noon	正午	shogo
midnight	真夜中	mayonaka
today	今日	kyo
yesterday	昨日	kino
tomorrow	明日	ash'ta
this morning	今朝	kesa
this afternoon	今日の午後	kyo no gogo
this evening	今晩	konban
every day	毎日	mainichi
month	月	getsu/ts'ki
hour		ji
time/hour	時間	jikan
(duration)		
minute	分	pun/fun
this year	今年	kotoshi
last year	去年	kyonen
next year	来年	rainen
one year	一年	ichi-nen
late	遅い	osoi
early	早い	hayai
soon	すぐ	sugu